City of Omens

CITY

OF

OMENS

++++

A SEARCH FOR THE
MISSING WOMEN OF THE
BORDERLANDS

DAN WERB

BLOOMSBURY PUBLISHING

NEW YORK · LONDON · OXFORD · NEW DELHI · SYDNEY

BLOOMSBURY PUBLISHING
Bloomsbury Publishing Inc.
1385 Broadway, New York, NY 10018, USA

BLOOMSBURY, BLOOMSBURY PUBLISHING, and the Diana logo are trademarks of
Bloomsbury Publishing Plc

First published in the United States 2019

Image on pages ii–iii: Guillermo Arias/AFP/Getty Images

ISBN: HB: 978-1-63557-299-5; eBook: 978-1-63557-300-8

LIBRARY OF CONGRESS CATALOGING-IN-PUBLICATION DATA

Names: Werb, Dan, author.
Title: City of omens : a search for the missing women of the borderlands / Dan Werb.
Description: New York, NY : Bloomsbury Publishing, 2019.
Identifiers: LCCN 2018055631 | ISBN 9781635572995 (hardcover)
Subjects: LCSH: Epidemiology—Mexico—Tijuana (Baja California) | Women—Mortality—
Mexico—Tijuana (Baja California) | Women—Mexico—Tijuana (Baja California)—
Social conditions. | Women—Crimes against—Mexico—Tijuana (Baja California) |
Violent crimes—Mexico—Tijuana (Baja California) | Prostitution—Mexico—
Tijuana (Baja California) | Public health—Mexico—Tijuana (Baja California)
Classification: LCC RA650.55.M52 T548 2019 | DDC 614.40972/24—dc23
LC record available at https://lccn.loc.gov/2018055631

2 4 6 8 10 9 7 5 3 1

Typeset by Westchester Publishing Services
Printed and bound in the U.S.A. by Berryville Graphics Inc., Berryville, Virginia

To find out more about our authors and books visit
www.bloomsbury.com and sign up for our newsletters.

For Susi

Perhaps the easiest way of making a town's acquaintance is to ascertain how the people in it work, how they love, and how they die.
—Albert Camus, *The Plague*

Contents

PART I

The Host

CHAPTER I

Welcome to El Bordo

I stood in the middle of the Jack in the Box parking lot, looking around anxiously, sweating under the desert sun. I had worn "slum-appropriate" clothing, or at least a facsimile of what I thought that meant: blue button-down shirt, jeans, and cheap sneakers. The plan, I had been told, was to blend in. All around us were slow-moving cars, slow-moving pedestrians, and the sustained clatter and low horn blasts of the trolleys heading in from downtown San Diego, filled with people crossing the border, all with their reasons. Everybody looked at home in the sun, belonged to the space, while the heat beat down on me relentlessly.

Leaning against a Mercedes, Argentina, in pale immaculate makeup, didn't care whether she blended in or not. In stiletto heels, tight white pants, and a white fur shawl, she scanned the small parking lot, cased me right away, and shook my hand impatiently as we got into the car and then set off for Mexico. She was a young Mexican medical doctor and had been asked to transport me safely across the border and hand me off to those who would take me into the canal. We sat on chestnut leather seats as we sped through the border line and into Tijuana. We were waved through quickly, and as we entered Mexico, hundreds upon hundreds of cars and people came into view, stacked interminably on the other side of the wall, all waiting to be let into the United States of America.

It's the first thing you see once you pass through the border line: the abandoned Tijuana River Canal, stretching north past the border fence and south through the city until there is no city left. There's no way to avoid it. If you want to get downtown, you have to cross a bridge to get over it. If you want to skirt it, you have to drive down a highway, the Vía Rápida, which snakes along both its sides for miles and miles, all the way to the city's southern limit. It's a barrier, a listless concrete space, appearing empty except for garbage and a thin trickle of sewage, engineered to be as inconspicuous as possible. As Argentina and I zoomed across a bridge in the white Mercedes, I let my eyes follow the wastewater seeping north along the canal floor below us. From my vantage point, I could see the brackish and brown pollution, just barely water, flashing under the white sun, but I could not tell where the stream flowed after the canal abruptly hit the border wall. The whole place looked like a no-man's-land, a static and determinedly empty negative space, the architecture devoid of shelter. And then something way down amid the concrete and refuse caught my eye: human beings.

Dr. Steffanie Strathdee, chief of the University of California's Division of Global Public Health, had told me about the canal before I came to visit, and about its peculiar ecosystem. She was investigating how an HIV epidemic was spreading through the hundreds and perhaps thousands of people who inject drugs and live in rough encampments along the space's low sloping walls. My job, she had explained, would be to help delineate the contours of the epidemic so that she and her colleagues could understand its spread and develop programs—behavioral interventions, social services, infrastructure, or some still unknown approach—to contain it.

I had come to the border from Vancouver, Canada, where I was finishing up my PhD in epidemiology and biostatistics after a short stint as a freelance journalist on the drug addiction beat. My graduate studies were defined by the behavior, tracked over eight years, of a sample of people who inject drugs in Vancouver's Downtown Eastside neighborhood, a place that is home to one of North America's largest open-air illegal drug markets. I had published some scientific findings about the neighborhood and the people who lived there, most of which focused on the destructive impact of policing among the sample's drug-injecting participants, which ratcheted up their risk of sharing contaminated needles and becoming infected with HIV. I was proud of the work, but I was also itching under the steady hands of my mentors and searching for my next move. It felt like I had taken research on my hometown as far as it could go.

I had first met Steffanie in 2006, the year I started working as an assistant at an HIV research center in Vancouver. At the time, my desk was in a dead-end hallway far from my colleagues. It was lonely there except when Steffanie and her husband, Tom Patterson, breezed in, every two months or so, to do some kind of consultancy work with my superiors. On one of those visits we got to talking and—in the scholarly equivalent of a first date—I asked Steffanie if she'd co-author a scientific manuscript I was writing (she agreed). She was smart, but more important, she was supportive, and she never seemed stressed out. I liked that combination. As the years progressed and I thought about my next career move, the idea of working more closely with someone as breezy and relaxed as Steffanie, and doing it in the sunshine of Southern California, became more and more appealing. By 2012, when I was a year away from finishing my PhD, we started talking seriously about me joining her team after I defended my thesis. Before I made up my mind, though, she wanted me to come down to Tijuana.

By that point, I was familiar with shock tourism, having lived or worked in Vancouver most of my life. People come to the Downtown Eastside to feel the thrill of outsider existence, of experiencing by osmosis the desperation and poverty of the people who live there, many of whom inject drugs in the neighborhood's chaotic alleys in full view of passersby. I've felt it myself: that yearning to parachute into a place where cops are ubiquitous, neck injections with dirty puddle water are the norm, and optimism is scarce. I understand the urge to step out of a car and wander around a place you don't understand for an afternoon (but not a minute longer). It is, of course, nothing more than a fantasy of belonging. But it's hard to resist the feeling that a kernel of truth has been passed from those who are suffering to those who have come to watch them, as if mute observation is an act of charity. When I took Steffanie up on her invitation, I vowed to avoid the temptation to treat Tijuana like a dark and titillating ride, and instead recognize the visit for what it was: a scientific excursion into a field research site beset by a public health crisis.

Perched above the Tijuana River Canal in the Mercedes, I tried to decipher what the small human shapes moving below us were doing, but Argentina revved the motor again and we were quickly away. We maneuvered off the bridge, cut into a busy road, and zigzagged across downtown Tijuana, the traffic moving against pedestrians with predatory intent. As we pulled into the driveway of a health clinic where Argentina was a volunteer, it hit me that I had completely lost my sense of direction.

With the border wall having receded from view, I stepped cautiously out of the car, trying in vain to find some touchstones. Before I could get my bearings, Argentina gave me a quick wave and promptly roared off, starting her day in earnest, the delivery complete. She had more important things to do. I was handed to someone else whose name I don't remember, escorted into another car full of people, and shuttled off again. We were finally heading to the field research headquarters for Proyecto El Cuete (the Needle Project), Steffanie's research study, in the heart of the Zona Norte, the neighborhood that is pressed up against the border fence and encompasses Tijuana's red-light district and the northernmost portion of the city's canal.

We parked along a narrow street and made our way up a staircase and into a dilapidated office where Dr. Patty Gonzalez, an easygoing Tijuanensis doctor, introduced herself as Steffanie's research coordinator. Patty was one of the few present who spoke English, and she exuded a weary kindness as she described the continual chaos of her work, most of which involved ensuring that the participants of the El Cuete study were being interviewed systematically and their behavioral data recorded for analysis. Next to her stood Susi, a short Mexican woman with shifting, impatient eyes. She was Patty's outreach worker, meaning that she was tasked with exploring Steffanie's laboratory—the city of Tijuana—to find study participants, a job that she was uniquely qualified for, having lived and injected drugs in downtown Tijuana for decades. Her job consisted of searching for people who injected drugs, many of whom had no interest in being found, and convincing them to enroll in Proyecto El Cuete so that Steffanie and her team could study their risk of acquiring HIV.

We left the office and walked a few blocks through narrow downtown streets to a rooftop parking lot covered in cracked asphalt. I tried to look at ease, with my hands in my pockets and a consciously relaxed stride. My "slum-appropriate" clothes, I realized, weren't helping me blend in after all, though it was becoming apparent that regardless of what I had worn, my pallor and lack of Spanish would have given me away. As a white Canadian, I felt the sun like a spotlight shining down on me and me alone.

The timeline for the day, Patty said, was fluid. While her only agenda was getting out into the field to recruit participants, I was intent on making a good impression on everyone I met, in the hopes that I could secure a spot with Steffanie's research team as a postdoctoral fellow. In Patty's office, though, nobody cared about why I was there. Everything seemed to be moving at its own slow speed and, as I would soon learn, the decisions for how we were to spend the rest of the day were being set by people out in the city whose needs dwarfed our own.

We climbed into a beat-up minivan with a faded University of California San Diego logo on its side and a series of heavy dents and scrapes marking the chassis. It roared to life in a billow of black smoke, and we chugged—five of us—into traffic. The mood was light, everybody laughing at the state of the van and the hairpin turns, sudden reversals, and radical lane changes our driver was making as he navigated us out of the Zona Norte. A young medical student next to me seemed to be especially excited, and he confided in me that even though he was born and raised in Tijuana he had never set foot in the canal. Everyone spoke together and at each other in Spanish, with Patty shouting brief translations to me from the front seat and apologizing for the jokes that couldn't make it through the language barrier. We approached a highway—not the one Argentina had taken, it seemed to me—and the border appeared dead ahead. I studied it with some relief: here was the only marker I had for where I had come from, and if it was in front of us then we must be heading north. As we entered highway traffic, the minivan finally started outracing the black smoke pouring from its exhaust and Patty passed around neon work vests.

We took the highway, called the Vía Internacional, eastward, the wrought-iron- and steel-slatted border wall running parallel to our left, darkening and dwarfing the road. I couldn't shake the anxiety of not knowing where we were going or what people were talking about; of not being in control. I wanted to be back at the hotel Steffanie had arranged for me across the border in safe and staid San Diego. And then, all of a sudden, the highway curved south and the canal came into view. Patty looked over her shoulder and caught my eye. "There are a lot of accidents here," she said over the noise of the engine. "People from the canal run into the road when they're trying to get away from police. They get hit by the cars and there's a lot of death." I nodded, trying to take the words in.

As the highway veered south, the border wall receded behind us. Meanwhile Patty and Susi chatted in a hard-edged Tijuana slang, their frustration growing as they scanned the cityscape outside the van's windows. We were driving alongside the canal, and it became obvious that they wanted to somehow get the van inside but couldn't find a way in; though I wasn't catching all the words, it seemed like a reliable entry point had recently been shuttered. Eventually, Patty became exasperated and we turned off the highway again to meander through a quiet neighborhood full of auto-body shops and faceless gray buildings, Spanish words hand-painted in uncertain yellow and red letters on their chipped concrete walls. At Susi's suggestion, the driver navigated us down a dead-end street that abutted a small paved plaza, and we pulled to a stop near a group of men loitering noiselessly in the heat. We idled, the van belching thick exhaust, and Susi jumped out and ambled toward the group. She talked loudly at a rapid clip as she got close, and we watched as she quickly grabbed one of them by the arm and hurried back to the van with him in tow. He was a slow-moving lanky guy in his late twenties wearing a black long-sleeved T-shirt and ripped-up cargo pants. He called himself Chango: Monkey. Susi explained that he lived in the canal most of the time and did drugs there. His manner was lucid and polite, his conversation slowed by opiates.

I couldn't tell if Chango and Susi knew each other or if their intimacy was a product of having both injected drugs in the city. They talked at our driver as he guided the van back onto the road, across a bridge, and up the highway running along the canal's eastern wall. We drove north, the border wall materializing in front of us again in the distance while everyone continued looking for a way into the canal, craning their necks out the windows for off-ramps or openings. I just stared out at the city, trying my best to take it all in. Rows of squat, yellow-painted dwellings blurred into each other as we picked up speed.

Chango saw something and signaled; our driver pulled tightly onto the narrow shoulder of the highway and flipped the hazards on. We sat idling for a moment against the canal wall, the van rocking gently each time a car or truck whizzed past us on the right. The silence lasted a few minutes while Patty stared intently through the rear window at the highway behind us. Then: "Okay, okay!" Our driver slammed the van back into gear hard and we sped in reverse the wrong way down the highway, narrowly avoiding the cars rushing past us, before veering sharply backward at an angle into the canal wall and up a hidden ramp, only accessible, apparently, by driving against the flow of traffic along the Vía Rápida. As we mounted the top of the ramp and came to a stop atop the canal wall, everybody laughed with relief, a frenzied energy circulating among the six of us. Though the whole exercise had taken ten seconds at most, my heart was pounding. "Driving in Tijuana," said Patty, shrugging her shoulders, as I pulled myself shakily out of the van's back seat.

We collected ourselves and put on the neon vests, then walked north as a group along the high edge of the canal in the direction of the border.

It was still early in the day, but I could already feel my skin burning. Patty pointed at an encampment of people down at the floor of the canal a few hundred yards ahead and we slowly skirted the gentle concrete slope to reach them. A bracing stink rose to meet us. As we approached the encampment we passed a solitary man in the center of the canal, shirtless in the sun and standing ankle-deep in the noxious brown wastewater. His old pants were cinched up above his knees and slick white foam spread in clumps along the water's oily surface and circulated around his bare legs. He leaned down, drenched his T-shirt in the sewage, and splashed it across his bare chest.

The camp ahead of us spread along the western wall of the canal, affording little shelter beyond mounds of debris and short pillars of polluted claylike mud under which, presumably, its residents found some refuge from the heat. But as we approached I saw other people, silhouettes in the high sun, seeming to move in and out of the canal wall itself. Patty saw me looking. "There are big drain shafts there," she said, "for when the rains come." The shafts, she showed me, were accessible through shadowy vents that looked like half-raised garage doors cut into the canal wall.

It hardly ever rains in Tijuana, but a few times a year it bears down in sheets, Patty explained, the desert landscape prone to flash floods and erosion. The Tijuana River Canal was designed to make sure that the destructive power of the floodwaters was contained, so it was built along an estuary that stretches from Tijuana's high canyons and across the border into the United States, where the concrete structure eventually meets the Pacific Ocean. To stop the seasonal floods, the hollow canal walls fill with water when the rain comes too strong, safely shunting it away from the city proper. "But people sleep in there," said Patty, "do drugs in there. If it rains all of a sudden they get trapped by the water and can't get out, and drown."

We kept walking and the small band of people, forty or so, looked our way, stood up, and prepared themselves for a visit. Susi and Chango walked at the head of our group, calling out joyfully to the men. Some stayed immobile, warily eyeing us. Others got up and walked over, everyone's movements dulled and overly slow. They greeted us listlessly, talking without pretense or enthusiasm.

This was my first dive into the purgatories Tijuana could produce. I did my best to blend in with the rest of the outreach group while simultaneously trying to mentally record as much of the scene as I could.

Epidemiologic field research is often imbued with this feeling of being at cross-purposes, because our discipline uses population level data to stop epidemics rather than working to cure specific individuals. We're scientists with laboratories that just happen to be located in the real world. As I was confronted by the raw unmet needs of the people who lived in the canal, that larger purpose—the one that I was clinging to in order to make this trip as useful to my scientific practice as possible—was obscured by a deep ache for the inhumane situation they had found themselves in.

Once the bottles of water and basic first aid kits had been passed out, there was little else to provide the group, so about half of the forty men turned and wandered away, some lazily picking their way through the piles of garbage and detritus that spread out across their camp, others lying back down on their sides against the sloping canal walls. The heat of the day was visible in the distance where the canal met the border, making both appear to melt into each other a half mile north of where we stood. None of the residents of the encampment seemed too disappointed that we had come practically empty-handed. It was just another familiar moment of quiet despair, under a relentless sun stealing the color from the landscape.

We stood around for a while. Patty, the medical doctor, asked the remaining men about their health. Susi grabbed people roughly, peering closely at the crooks of their elbows then bringing them over to Patty to examine. Many had abscesses and black infections on the track marks that dotted their arms; one man raised a pant leg to reveal a giant, cankerous wound, pink and brown, that had spread feverishly across his shin and calf. I thought about the man we had passed moments earlier, bathing ankle-deep in raw sewage. Another man, older, with a dark, deeply lined face and graying hair, came toward me holding his blistered arm up to my face, thinking I was a medical doctor, thinking I knew the language, and assuming I could help him somehow. I shrugged and wordlessly communicated to him that I was unable to help. He smiled wanly and walked away.

In Vancouver, I was familiar with the scenes in the alleys downtown, dense groups of people injecting openly, many young, mentally ill, and bursting with frenetic, unchanneled energy. But in Vancouver I would also see health workers systematically scouring places where they knew people congregated, and in recent years the Vancouver Police Department had even begun to accept that the practice of distributing clean needles could prevent HIV among the people who injected out in the open, which would ultimately make the neighborhood safer for everyone who lived there.

Here at the bottom of the canal, a few hundred yards from the world's busiest border crossing, there was no energy at all. The place felt entirely deserted. Were Patty and her crew the only line of defense? Were we the only friendly visitors the people here would meet today, or this week? These were sick men, sick and forgotten. Or, sick people. I noticed one woman, watching us from the entrance to the drain shaft, about a hundred feet away. She refused to come close. It seemed odd to me that there would be no other women among the dozens of people living here, but all evidence suggested she was alone. By the time I looked for her again, she had slipped into the drain shaft, hiding under the unstable protection of the canal's wall.

While statistics vary, about 5 percent of people who inject drugs in Tijuana are believed to be infected with HIV. That meant that, of the forty or so people we met in the canal, two of them were probably HIV-positive (though practically all of them were likely infected with hepatitis C). One needle might serve the whole group's daily injecting needs. It would be well hidden under a crevice in the canal floor or between some dusty rocks, and rinsed only in the trickling wastewater, if at all. There was one person there, though, who I knew was more likely than anyone else to be infected with HIV: the woman who had fled into the canal wall as we had approached. About half of Tijuana's drug-injecting women have reported that they trade sex for drugs. Among that group, 12 percent are believed to be HIV-positive. In this encampment, with so little currency to offer, it was likely that she would have both traded sex and injected drugs, a victim and vector at multiple crosshairs of HIV.

Meanwhile, we were outstaying our welcome. It was time to go. We waved goodbye and the remaining men wandered away, Chango among them. He had decided to stay at the camp to fix.

*

Susi's wrist is circled by a bracelet of fibrous scars running halfway to her elbow, raised and stiff. It is a legacy of a life in the Zona Norte, a cue to the many years she spent injecting drugs here. Scar tissue builds up around veins when puncture wounds get infected, a common problem among people injecting on the street, where dirty water is used to dissolve drugs and clean needles aren't available and get reused. With each repeated hit the needle becomes blunter, making injecting an increasingly difficult and bloody prospect, especially if the needle has to be guided into veins that are collapsing from overuse. When police are patrolling those dark and public places where injectors congregate, it becomes even more difficult to avoid damage; the anxiety of being discovered with a needle during a police raid makes people rush the process rather than carefully choosing a vein and separating the skin in a gentle motion. Instead, the injection becomes a panicked ritual, body parts sacrificed in a hurry to avoid a confrontation with the police, who emanate a threat of violence much more immediately dangerous than the bloom of scar tissue in needle-damaged skin. I had seen the effects before in Vancouver, where in the mid-2000s police stormed into the tall and greasy alleyways of the Downtown Eastside to capture people and destroy their needles, sending groups running into the night. A similar kind of police work was happening here in Tijuana, though it appeared to be much more ruthless.

Later that day, I walked with Susi and Patty through the Zona Norte, the broken concrete sidewalk dipping under our feet. Susi had spent decades in this neighborhood, and its rough and informal energy was as much without as within her, while the scars gave her away as a longtime resident. She was never a sex worker, but she managed to parlay her injecting experience into a bit part in the vernacular economy of the red-light district. She was a "hit doctor," someone highly skilled in injecting other people, and she did it for money and drugs. Mainstays of injecting scenes, hit doctors play an important role tending to the needs of those who cannot fix themselves. After years of injecting have caused the most accessible veins to collapse, and it is time to search your body for other closed paths, more intimate, strange, and arcane—like the groin, the space between the toes, the armpit, or the jugular—a hit doctor can help you with that. Or perhaps, like so many women, you were never taught how to inject yourself and are forced to rely on boyfriends or johns to do it for you. A hit doctor can help you with that too. Susi helped all comers, but her clientele were mostly the Zona's sex workers.

Eventually we sat down in an open-air taco shop on a busy corner and Susi talked at me in a barely comprehensible Tijuanensis slang, with Patty translating on the fly. Out on the street there were people everywhere, innocuous vendors and old men on makeshift seats watching tortillas being fried on street corner grills, lazily turning their eyes to the sex workers, drug users, and police patrolling the streets. Susi described experiencing the kind of vulnerability that I spend my days aggregating into cold, quantifiable statistics. An ID card on a lanyard hung over her loose T-shirt, and she stared at me with large brown eyes that, while full to the brim with emotion, nevertheless remained opaque, concealing her true thoughts. She shifted in her seat, impatient, talking in a long stream-of-consciousness ramble while the slow grimy chaos filtered in, heavy particulates floating in the heat and grease. "My friend Angie was a sex worker for nine years," she said at one point. "She was an American that worked here." I could hardly hear her over the corrido music blaring from speakers propped up against the shop's walls, the plodding polka rhythms and mariachi horns mixing together to tell another Tijuana story. Angie, she explained, was a friend and injecting partner, and she and Susi had worked together robbing American tourists. "She called me 'Auntie,'" Susi recalled with a smile.

Susi's arrival in Tijuana came just on the cusp of the 1980s, at the dawning of the era of AIDS. It was a time when the border was as porous as soft skin, before the fencing and the most recent explosion of mad paranoia about "illegal aliens" had gripped America. HIV changed all that. No sooner had she arrived than the world began to turn its attention to potential reservoir populations (groups of hosts within which an infection can lurk and replicate) as it became clear that the virus was killing absolutely everyone who got infected. It was a time when a city's reputation could be left in tatters by the mere suggestion that it was harboring a homegrown outbreak.

Tijuana was more vulnerable to the destruction wrought by HIV than most other places in North America: it is and was a city built on sex and drugs, its economic success propelled by the human appetite for risk. Nowhere has this appetite been more efficiently monetized than in the Zona Norte's red-light district. Viruses can cross borders as easily as people, particularly if there is a reservoir population to welcome them. Tijuana, home to vice economies reliant on intimacy, in which people are bound to one another by sex and needles, had ideal reservoir populations for HIV, with the upshot that new potential hosts, in the form of migrant women entering the sex trade, were constantly replenishing the pool. The potential impact of HIV here was neatly summed up by a local health official interviewed in 1989, who stated that "prostitutes who work in Tijuana often cross the border and have sex with migrant workers in California fields. Most of these women don't know a lot about AIDS and they usually don't use condoms. If we don't do something, this might explode someday." This was the worst kind of press a city dependent on selling sex could acquire.

Susi, despite being at the epicenter of the HIV epidemic in Tijuana, only heard about the virus in the early 2000s, and even then none of her friends would take her concerns seriously. A drug user embedded within a sex work scene, Susi dealt with what scientists like me would detachedly describe as "multiple risk factors," epidemiologic shorthand for a life rich in complexity, one in which days are spent moving toward and turning away from the thing that you need, the thing that might kill you.

"Nobody gave syringes away. I picked up syringes that had been thrown away, dirty. I washed them with water or I burnt them with a lighter to make a syringe out of other syringes that I picked up. I would make my own syringes because they didn't use to sell them," she explained. "Well, they would sell them to us sometimes, but only in veterinary clinics, already used to inject chickens or little animals in the clinic. We would buy them for five pesos." Susi put her right arm on the table, her fingers running along the thick, discolored mass on her wrist. "These are scars that I have from all of the drugs I did," she said; scars from the morbid instruments she was forced to assemble.

Susi moved without pretense, with energy flowing off of her all the time, chaotic Tijuana energy: shifty, forthright, but also hidden, though perhaps only because I could not yet read the signs. Her mind constantly raced to new destinations, and it was up to whoever she was talking with to fill in the missing steps. "Sometimes I would walk up to the Bordo at dawn," she said suddenly, "or because I lived on the far side of La Línea (the border fence east of the canal), I would walk on the bridge at four or five in the morning." I could see the scene: Susi, exiting a sex club in the Zona Norte at dawn after helping the women inject themselves, intending to find her way home only to be drawn back to El Bordo, the familiarity of the abandoned canal, as she crossed a bridge above. "Sometimes if I didn't have money, well I had to rob someone or something for the chills, for the morning." I pictured her looking down from the same place as my first crossing, where I had scanned the space below from the safety and leather of Argentina's Mercedes. It was obvious that I did not know night work, hit doctoring, and thieving, Tijuana style. I could see why Susi would want to keep her distance from me.

Her fierce eyes were fixed, the tumble of words surging with their own momentum. I had a long list of questions I had prepared that day, a systematic line of reasoning that would fill in the blanks and help me do the work I was here to complete. The interview, though, had gone awry. I was used to talking to people enrolled in HIV studies who were what we call "experienced participants," people who had answered the same standardized questions about their lives to scientists in exchange for money so many times that their patter had been edited down to its bare essentials. Listening to Susi's uninterrupted flow, I realized with a twinge of shame that what we really meant by experienced participants was docile subjects. The conversation was supposed to move linearly under the interviewer's control, the direction as fixed as fence posts hammered into the earth. Susi did not care what I thought was important. I ate; she talked. I tried to interject with Patty's help but it didn't make much difference. Now Susi was running through a list of clubs that had illuminated Tijuana's downtown strip, marking them off one by one on her fingers.

"The soldiers came to Avenida Revolución, to Calle Primera. They used to hang out at a place called La Redacción. El Chicago is still there; El Molino Rojo used to be there but not anymore. They used to go see the dancers or to have sex with the *paraditas* or with the *baquetonas* from El Gusano; soldiers used to hang out there too . . ." I looked at Patty meekly for explanation; *paraditas* were sex workers who stood on the street, the literal translation meaning "women who stand." *Baquetonas* were a different breed: a *baquetón* is a thief, and in Susi's world, baquetonas were women who worked in the sex trade and held up other women.

"Did having the soldiers in the neighborhood make it more dangerous?" I asked, thinking about how hard it is for women who work in the sex trade to control their bodies when they're in the hands of clients who can act with institutional impunity.

"Well, many women got killed in those years," Susi said, referring to the late 1990s and early 2000s. "La Paloma, La Paniqueada, La Osa, La Lobita; those were all my friends. They would pick them up and many of them didn't come back."

"Who picked them up?" I asked.

"Well, men picked them up for a job and then they wouldn't come back." Susi groaned at the memories and then started to cry. Instinctively I looked around; nobody at the taco shop seemed to care about her sudden burst of emotion.

I sat there on the high-backed chair and looked at Susi, processing. So much had happened here, in this small downtown core and in the small parcels of land in El Bordo, the canal, just a few blocks away, so close to the border wall that its shadow loomed over the low-slung walls. I knew about the dynamics of HIV transmission. But what Susi was describing was another epidemic entirely: the mass murder of women.

*

A Greek word meaning "upon the people" (*epi* = upon; *demos* = people), an *epidemic* can be defined as some kind of outcome—like measles, obesity, or frogs raining from the sky—occurring at a higher rate than we'd normally expect. One byword of epidemiology is that even the appearance of as few as two cases of some strange new disease like AIDS can be classified as an epidemic if the expectation is that there should be none at all. The upshot is that every epidemic, by definition, is abnormal until that moment when it has infiltrated a population so profoundly that its occurrence is no longer unexpected. That's when it becomes *endemic*, another Greek word, meaning "in the people," at which point we just have to live with it, like chicken pox in the United States, malaria in sub-Saharan Africa, or cholera in South Asia.

Epidemiology, then, is the exploration of what causes epidemics to form, expand, and either settle into stability or shrink away into nothing. For that reason, it is a scientific discipline deeply tied to what happens in the real world. Unlike laboratory or basic science, where experiments are undertaken in sealed environments and every minute difference can be controlled for, epidemiology tracks the behavior of individuals and groups as they move through their natural habitats. Epidemiologists set for themselves what is, effectively, an impossible task: quantifying how the countless choices, interactions, and situations that a person encounters throughout their life place them at risk of being a victim of an epidemic. The only way to do that is through rigorous and systematic analysis of group behavior. The raw material of epidemiology, then, isn't a beaker full of bacteria or a petri dish of viruses. Rather, it is the behavior of individuals and the clinical changes occurring in their bodies, which are then recorded, turned into numerical information, and aggregated into data on a spreadsheet so that they can be analyzed statistically. In its simplest form, epidemiology is survey work, with scientists asking a set of standardized questions—How old are you? What is your gender? What neighborhood do you live in? Who have you had sex with in the past six months? What drugs do you use?—of hundreds or thousands of people to glean whether those who report certain risk factors are disproportionately likely to acquire some kind of condition.

These standardized ledgers are then mined using a scientific road map that investigates three basic phenomena. The first is the host, which is defined as any living organism that carries a pathogen and, in the words of John Last's *Dictionary of Epidemiology*—the discipline's bible since the 1980s—"affords subsistence or lodgment" to it. While that's a straightforward definition, it can get complicated when the life cycles of pathogens require them to inhabit multiple hosts. Plasmodium, for instance, the eyeball-shaped parasite that causes malaria in humans, first matures within a mosquito, making the mosquito its primary or definitive host. Only after the plasmodium spores have burst out of sacs planted in the mosquito's guts do they travel through the insect's body and into its salivary glands. During this journey the plasmodium parasites become ready for sexual reproduction, though to engage in the act they must first migrate into a human's bloodstream. The eventual transfer of plasmodium from mosquito to human is what makes us the parasite's secondary or intermediate host (though compared to the mosquito, we are the species that suffers the greatest from its presence).

The second is the environment. In the words of the *Dictionary of Epidemiology*, this is "all that which is external to the individual human host." Captured in that broad statement is the understanding that no epidemic arises spontaneously from the interaction between pathogen and host; as with an artist and her paints, there must be a canvas upon which the drama plays out. The constraints and textures of the environment and its constantly shifting form as we move through time create variations in the relationships that lead, inevitably, to new epidemics.

The third and final feature of every epidemiologic investigation is the pathogen: this is the infectious agent causing the sickness at the heart of an epidemic. In its simplest definition (again from the *Dictionary of Epidemiology*) a pathogen can be defined as "any organism, agent, factor, or process capable of causing disease (literally, causing a pathological process)." While viruses, bacteria, and parasites are the most common pathogens, they're not the only ones. Literally anything that can be spread from organism to organism and do harm can be defined as a pathogen.

These three factors—host, environment, pathogen—are known as the epidemiologic triangle because every single epidemic's expansion and spread can be described by their interaction. More to the point, every epidemic starts with a shift in the relationship between the three that has upset an equilibrium and allowed the spread of some fearful new condition. An epidemic could arise because the host population somehow becomes weakened and more susceptible to pathogenic intrusion, because environmental changes lead a host population to come into contact with a heretofore unknown pathogen, or because a pathogen mutates into a more virulent and deadly form. Whatever the causes of any particular epidemic, the gaze of the epidemiologist never wavers from this holy trinity of host, environment, and pathogen. Within that trinity lie the secrets propelling transmission, the key to stopping the relentless spread of infection and victimhood, and the drama of life and death played out on a mass scale.

All epidemiologic investigations start as mysteries. Clues—variables—emerge, allowing epidemiologists to build the theory of the case until they can point to specific factors propelling the interaction of pathogen, host, and environment. That process is repeated over and over until it produces a murderer's row of variables responsible for the epidemic's spread. Steffanie and her team were working in Tijuana to define an HIV epidemic so that they could counterattack and control it. But Susi's scarred wrist and the story of her lost friends made it clear that other dangers beyond the HIV virus were plaguing the denizens of the Zona Norte. How did those dangers fit, if at all, into the pattern of an epidemic?

*

The doleful corrido faded out abruptly. Susi stared at me. She had been talking as if I understood every word, rarely pausing for translation. Just as abruptly, the speakers returned to life with the sound of horns and guitar, mariachi music this time, the party continuing as the clatter of cutlery and plates piled high with big TJ-style tacos ricocheted around the restaurant.

That evening we drove across the busy streets and back toward the red-light district. Everywhere we went competing music—techno, corrido, mariachi, American pop—blared from speakers mounted outside bars and pharmacies, a frenzied jumble of percussion tracking us through the downtown core. Inside the van we sat in muted silence, at one point slowing to pass a police pickup stopped haphazardly in the middle of a busy street in the Zona. I looked out the window at a dozen men being loaded brusquely into the flatbed. A small squad of officers with automatic weapons in hand casually oversaw the spectacle. As we passed, Patty looked over and let out a wincing sigh. In the middle of the truck stood

Chango, hunched over and despondent. He watched us roll by, held our gaze, and threw his hands in the air as we drove away.

*

The goal of every epidemiologic investigation is to reveal a relationship between the factors causing an epidemic to spread, and then to disrupt it. That usually entails comparing the prevalence of an outcome across two groups that differ based on a single risk factor. It's a key function of the discipline, but even more critical to epidemiologic work is describing uncertainty. Depending on how robust the statistical relationship is, an epidemiologist might be comfortable saying that one variable is correlated with another, but only with a certain degree of confidence. When studies hit the news cycle, though, their findings have a funny way of somehow becoming sturdier: a mere association between two variables in a tiny sample of people suddenly turns into scientific proof of a new causal relationship. What such reporting misses is that the true elegance of epidemiology is its capacity to quantify the gap between statistical models and the real world.

Epidemiologic models are just that: models. A model airplane has wings, wheels, and a little cockpit with a tiny plastic figurine inside. We know just by looking at all these components what they are meant to represent: a working life-size aircraft. We can even hold the model up in the air and simulate the flight path of a real-life airplane to get a sense of how the real thing might move in the air. But a model plane should never be mistaken for the real thing. That's why epidemiology requires another part of the story to put everything in its proper perspective.

Statistical models generate associations, but they also generate measures of uncertainty that give you a sense of the spectrum of potential relationships between a variable and an outcome. These measures are most often presented as what statisticians call "confidence intervals." While uncertainty is often lost in the retelling of results, it's more important than anything else that epidemiologic science can generate. Take the following statement, which is based on the actual results of an epidemiologic study: people who drink coffee have twice the risk of developing heart disease. That's a pretty bold claim, and taken at face value means some pretty radical behavior change is in order for those of us who drink coffee daily. But what if you were also told that scientists weren't exactly sure about that relationship—and that in fact (as other, equally real studies have found) coffee might actually decrease your risk of heart disease by half or raise it as much as fourfold? Confidence intervals describe the range of the potential impact of your variable of interest (coffee) on your outcome (heart disease), making them a nuanced way to present scientific evidence with the uncertainty baked in. In this case, the upshot is that coffee might either cause heart disease or be among the better defenses against it.

The overwhelming amount of data we generate has created a scientific shorthand in the news cycle. It's an irony and a natural result of the information age: even as our statistical models become more complex and exacting, the space to explain them keeps shrinking. But without knowing the level of uncertainty inherent to scientific models—how comfortable would you be trying to fly this model plane?—we can't say anything meaningful about our results. We need to know how confident scientists are about their own findings before we can make up our own minds.

That obsession with uncertainty is the reason that, the day after my trip to the canal, I found myself back on the U.S. side of the border in a hotel room in San Diego searching reams of statistical code for errors. Earlier that day, I had engaged in the familiar ritual of academic recruitment: prospective hires come before an assembled university department to describe their work and, perhaps, reveal who they really are. It's typically an anodyne affair, the young visiting scientist earnest and obsequious, the audience quiet and respectful, and everybody withholding judgment (until the prospective hire leaves the room, of course). Steffanie had pulled out all the stops for me so that the presentation would go smoothly. But her husband, Dr. Tom Patterson, a scientist with an outsize reputation for rigor, wasn't interested in a warm and fuzzy welcome.

"Something's wrong." Tom sat at the back of the room, arms folded across his barrel chest, his words without rancor. "Your confidence intervals just don't make sense . . . Why are they all so narrow? Something is making them unnaturally compressed." The thirty or so faculty members and students of the Division of Global Public Health stirred uneasily. Tom was leaning back in his chair, his gray mane flopping over his ears as his head rested against the back wall. Even sitting down, he towered over everyone else. I flipped my presentation slides back and squinted at the projector screen, mentally reviewing how I had constructed my statistical analysis. One slide showed a table of results representing the culmination of two years of research I had done tracking whether the number of needle distribution sites in Vancouver influenced whether people were more or less likely to stop injecting drugs altogether. It was work that I thought might have an impact. The model I had developed showed that a higher number of sites actually increased the likelihood that people would cease injecting drugs, meaning that trying to prevent HIV infection by supplying sterile injecting equipment could go hand in hand with efforts to wean people off of injection drugs. I was proud of it, which made Tom's concerns about the confidence intervals troubling.

What Tom meant when he said my confidence intervals were "unnaturally compressed" was that my model was impossibly sure of itself to the point that it assumed no uncertainty at all. The coffee–heart disease model I described above has confidence intervals ranging from a 25 percent reduction to close to a fourfold increase (written like this: 0.75–3.70, with 1.0 representing no relationship, less than 1.0 representing an inverse relationship, and more than 1.0 representing a positive relationship. Confidence intervals that cross 1.0 are statistically insignificant). My model assessing the impact of clean needle distribution on injection drug use cessation had confidence intervals that looked like this: 1.04–1.05. That meant I was confidently claiming that for each additional clean needle distribution site established in Vancouver, the likelihood that study participants would stop injecting drugs went up by between 4 and 5 percent. That is a ridiculous level of exactitude for a study that included only about a thousand participants. When you are making a model based on the behavior of people in the real world, especially when those people live in poverty and are addicted to drugs, you almost never have the right to that level of precision. Essentially, I was claiming that my model plane was the real thing, down to the four jet engines, first-class seats, grumpy flight attendants, and tiny bottles of wine. I was saying that what I had created wasn't a model but reality itself.

Back at my hotel room later that evening, I listened to drunk revellers walking the streets outside while I lay in bed reviewing my statistical code. The model shone in cold fluorescence on my screen and I searched its architecture for the flaw: Was it the way it accounted for the impact of confounding variables? The approach it took to measuring the passage of time? Or was there something wrong with how it clustered participant data? It was when I investigated this last question that I finally discovered where I had gone wrong.

All of the data in my study came from people who were injecting drugs and who had been interviewed every six months for more than ten years. At each interview, the people answered the same questions, mostly about their drug use and injecting habits. Naturally, every time someone showed up for another interview, their responses were linked to their previous interviews. When constructed correctly, the model should have recognized that the additional interviews were from the same person returning multiple times and adjusted its handling of the data appropriately. But I had coded the model to treat every single follow-up interview as if it were capturing data from a unique individual. So, if someone had shown up for twelve interviews across the study's ten-year period, the model treated them as twelve different people. Twelve different people with identical backgrounds, identical lifestyles, and identical outcomes. I had created an army of duplicates, all nodding in unison in response to the same question. The uncertainty in the model evaporated because all these doppelgängers were answering questions the same way every time, amplifying the message until it sounded like a chorus all singing together when it was actually just a soloist returning for an encore. The error in my code had caused me to drown out the natural differences that existed between people. It was a critical mistake.

The cars sped down Washington Street all night. I was wired and lay awake for hours, my error running along a toy track in my mind, circling, circling, speeding, slowing but never stopping. While it felt good to have finally identified the flaw, I couldn't shake the feeling that I had let the study's participants down. They had been willing to share intimate parts of their lives, and I had been too cavalier with their trust. That night, I promised myself that I wouldn't make the same mistake again. Especially not in Tijuana, where the stakes were too high to produce shoddy science.

The lazy heat started to build in the early morning, and I packed my bags for my trip back to Vancouver and called down to the front desk for a cab to the airport. It was a short ride through the outskirts of downtown San Diego, and as we neared the airport, I watched planes dip down between the skyscrapers, rattling buildings as they came in for landing, a city stunned and quieted every couple of minutes.

Would Susi be making her way across a pedestrian bridge, looking down at the Tijuana River Canal, on her way to work in the red-light district? At the airport, I checked my bag then waited impatiently in the security line thumbing my passport. Would Tom and Steffanie be awake already, watching the ocean surf build along the coast? I wanted to understand their mastery and the science they had nurtured together.

As an epidemiologist studying drug-using populations, I take a handful of factors—for instance, age, gender, ethnicity, and place of residence—to explain seemingly irrational behavior. From this professional vantage point, it becomes easy to sketch out a story about statistical risk and probability that makes the choices that people make seem almost irrelevant to where they eventually end up, swept away as they are by the greater population-level forces at play. Susi and the rest of us take a life's worth of decisions and paint coherent self-portraits, stories that make sense; epidemiologists try to paint landscapes, showing how patterns repeat across individuals. It's an effective scientific tool, but it also makes us limited in our scope of vision, and most myopic when we try to justify our own chaotic paths.

The plane took off and gained altitude then looped lazily around, tilting its wing over the Pacific Ocean, an endless hazy blue outside my small window. We headed south for a moment, free to pass the border wall, and I saw the tensions of the two cities writ large. Tijuana's southern mesas were covered in boxy concrete dwellings, industrial plants, endless traffic, and colorful billboards. The urban mass pressed up against and along the wall for miles in both directions, ready to spill over, the border fence appearing almost crushed under the weight of this frenetic, barely contained latticework. For all the indignities it exacts upon visitors, the unyielding border wall is the thinnest of barriers, and the whole city seemed to be leaning against it for support. I cupped my hands against the tiny airplane window to shade my eyes from the sun's glare. At the American side, the sprawl ended abruptly, evaporating into the desert, with just the diminutive suburb of San Ysidro funneling into a single entry point at the border, as narrow as possible, as if the city were fleeing its Mexican neighbor. The straw-colored hills north of the border were jarringly barren, their sameness juxtaposed against the chaos of the concrete and paint-covered hills abutting the wall from the south, covered in human dwellings without any space left to exploit. The plane completed its loop and we started to head north. I followed I-5 and watched San Diego unfurl itself, expanding into neighborhoods and communities a safe distance from its sister city.

Further north we passed from desert to mountains and then long stretches of flat plains. I kept thinking about Susi's wrist and the way time turned stagnant and deadly in the canal. I thought about my faulty model and the ferocity of Tom and Steff's brains. Down in the Zona Norte, women were injecting with men, with each other, with women like Susi, and—through nostalgia and circumstance—were finding a path back to the canal, spooling the virus from one place to the next, drawing

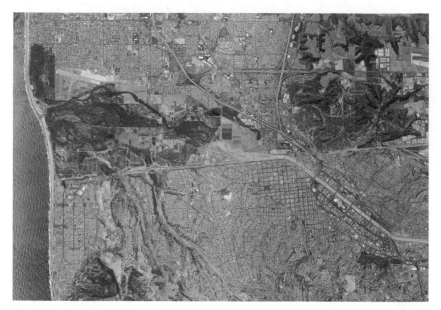

Aerial view above the Mexican American border. (Aerial Archives/Alamy Stock Photo)

populations dangerously close together. There were so many moving pieces to the spread of HIV, and though the culprits seemed obvious, there was a reason that the virus was continuing to spread, particularly among the city's women.

Among the forty or so people living down in the canal, the only woman I had caught sight of was the one moving furtively in and out of the vents along the canal wall. I knew from the data collected to date that thousands of women injected drugs in Tijuana, and thousands more worked in the street-level sex trade. There were more men than women injecting drugs in Tijuana—the ratio was about 65 percent men to 35 percent women—but even so, based on the data, I should have seen more women at the canal; many more. Yes, it was a single visit into the field, so maybe it meant nothing. But maybe there was a reason why only one woman was in that camp, keeping her wary distance from us. I couldn't shake the feeling that at some point there had been women present, and now those women were missing.

The names Susi had spoken like a mantra two days before came back to me. La Paloma. La Paniqueada. La Osa. La Lobita. From what I knew of how HIV moves through sex worker populations, they would all have been at risk of getting the virus. From the little I saw of the desolation experienced by women at the fringes in Tijuana, I figured they would also likely have perished from it. And yet, according to Susi, they hadn't. Though they occupied the statistical epicenter of the HIV epidemic I was here to study, these women had died before the virus could even take hold. Instead, they had been taken away on a job and were never seen again.

There is a term for this situation in epidemiology: competing risks. It describes how an epidemiologic investigation can be hampered when the population of interest dies of some other cause before they succumb to the outcome you're tracking. Susi had given me a tiny glimpse into what appeared to be a set of competing risks to HIV unfolding in Tijuana, and what she said was consistent with what I saw in the canal, where the virus moved freely but women appeared missing before the infection could flourish. So what were the competing risks? If HIV wasn't the primary cause of death women in the city faced, what were the other risks? And could they all be related somehow? The plane shook slightly as we passed through some turbulence. It dawned on me that the spread of HIV I was signing on to study might just be a symptom of a larger epidemic ensnaring Tijuana's women.

Perhaps epidemiology could reveal the hidden structures lurking just beyond reach, like asbestos behind wallpaper. Those structures might manifest as cruel calamities—car crashes, murders, HIV infections—that at face value appeared unrelated. If that were the case, these women were not victims of a textbook epidemic, driven by an infectious agent that could be placed in a petri dish under a microscope. There was another pathogen lurking here, protean and murderous, distributing itself across this border town's strange environment. I flew north but already I was desperate to return, to understand this place, to tell the story of an epidemic that I could not yet even name.

CHAPTER 2

The Price of Something Purchased

The room in Tijuana was white, small, hot. The sounds of the street below drifted in through the window on an endless loop: slow winding trumpets, an accordion vamping, the corrido blaring fuzzily from small tinny speakers, making it sound like a pile of dirt had been kicked over the band. Rosa, the woman I was interviewing, stared at me, flinty and impatient, with thick black eye shadow and raven hair falling past her shoulders. She chewed on her fingernails while she talked, no matter the question, speaking in the same arrhythmic cadence, the words speeding and piling into each other like the beat-up taxis outside, then suddenly slowing and trailing off into nothing. There was no excitement or pretense, just words and memories told one after the other. Rosa was fifty years old. She had about three clients a day. They usually paid her one hundred pesos each, about $6.50.

"Well *mija*," Rosa said to my interpreter, "there were so many clients I used to be able to choose between them. I robbed a lot too, wallets, money . . ." There was no joy in her voice. In the 1980s, Rosa explained, she made a good income and avoided dangerous clients, easy enough when the supply of johns flowing in from the United States was so plentiful. This was a time before the collapse of the Colombian cartels, when Mexico was relatively peaceful and the border hadn't begun to harden like cement. Money still flowed freely from north of the border into the city. Within the base economics of Tijuana's sexual market, Rosa was young enough to attract a lot of clients but old enough to know how to satisfy mature men. The clubs on Calle Coahuila, the red-light district's main drag, were booming. It was a time of excess. "Well, you could find drugs anywhere and of better quality," she said. "There were people everywhere . . . and you could see people pulling necklaces from women's necks, stealing and robbing in the middle of the day, a lot of violence everywhere." Thirty years later, I met Rosa in the field offices of Proyecto El Cuete; she was one of the hundreds of women participating in Stef-fanie's study of drug-injecting populations in Tijuana. The longer Rosa talked, the more I noticed her jerky eye movements and anxious hand-wringing. There was a time limit to this interview. I wondered how long it would be before she needed to find her fix again.

*

Rosa's journey to the Zona Norte mimics the larger path Mexico took as it became home to Latin America's most powerful drug traffickers. Before she came to Tijuana, Rosa was introduced into the sex trade in Guadala-jara, in Mexico's southwest. At that time, the city was being used as a labo-ratory to create Mexico's first modern cartel. Guadalajara in the 1970s was like today's Tijuana, a town exploding under the pressure of migrants from all over the Americas. Mexico's second largest city—La Ciudad de las Rosas, La Perla del Occidente, a hyperbolically beautiful place—is also the capital of the state of Jalisco, a mountainous southern Mexican state that has long served as a key transit hub linking Andean cocaine to North American consumers. The city is far from the U.S. border, nestled near a lake safe up in the mountains, remote and untouched, or at least it was; today the city groans under the weight of violence, the corruption and drug trade powering a cycle of homicides by members of the Sinaloa Cartel and the police, bullets catching innocents every so often. Before all that, though, back in the 1970s, Guadalajara was largely peaceful. There was little to indicate that it would soon become the place where the blue-print for Mexican cartels as we now know them—fearsome, powerful, and utterly cruel—would be developed, in the form of the Guadalajara Cartel.

The Guadalajara Cartel emerged as a power player in 1980, but its formation wasn't an accident of fate or a case of a town simply backsliding into criminality. Guadalajara was chosen by powerful people as the setting for the intentional fashioning of a new breed of criminal organi-zation. In the late 1970s, the U.S. and Mexico were embroiled in

Operation Condor, a bloody military campaign aimed at drug traffickers living in the mountain villages of Sinaloa, a state north of Jalisco along the Sea of Cortez. The mission of Operation Condor was to destroy the drug traffickers' infrastructure and product, and to kill any traffickers they came across; the campaign is remembered for its uncompromising barbarity. While it temporarily weakened the trafficking networks being cemented from Colombia to the United States, it also led to the spread of the drug trade across Mexico's southern states, including Jalisco, which suddenly saw itself becoming a magnet for displaced narcos seeking a home remote enough to allow them to elude the government's grasp.

It was the responsibility of the Dirección Federal de Seguridad (DFS), a famously corrupt Mexican intelligence agency created in 1947, to keep the peace within the country's borders. When the bloodshed from Operation Condor caused drug traffickers to scatter through the Sierra Madre mountains in the late 1970s, the DFS was tasked with finding them and shutting them down. By this time, though, serious mission creep had shifted the DFS from its original mandate—"preserving the internal stability of Mexico against all forms of subversion and terrorist threats"—to dabbling in torture, assassinating journalists, and profiting handsomely from the international drug trade.

Instead of moving against the interlopers, the DFS decided to embrace them as potential assets. The agency's plan, which was executed brilliantly, saw DFS officials relocate major traffickers from the mountains of Jalisco and into the city of Guadalajara, where they were provided resources to collectively form a new organization, dubbed the Guadalajara Cartel. The DFS then aggressively pursued minor players in the drug trade, clearing the field for the new cartel to operate unchallenged by rivals, including Mexican and American counternarcotics agencies. In exchange, the DFS commanders orchestrating the scheme were paid 25 percent of all profits, a sum in the tens of millions.

The formation of the Guadalajara Cartel by the DFS represented the last audacious act in a saga of corruption that had begun decades earlier. The founding of the Republic of Mexico in 1920 and a subsequent decade of unrest eventually ended with the Institutional Revolutionary Party (PRI) in power, where they would stay for seventy-one years. While this continuity kept the nascent republic shakily moving forward, it came at a price. With a perennially weak central government unable to quell organized crime, the PRI chose instead to cut a series of deals with local power players to maintain the illusion of functional governance and keep its hold on power. These deals became the basis for the plaza system, an unwritten agreement between the state and the country's drug traffickers. Under this system, Mexican drug cartels submitted themselves to light taxation and regulation (unofficially, of course) in exchange for broad discretion to traffic drugs. The deal relied on three basic tenets: First, the cartels would limit violence among civilians and in public places. Second, they would never threaten PRI officials. Third, members of the PRI—mayors, police chiefs, governors, even presidents—would get their *mordida*, a bite of the action. While the plazas, or areas, allotted cartels were inviolable, everyone who was in on the action could enrich themselves. Of course, this meant that civilians unlucky enough to live within the boundaries of a cartel's plaza were often dependent on narcos to provide their daily security. It was a hollowing out of state control, and it functioned only as long as all of the actors in the drama—federal PRI officials, the cartels, and local political and enforcement leaders—remained in total control.

*

As the Guadalajara Cartel rose to power, it found its way to Rosa and other Tapatías. *Tapatía* is an old word for female residents of Guadalajara, its etymology lost, though a sixteenth-century Franciscan priest and grammarian named Alonso de Molina claimed that it was a bastardization of an indigenous Nahuatl word. For the Aztecs, Molina wrote, *Tapatía* meant, "the price of something purchased."

"Well, I was like fourteen years old," said Rosa, "and a *joto* [gay man] got me in; he started to dress me and all that. And then he took me into a *casa de citas* [brothel]. He told me that he needed help in the kitchen," she explained, "but the casa de citas was next to the restaurant so that's how I started to work there, when I started to sell myself."

This is the story Rosa tells of her teenage years in Guadalajara's sex trade in the late 1970s. I asked her if she remembered the narcos. "Yes, yes," she said, nodding to me, "they came with rifles over there in Guadalajara; they would go and choose a girl and they would take us whether we wanted or not. They didn't give a shit." It was there that she first learned about weakness and strength, about the cold brutality of negotiation—as a girl, facing men with guns, the price of something purchased being worked out in the back rooms of the casa de citas. It was a lesson that she carried to her decades of work in Tijuana's Zona Norte.

"In Guadalajara, they had guns and they did whatever they wanted with us," Rosa said. "I told one of them that I had an STI to try to avoid having sex with him, and he hit me so bad. So we had to have sex with them. This one time we went to a hotel and I was able to take a glass bottle and defend myself—he wanted to kill me, but at the end we were able to escape."

The lawlessness that Rosa experienced firsthand was a symptom of a greater collapse of Mexico's social and economic order. In 1982, the PRI's endemic corruption eventually became too much for the state to bear and the government went bankrupt. In response, the administration of President Miguel de la Madrid nationalized the country's banks and established strict monetary exchange controls in a vain effort to stop the hyperdevaluation of the peso. When that effort failed, de la Madrid then sold off a number of government entities to raise the capital required to keep the creditors, most of whom were U.S. banks, at bay. But even that wasn't enough. With the country's reserves gone and inflation out of control, de la Madrid found himself at the mercy of an international economic order that demanded free market reforms before it would agree to halt the country's full financial collapse. Out of options, de la Madrid was forced to cede control of the country's economy to the World Bank, the International Monetary Fund (IMF), and the United States of America in exchange for massive infusions of cash.

This decision marked the beginning of the end of the PRI's tenure as the governing elite. While the party would hang on to power until the year 2000, the aftermath of the restructuring and economic controls sapped it of its capacity to govern effectively. That had direct repercussions for the plaza system, which had required a consistent set of players as well as a government powerful enough to ensure that the plaza system's rules would be respected. With the World Bank and IMF essentially running Mexico's economy and new cartels vying for market share, both of those preconditions were absent.

In retrospect, the timing of this breakdown could not have been worse. The U.S.'s success in dismantling Colombia's two major cartels (the Pablo Escobar–controlled Medellín Cartel and its main rival, the Cali Cartel) by the mid-1990s left a massive void in the Latin American drug market. At the height of their power, the Colombian duopoly had controlled the cultivation, production, and export of cocaine from the Andean region, with Mexico's cartels acting as mere go-betweens, tasked only with the final leg of trafficking into the United States. With the Colombian cartels' demise and the power vacuum that ensued, the junior partners in Mexico—recently emboldened through the Guadalajara

Cartel experiment—expanded their operations exponentially; by the early 2000s, Mexico had eclipsed Colombia to become the central hub of cartel power in the Americas.

So, as Rosa was told to put on a dress and walk to the very back of the restaurant, glimpsing the city's violence throb from within the casa de citas, she was standing at the precipice of an epic period of lawlessness. While she eventually found her way out of Guadalajara in the 1990s, ultimately ending up at the border, others didn't survive the city's cruel evolution into a cartel underworld. Enrique "Kiki" Camarena, an undercover U.S. DEA agent, was tortured and murdered in 1985 after the burning of a twenty-five-hundred-acre marijuana farm owned by Miguel Ángel Félix Gallardo, El Padrino (the Godfather), founder of the Guadalajara Cartel. Guadalajara's archbishop, Juan Jesús Posadas Ocampo, was assassinated in the city's airport parking lot in 1993 after sermonizing against the relationship between Mexico's emergent drug-trafficking organizations and the PRI. The official explanation of his murder was that it was a case of mistaken identity, and that the real target had been Joaquín "El Chapo" Guzmán (who was present at the shootout but survived to emerge as Mexico's most powerful crime lord until his capture and extradition to the United States in 2017). But recent evidence suggests that Ocampo's murder was undertaken by a federal police commando unit. The shamelessness of those murders presaged the start of an epidemic of violence that would increasingly target the most vulnerable. Between 1997 and 2015, 1,344 women were murdered in Guadalajara and across the state of Jalisco, those numbers swelled by Tapatía sex workers, their pain scoring the city and emanating across the rugged state.

*

In 2013, the year I arrived at the border, Tijuana had only recently begun to relax again, cautiously, after a sustained spasm of violence that had first flared up in 2008. That was the year when the Mérida Initiative, a militarized show of friendship between Mexico and the United States first announced in 2007, was signed into law. In U.S. president George W. Bush and Mexican president Felipe Calderón, North America had two leaders who shared a common and aggressive neoliberal vision of the future of the region: unfettered access to regional markets, participation in a global economic system governed by institutions like the World Bank and the World Trade Organization, and the spread of democracy through military force. It wasn't long, then, before Bush and Calderón sought to test the limits of that vision by scaling up Mexico's fight against the North American drug trade. Basically, the United States would provide funding, intelligence, and expertise, and Mexico would provide the muscle to move against the country's drug traffickers. But as military operations against the cartels expanded across all of Mexico's major regions in 2008, the folly of the pact became evident.

The Mérida Initiative was billed as a surgical operation to dismantle drug cartels. What the agreement failed to take into account, though, was the scale of the institutional rot that had set in through the plaza system, which bound Mexico's cartels directly to government institutions. That meant that achieving the initiative's objective required no less than reorienting the country's entire political and economic apparatus; ending the cartels meant stopping the crushing weight of a million handshake deals refined to perfection over decades. The PRI had so accommodated organized crime during its intergenerational tenure that, by the time the initiative was launched, the only way to win was by waging war on the state itself.

HIV, once it finds its way into a host, will immediately establish reservoirs in the lymph nodes, the gut, the spleen, and the nasal cavity. While the virus in the bloodstream can be mostly eradicated through a steady course of antiretroviral therapy, viral reservoirs—hidden, tenacious—remain, ensuring that no matter the course of the medication, copies of the virus will persist somewhere within the system. Likewise, the Mérida Initiative revealed the resilience of the reservoirs the cartels had created, and how impervious they were to state power. I would soon find out what that meant for those who lived within their zones of control.

*

After I defended my PhD, Steffanie made me a formal offer to join her group at UC San Diego. From Vancouver, I flew back to San Diego with two massive suitcases bursting at the seams and spent a few days exploring the city, which struck me as an exceptionally quiet place compared to the constant thrum of activity in Tijuana. It was November 2013. Steffanie found me a windowless cinder-block office space close to the Hillcrest neighborhood; it was off campus but closer to the border. I met Rosa in the small room in the Zona Norte shortly after that.

Everything was new. The sun moved through the sky, but the weather was devoid of that inclement waxing and waning that I had grown accustomed to at home. Instead, day in and day out, the dry heat beamed down consistently until the light winked out, after which it suddenly vanished. Cloaked by vast lawns and side streets wider than the housing lots, the desert eluded me at first. The succulents and palm trees that dotted the city, along with the eucalyptus pungent like woodsmoke, appeared like ornamentation next to the verdant green spaces fed by San Diego's scant water supply, grown in defiance of the ever-present threat of drought. And yet for all of the city's concealments, that desert nothingness imposed itself on the urban landscape as a feeling of stasis, lifting rarely only with the rain, which the city drank down greedily in great gulps before returning to its cocoon state.

Prior to her offer, Steffanie and I had agreed in principle on how I would spend my time during my three years of postdoctoral research. Epidemiology is about the ever-shifting triad of host, environment, and pathogen, and the environment in Mexico had undertaken a potentially seismic shift. This shift wasn't the military scale-up of the Mérida Initiative of 2008, but a policy change that was announced shortly after. In 2009, one year after the formal launch of the Mérida Initiative, Mexico was moving perilously close to what amounted to a civil war, with military strikes taking place in every major region of the country. Meanwhile, the country's criminal justice system was buckling under the weight of the arrest and prosecution of thousands of people involved in the drug trade. It was within this context that the government of President Calderón passed a radical new drug law called the *ley de narcomenudeo* (drug trafficking law). Without any hyperbole, the ley de narcomenudeo held the very real promise of ending the cartels altogether. It was one of those transformative policy shifts that happens once in a lifetime, making it the perfect backdrop for a research project at the border.

The passage of the law effectively decriminalized drug use and possession in Mexico. For the first time, it was no longer a federal offense for Mexicans to carry or use illegal drugs for personal use. While people were still subject to warnings if they were caught with drugs, repeat offenders were given the option of entering into drug treatment rather than being prosecuted and sent to jail. It was a radical public health approach based on a model developed in Portugal. Portugal's problems and the solution it landed on amount to an ideal road map for the future of our response to drug use.

In 2001, Portugal was facing a crisis: drug addiction was on the rise, with increasing numbers of young people turning to heroin, which was being shipped in from Afghanistan through new drug-trafficking routes that had opened up in nearby West Africa. A high-level government commission was convened to study the problem, and it concluded that the drug situation in the country had become out of control because criminal law had made drug-addicted people too scared of being arrested to seek treatment. The solution the commission came up with was simple: decriminalize all drugs. Under this new law, Portuguese police would still have a role as a first point of contact for drug-dependent people. Instead of arresting them, though, officers would refer them to Orwellian-sounding Commissions for Dissuasion of Drug Addiction, which would then meet with individuals to assess their needs. The person would then be offered a slew of services including social assistance, addiction treatment, and housing.

What's astounding is what happened next. There was no spike in the use of drugs among Portuguese citizens, nor did drug tourists come flocking to the country to exploit the new lax policy. Instead, almost two decades into the decriminalization regime, the overall level of drug use in Portugal has remained basically the same as in the period before the law reform. This suggests, of course, that of all the reasons people use drugs, their legality may be among the least relevant.

Dig into the data a little deeper and the story becomes even more intriguing. Among young people aged 15 to 24, the use of heroin dropped by about 25 percent in the first few years after decriminalization. Over the next decade (2002–13), the overall demand for heroin addiction treatment dropped by 37 percent, while the proportion of heroin-dependent people engaging with treatment nearly doubled. In other words, more of the people who needed treatment were making use of it, even as the total number of addicted people decreased. By 2008, the proportion of cases of heroin addiction sent to Dissuasion Commissions had dropped 60 percent from 2001, meaning that significantly fewer people were becoming addicted to the drug after decriminalization. Finally, the country saw sustained reductions in the rate of drug overdoses and HIV transmission among people who injected drugs, as well as an uptick in their sense of general well-being.

Portugal's experiences confirmed my own sense about the relationship between drug policies and the dangers of drug use. Heroin is a good example, as it's widely perceived as a drug that carries all manner of risk, especially when it's taken by injection. But if a known quantity of pharmaceutical-grade heroin is injected slowly into the bloodstream with a clean needle by someone with the skills to do it without injuring themselves (someone like Susi, for example), the risk of overdose, disease transmission, abscesses, and blood poisoning all but disappear. If the heroin is also provided for free, people don't need to generate money to buy it, which means they can avoid stealing, begging, grifting, or trading their assets; the violent scramble to satisfy the addiction can be set aside and the work of building a life can take center stage. Yes, heroin is addictive, and injecting it can be hazardous. But it's the ecology of laws around heroin use that transforms it from a risky activity into a variegated set of unavoidable, and often lethal, dangers. Make heroin legal and regulated, and much of what we consider inherently dangerous about it will disappear as well.

That's why I was so intent on working with Steffanie to quantify how the ley de narcomenudeo was changing drug use at the border. We had the opportunity to test a hypothesis that could save thousands from untreated addiction across Mexico, while also potentially ushering in a new kind of public health system that could end the nation's drug violence. Based on the data from Portugal's experience with decriminalization, Steffanie and I hypothesized that the ley de narcomenudeo would cause the risk of HIV infection to plummet among people who injected drugs in Tijuana. With the new law in place, addicted people in the city would be connected to treatment instead of being caught in an ongoing cycle of thirty-six-hour imprisonments, after which they would be released back onto the streets and into the canal. With the ley in place, the police would be disempowered from acting with impunity, meaning they could no longer crush needles under their boots in a misguided attempt to stop people from using, a practice which I had learned in Vancouver only led to more syringe sharing, with rates of HIV infection rising as a result.

In principle, the best way to test the hypothesis was to tap into the Proyecto El Cuete research apparatus, which would allow me to analyze how the behaviors of people who injected drugs in Tijuana changed as the law came into effect. In principle . . . The problem was that when I finally arrived at the border to start the work in earnest, the effects of the ley still hadn't materialized.

Steffanie's office is crammed with framed degrees and awards, alongside pictures of her and Tom on vacation. From early on she had warned me that we probably wouldn't have the kind of "before and after" data that I could use to neatly quantify the new law's impact in Tijuana, because she and her team—and really, the whole country of Mexico—were still waiting for the "after" to show up. We had been having versions of this conversation during scattered phone calls over the previous few months, so I should have known what was coming. But ever the optimist, once I landed at the border I asked her once again about the status of the law. She was blunt. "The data we're collecting still hasn't picked up anything. We need to find something else for you to work on." I offered that perhaps it was just taking time for the law's effects to trickle down to the street; maybe the whole process was still going to reach the people that were enrolled in Proyecto El Cuete. Steffanie shrugged. "Sure," she said, growing impatient. "Maybe. But we've been waiting for five years and the implementation hasn't even started. There's nothing to suggest anything is going to change, and you've only got three years of funding. You need to think hard about what else it is you can look at while you're down here. We have lots of data so don't worry—we'll find something for you."

While I should have seen it coming, it was still a blow. Sure, my research project would have to change, but that was nothing compared to what would happen to the people who were participating in the research on the ground in Tijuana. The ley could have changed their life in the city by helping to treat their addictions, thereby making them less likely to inject with others behind crumbling half walls, jamming a needle into their arm, one eye scanning for the police. The ley would have made the police's daily hunt for drug injectors irrelevant. Instead, Tijuana was going to be as wild as ever.

I left Steffanie's office and walked out of the Institute of the Americas, the home of the Division of Global Public Health. The sun was shining, as always. I stood there and gazed at the beautiful old Spanish colonial–style edifice, built around a courtyard that looked out over the Pacific Ocean. An ornate fountain bubbled genially. I basked in the stillness and stared out at the view, the only sound the gentle splashing on knockoff porcelain, wasted water in the desert, circulating ad nauseam.

*

Host, environment, pathogen. As connected as the three sides of a triangle, and obeying natural laws akin to Pythagoras's theorem—$a_2 + b_2 = c_2$; if you can define two of the sides then the third will reveal itself. If an epidemic isn't spreading because of a change in the vulnerability of a host, then it must either be because of a shift in the environment or an increase in the virulence of the pathogen. In one classic example of this phenomenon, we have a subtle environmental change to thank for the tenacity of the global influenza pandemic (Greek for "all the people"), which most of us know as the seasonal flu. In the mid-sixteenth century, improvements in Chinese farming techniques went through a technological leap that radically increased productivity. The trick was adding ducks to rice paddies, where they would eat the insects and crabs feasting on the crops but leave the grains alone, thereby increasing the quantity of yields. Ducks became a regular feature of Chinese farming life, which already sometimes involved pigs sleeping side by side with people. However, the duck's unique biology makes it a generous reservoir for a vast number of viruses, while the particular genetic makeup of pigs makes them uncannily effective mixing vessels for new viral strains that can then be easily passed to other mammals. Breeding these two animals in close proximity on a mass scale created optimal conditions for the production and propagation of new diseases: with the animals rubbing together in close quarters, it was only a matter of time before viruses harbored inside ducks jumped the species barrier to pigs, where they merged with other viruses into new and highly virulent pathogens—hybrid pig-duck influenza strains that have been tormenting humanity ever since, leading to tens of millions of deaths.

Sitting in my cinder-block office, I tried to follow these first principles back to a solution for my now defunct research project on the impact of the ley. I had been recruited to find out how the spread of the HIV virus (the pathogen) throughout a population who inject drugs in Tijuana (the host) was affected by a change in drug laws (the environment). The hypothesis was that this change would be the beginning of the end of the HIV epidemic: while the pathogen would remain just as virulent, the shift in the legal environment would lead to a less vulnerable host. Under the new law, people who injected drugs wouldn't need to rush their drug use, they could carry syringes without fear of police reprisal, and instead of being forced to use in makeshift encampments along the sloping expanse of the canal, they could be connected to addiction treatment. All of these changes would make them less susceptible to acquiring HIV. But as yet, the environmental change was still only a hope. The lives of those few I had met and the many whom I knew only by peering at datasets that listed their risk factors—homeless, female, uses black tar heroin and cocaine in combination, shares syringes, works in the sex trade—would be as vulnerable as they ever were.

Rosa fit that profile. Susi's friends—all dead—did too, from what she had told me. La Paloma. La Paniqueada. La Osa. La Lobita. Angie. All women, all Tijuanenses, denizens of the Zona Norte, working the red-light district. They were fixtures there until they died, a group of friends walking a daily line between sex, drugs, money, and death, until the moment when they were killed. What surprised me, though, was that their deaths appeared to have come via competing risks before AIDS could take them.

Susi's situation—her entire group of friends, all women, wiped out—was as improbable as it was horrific, but its very improbability put it squarely in the realm of epidemiology. That byword again: the appearance of even two cases of some strange new condition can be classified as an epidemic if the expectation is that there should be none at all. And so, as I thought about the deaths of Susi's friends, I started to piece together a new hypothesis. There was an epidemic in Tijuana propelled by a hidden force (a pathogen that I could not yet define) that was killing a specific group of women here (the hosts); and the roots of this epidemic could be traced back to a shift in the city (the environment) that made the hosts more vulnerable than usual. Without the protective shift that the ley de narcomenudeo would have brought to the environment, this epidemic—whatever it was—would continue.

From this patchwork outline a flood of questions emerged, familiar and systematic, based on protocols I'd learned during countless hours of studying. There were certain questions that you could pose to advance an epidemiologic investigation, regardless of the little you might know about what it was you were chasing. What was the population at risk? How were the deaths of the hosts connected? Was there a single pathogen driving those deaths? If so, where was it harbored? How deadly was it? In short, could the source of the horror that Susi described—in a way that made it seem like part and parcel of a woman's life in Tijuana—be uncovered using epidemiologic tools?

*

Susi had told me that much of Tijuana's predatory policing, the most visible manifestation of drug criminalization, took place in the city's *picaderos*. Known as "shooting galleries" elsewhere, picaderos are abandoned buildings and semiprivate venues where people inject drugs together, shielded at least partially from the ravages of the street. You can find them in pretty much every city or town in one form or another; they're places where HIV and other diseases are transmitted as people move in and out all day and night, injecting with various partners because they have nowhere else to do it. After my first interview with Susi, I had joined her and Patty as they visited one of these sites.

When we came upon the abandoned building near the border fence, its faded footprint was barely visible. At one time it had been some kind of low-level commercial development, perhaps, or a network of small one-room apartments. Whatever it once had sought to be, that dream had died, leaving wooden debris, rebar, and fallen concrete walls crumbling on the ground around me as I followed Patty and Susi through the site's remains. We were steps from the Vía Internacional, the highway running along the southern side of the border wall, each vehicle passing so closely that it stirred up dusty wind from the decaying site. This was Las Palmitas, Susi said, one of Tijuana's main picaderos. She pointed to the highway and with her fingers mimed someone running into the middle of the road and into the blur of the passing cars and trucks.

While it looked to be nothing but abandoned debris, the site was actually cleverly designed to both conceal and protect. There was a natural camouflage afforded by the ruins; if you looked at the site from the street, even if you were specifically looking for an injecting space, the only thing that jumped out at you was the rubble. Las Palmitas was on a corner lot, and Patty explained that the picadero itself, the space where people came to inject, was set back from the street. Piles of industrial waste lay dormant on the site, with a driveway leading up to a nondescript outbuilding. Susi knew exactly where to go. We followed her, carefully picking our steps to avoid broken glass, rusty nails, and the rebar that was thrust up to the sky like cacti. Though I stared at the ground, in the periphery of my vision I was vaguely aware of a man, in his midtwenties, purposefully running ahead of us, deeper in. The driveway ended at a makeshift fence with a wooden gate lying delicately at an angle. Once there, Susi and Patty started calling out loudly. Eventually an older man shuffled slowly over and peered cautiously out at us. Susi, in a boisterous mood, happily led the negotiations and eventually the man let us through.

The driveway continued on the other side of the gate, beyond which it opened up into a stable of sorts, with stalls organized side by side. While we were only about fifty feet from the highway, the interior of Las Palmitas felt like a totally different universe, self-enclosed and deathly quiet, the speed of the cars replaced by the ponderous movements of our old guide and the self-conscious stares of the handful of other men hanging around. There was no roof; it had started out a hot day and had only gotten hotter as the afternoon progressed, and I could feel my skin burning.

Patty and Susi charged ahead, closely following the man to one tiny room set in front of the others, enclosed by a small wooden door and crumbling dusty walls. I followed timidly a few paces behind them. Though there were no windows, cracks of warm light pierced the door's weathered slats, spilling out and evaporating in the bleak sunlight of the day. The man knocked delicately and called softly inside, his cheek resting on the rough wood of the door. There was a muffled sound, and then he ushered us inside while he lingered at the threshold, watching us pick our way through the cramped room.

It was essentially a crawl space, but it felt both larger than it looked from the outside and more crowded. In the far corner, under the light of a bare bulb hanging from a thin wire, an old woman sat in a busted-up recliner, a tabby cat dozing next to her, curled up tightly upon itself. The room was piled high with furniture and trinkets, and crude makeshift needles rested on an overturned box at her feet.

She was ancient, the woman, her face dark and deeply lined like cracked leather, and she wore a thin and dirty nightgown along with a small throw that covered her lap. She moved slowly, almost not at all, her subtle gestures the product of extreme age and physical weakness, or perhaps of opiates coursing through her bloodstream and into her brain. Patty asked her questions and she responded in a hoarse whisper, unable to raise her voice, her collarbone protruding from her thin chest. The man who had led us here stood dutifully on guard, with something like filial devotion radiating from his face. Patty leaned in toward the woman, Susi right behind her, straining to listen though careful not to get too close.

The woman ran Las Palmitas. How she did this, given her dire frailty, I could not fathom, especially when the place was frequented mostly by young and desperate men and women looking for a safe place to fix and the cadres of police officers sent to hunt them down. What happened when the cops arrived? While her clients escaped from their pursuers through the labyrinthine rubble, risking their lives dodging cars and trucks on the Vía Internacional in the shadow of the border wall, this woman would not even have been able to move from her chair without careful assistance.

In response to Patty's questions, the old woman slowly elaborated on what it was that she did here. Clients would pass through this room under her watchful eye, paying the entrance fee and availing themselves of the gear they needed to fix. She made sure there were enough clean needles or, at the very least, makeshift rigs that clients could employ to inject their drugs, and she did what she could to help those who didn't know how to inject themselves. As with shooting galleries around the world, clients came with money or drugs, or sometimes with their bodies as furtive collateral, though the woman mentioned none of that and Patty didn't ask. Instead, Patty mostly just listened, betraying no surprise at the woman's responses, and nodding sympathetically as details emerged, tentatively at first, about the changes she had seen here as the haven's sentry.

Things were getting worse, the woman said, staring vacantly ahead, not once raising her head to look us in the eye. Visits from the police had become more frequent and more vicious since the Mérida Initiative, which had spurred the narcos to enact acts of violence and terror too horrible to fathom. In 2010, for instance, two decapitated bodies bearing multiple gunshot wounds were hung from a bridge passing over the Tijuana-Rosarito highway, the city's main southern thoroughfare. Their heads, one of which was wrapped in baby clothes, were found in the back of a Toyota pickup truck nearby, along with a message from a cartel faction. Two years earlier, in 2008, twelve rotting corpses—some naked, some with their tongues cut out—had been left on the doorstep of a Tijuana elementary school; it was a warning to children, presumably, not to speak to the authorities about cartel activities. These and other acts had imposed a de facto curfew on the city, leaving residents scared to leave their homes or congregate in public spaces at night. For those that had no homes, like the drug users of El Bordo, the violence was harder to avoid.

Las Palmitas was supposed to be a refuge from all of that, a necessary haven in the larger ecosystem of drug running and injecting in Tijuana. Even so, according to the woman who ran it, whose memories of the ebb and flow of Tijuana's violence surely stretched back decades, it was getting harder to inoculate this rough oasis from the pressures of the street.

Like the shooting galleries I knew of elsewhere, Las Palmitas was a pragmatic solution to the basic risk of arrest and violence that people who inject drugs face in most cities around the world. Messy and chaotic, a spot to share needles and so risk infection, rife with violence and other predictable manifestations of poverty and addiction, these were poor places to hide from the dangers of the street but hiding places nonetheless, both public and private, safer than the corner in the short term, but more dangerous in other ways. Shooting galleries have been the subject of many scientific investigations into the spread of HIV because it became clear early on that they were epidemic epicenters, spaces from which the virus could spread efficiently within a core group and then across a larger population at risk. They are not only shelters, but also depots, one-stop shops where people come and go at all hours of the day and night to find drugs and the equipment that is needed to use them. And with many people looking to inject drugs and only a few willing to carry needles, sharing is inevitable.

From the corner of the crawl space where I stood, I peered at the syringes covering the upside-down box lying at the ancient woman's feet, the bare light glinting off the slim steel needles. I was lingering near the door, the old man and me a silent audience to the quiet negotiations of the three women before us. I squinted, trying to figure out if the needles were new or rentals; if this picadero only sold needles, the chances of HIV spreading among its clientele was low. If the same battered and bloodied equipment was rented to clients, even if it were briskly cleaned in boiling water or bleach, the virus could spread exponentially. If things were getting worse for this site and the woman who oversaw its operations, I wondered what that meant for the cleanliness and availability of those needles.

Ten years before I set foot in that crawl space and listened to the woman's hoarse whispers, Tijuana's picadero culture had been documented by field researchers fanning out across the city, who had followed leads down dirt roads and alleyways in nondescript parts of town. While many of these sites were located in abandoned lots in the Zona Norte, others were found in private homes, off of hiking trails in rural parts of the city, or within crevices along the sheer canyon cliffs that ran through many of Tijuana's *colonias*, or neighborhoods. At the time, the researchers found a loose understanding across two hundred or so sites in the city, including shared rituals for access, norms to reduce disagreement, and stable prices for service. One of these was the *sica*, a fee for entry that could be paid in either money or drugs. "The oldest one in the place is the one that charges the 'sica,'" explained a study participant at the time. "I go to a shooting gallery, I put my dose where I'm going to dilute it and before injecting that dose, I have to give [the equivalent of] ten lines of the insulin syringe to the person in charge of the shooting gallery, because he's in charge of maintaining the place, understand?" The coordinator would then sell the drops to other clients or keep them to use.

Like high-end organic grocery stores moving into gentrifying neighborhoods, shooting galleries also reflect the relative privilege of places.

As desperate as Las Palmitas seemed, it was not the worst of the worst: at least this place had doors, a modicum of privacy, a manager of sorts, injecting equipment for sale (or rent), and, in the piles of debris outside, an ad hoc system of safety, like locks on a canal, to keep the regular storms from sweeping everyone up. I knew that there must be grimmer spots, likely not so far from where we stood. Picaderos without even these bare essentials, perhaps just a half wall behind which a couple of people could crouch, a space known only to those that frequented it, its dimensions defined through silent agreement. The boundaries might have been understood as nothing more than a certain distance from a secret spot where a single needle had been used hundreds of times, becoming blunter with each plunge, and returned after each episode to a space between bricks where mortar had crumbled and the police would never bother to look.

But Las Palmitas was definitely not the best of the best, either: there were places in Tijuana, I was sure, closer to Calle Coahuila, with heat and locks on the door, and a polite doorman dressed in a suit, where clean drugs were sold and syringes bought from pharmacies—still in their original plastic packages—provided with every purchase. Places with pillows and even, maybe, ballads by Juan Gabriel, the Mexican Frank Sinatra, wafting from speakers set into the walls. There were, perhaps, girls there too, and alcohol and cigarettes and comfortable beds. Maybe their upscale clientele didn't think of these places as picaderos, but they provided the same basic services as Las Palmitas. All for a fee.

I stared at the gatekeeper, this woman sitting immobile like an ancient fading god on a mantelpiece, and pictured the sica she was given, drops of falling psychotropic substances flowing from one syringe to another, the price of respite from the trench warfare of the street. Patty's questions continued in a slow and patient patter, now about the woman's health; she muttered briefer and briefer responses until she faded completely into the background once again, her mouth clamped shut. She had never once bothered to look up, a habit perhaps learned from years of interactions with men where the intimacy of a locked gaze heralded, more often than not, horror to come. Patty and Susi turned to the old man; he nodded that the visit was over. We left the woman there and headed back out into the sun. There were more places to go.

*

The traffic and sirens of the red-light district bled into Patty's office as Rosa continued to tell me about her early days in the sex trade. She recounted a succession of heightened moments, incident stacked upon incident, each seeming distinct and impossible until enough of them accrued to define the pattern of her life. "I got pregnant after working a while in the casa de citas," said Rosa. Then she met a *padrote*, a pimp. She started smoking marijuana, drinking, and taking inhalants, which she called "cement." The pimp, she complained, took her money. Worse, she said, was the attention. "So all the time we would have issues with the police. That's why we came to Tijuana, but we started to have issues here too." She didn't elaborate. "So I dumped him and then he died, and I stayed here." She didn't mention the padrote again; he was a relic. Her sentences were whittled away to bare bones. Rosa had been twenty-two years old when she came with the padrote here, in the 1980s, to La Coahuila. She had already been working in the sex trade for eight years in Guadalajara.

Tijuana in the 1980s was still America's discotheque, a place to party and enjoy the headiness of the Reagan years, when Latin American cocaine was fueling politics, youth culture, and the breakdown of inner-city communities and Colombia was still the epicenter of the drug trade, far away from Tijuana. In 1986, the year Rosa arrived, *Billboard* magazine voted Tijuana's Oh! Laser Disco, on the city's Paseo de los Heroes, one of the top five best discotheques in the world along with clubs in New York, Paris, Rome, and Madrid. Clint Eastwood, Tina Turner, Neil Diamond, and Pat Benatar all reportedly partied at the club. It even had a slow-jam room devoted to bumping Lionel Richie tunes. Back then, the border fence was just a few rusted rods stretching to the ocean where it sunk into the waves. The canal was just starting to be home to human beings, and black tar heroin was flowing in greater quantities from Jalisco and Guerrero down south. The Guadalajara Cartel was on the verge of splintering, with Padrino Miguel Ángel Félix Gallardo's arrest in 1989 setting the stage for the birth of the Tijuana Cartel, which arose partly from the Guadalajara Cartel's ashes. Tijuana was entering what would become its modern era as a city of migrants, some coming for the day and others for a lifetime, all lured by the many promises of the border.

Listening to Rosa recount her story, I tried to picture the scene. And then she reminded me—it was when she arrived in Tijuana that she started using heroin. In the white room, I blushed, realizing that I had lost track of time and feeling instantly awkward at this breach of protocol. Like her sentences, Rosa's minutes got flintier the longer we sat together as she got closer and closer to her next fix. I thanked her for her time and

Rosa, clearly relieved, grabbed her bag, smiled politely, and rushed out the door.

Left unsaid was an acknowledgment of the stakes each one of us brought to the interview. Rosa left with her memories intact, the trauma of being forced at gunpoint to service narcos sexually and the sheer terror she felt brandishing a broken bottle to stop herself from being raped. Those memories, transmuted into a heroin addiction, forced her to flee the room in search of self-medication. I just left the room and walked away. Epidemiology is no different from other scientific disciplines: at its core, it is a project of the elite. It takes tremendous resources—years of education and grant money, for starters—for anyone to build the infrastructure necessary to undertake well-designed and rigorous epidemiologic research. That scientific architecture is critical to do the work, but it also amplifies the degree of disparity between epidemiologists and their subjects. Rosa fully owned her story; she was forthright and pulled no punches. But the only reason she told me anything was because of her involvement in Proyecto El Cuete, which paid her for every interview. Her pain and trauma were currency used to purchase the scientific discoveries made by Steffanie, Tom, and everyone else who worked here. I belonged to that group now too. Being a white man, a relatively wealthy foreigner, and a person with "PhD" after my name conferred a power that could become invisible to me if I didn't work to keep it in view. I held Rosa's pain for a long time that day but eventually let it go as the distractions of my own life took hold. That letting go was one more luxury I had that she did not. What I did with the currency she and other research participants provided me would define whether I helped to make their lives better or, through my inaction, further entrenched the forces that led to their sickness and death.

Later, after I conferred with Patty about the next steps for my work, Susi escorted me out of the Proyecto El Cuete offices. Out on the street, she hailed a cab and talked in a rapid clip to the taxi driver. "Take him to the border," she commanded in Spanish, "and don't charge more than five U.S. dollars." I got in, the door creaking as I slammed it shut, the thick smell of the city—frying oil, exhaust, desert dust—masked by the musty atmosphere inside. The driver was young, in his early twenties, with a frizzy Mohawk cut short against his scalp. He was wearing the jersey of Tijuana's local soccer team, the Xolos, named after a breed of hairless Mexican dog favored by the team's owner, an ex-mayor and notorious gangster. Up-tempo corrido blasted from the car's sound system while we talked, he in his bad English, me throwing out occasional Spanish words to assure him I understood. We passed through roundabouts, one with the sculpture of a tall indigenous man carrying some kind of spike; the next, a monumental Abraham Lincoln, defiant, broken chains held firmly in his outstretched hand. The driver was okay to take me to the border, he said, but there were such pretty girls in TJ. And my girlfriend wouldn't mind. Had I been to El Chavelas? Hong Kong? El Kun Kun? Had I drunk the beers and seen the girls in there? The girls, the girls, the girls . . . We circled the roundabouts without slowing, the car's drag pulling my body to the center of the back seat, the kid doing his best to keep me from leaving.

I laughed, shook my head, said thanks and maybe next time. He persisted, but only for a moment, not beyond what would set the mood on edge, and then we cleared the roundabouts, I fell back onto the seat, and we took the circuitous road toward the looming border fence, the night air clearing while the fluorescent lamps overhead illuminated the long line of people, mostly Hispanic, waiting to pass over.

We crossed over the canal. Before her job as guide to Tijuana's underclass of drug users, Susi would stop and look down from a bridge just like this one, dopesick and HIV-infected, her path leading from the epicenter of the Zona Norte to the diseased causeway of the canal. The most basic connection between those two places—the red-light district, with women and their clients, and the canal, with people using drugs and the police—was their shared violence. In its spread across the city there lay, potentially, a clue to gaining purchase on this nebulous epidemic.

We reached the wall and I could feel the crush of the border, the vague uneasiness of the orderly crowd, silent and castigated. Tijuana boasts that it is the world's most visited city, with 130,000 people a day crossing south over the border. It is a trick, like the donkeys painted like zebras on the Avenida Revolución, the city's fading tourist drag. Tijuana's daily visitors are really just its citizens, compelled to work on the other side of the border and return dutifully back home each night, obeying the unofficial curfew set by the U.S. Department of Homeland Security. These daily migrants denied the right to stay in the U.S. are used to burnish Tijuana's statistics, as if being forced out of the country you work in each day and feeling the eyes of armed guards profiling you skeptically before you eventually return home could ever be interpreted as a visit to the world's most popular city. The border is a lung breathing the same circulated air every day.

We looped around, the driver dropping me off on a dark hilly inter-section within walking distance of the pedestrian line. Here were small bars, bodegas, liquor stores, churro vendors, and a low-rent art gallery/gift shop that all travelers passed as they made their plodding way through U.S. Customs. At regular intervals, bored soldiers stood with difficulty, chafed by their armor and guns, heavy and awkward. A legless man sang dolorous songs to a Casio beat. All of it, all of it, pressed up relentlessly against America.

CHAPTER 3

The Threshold

On August 19, 1773, roughly three years before America declared its independence from Britain, a friar named Francisco Palou erected a cross on a rock near what is now Tijuana. The cross marked the spot where the domain of the Reverend Franciscan Fathers of Alta California (now the U.S. state of California) ended and where that of their rivals to the south, the Dominicans of Baja California, began. Despite this religious boundary, both Californias remained the property of the king of Spain until 1821, when the newly independent state of Mexico was founded. Despite this political change, Tijuana remained throughout this time as the southern edge of a set of economically integrated religious communities that stretched north all the way to Los Angeles. By 1848, though, when the Mexican-American War ended, much had changed. During the war, the United States had conquered California, severing Tijuana from the Spanish-speaking settlements to its north. The unassuming cross erected by Francisco Palou as a spiritual dividing line became the site of an international border. To survive, the city was forced to adapt to its sudden political exile by meeting the needs of its neighbors on the northern side of the border. It's a task the city has undertaken for over a century. Even as far back as the Mexican Revolution, a bloody decade-long civil war that began in 1910, the city's power brokers have sought to exploit Tijuana's proximity to the United States to drum up business. During the war, it was the city's resident socialist revolutionaries encouraging American tourists to come down to experience the conflict up close. Once they arrived, the spectators were all charged an entrance fee as they lined up to view impending battles from a safe remove.

This northward orientation speaks to why Tijuana and San Diego, for all their differences, have been interconnected for almost two centuries. Until recently, they were mirror images of each other in many respects: in 1990, according to data from California and Baja California state government sources, the murder rates of both cities were roughly 10 per 100,000 inhabitants, which is also the threshold the World Health Organization has defined as marking an epidemic of homicide. In the ensuing years, though, something happened to make the two cities diverge. By 2010, San Diego's murder rate had dipped to 3 per 100,000 inhabitants, making it one of the safest cities in America, with the feel of a city-size resort rather than a major metropolis. (Its sleepiness is nothing new; in 1923, a local business leader was already bemoaning the fact that the city seemed doomed to "miss the train.") Meanwhile, Tijuana's murder rate closed in on 90 per 100,000 inhabitants, thirty times higher than its neighbor, making it one of the world's most dangerous urban centers. In 2017, it would surpass that level, reaching 101 homicides per 100,000, meaning that for every thousand Tijuanenses that lived here, at least one had been killed.

Dig deeper into the specific numbers for women and the epidemic of violence Tijuana faces becomes even more chilling. Scores of women are found dead in the city each year, and while most of the deaths seem unconnected, their cruelty has led some to call it a "femicide" an epidemic of death visited upon the city's women solely because they are women. While usually used reductively to describe gender-based hate crimes, it is an apt way to describe the growing epidemic of death being visited on Tijuana's female population. In 2015, the murder rate for women in Tijuana was 40 per 100,000; in San Diego, it was 1.4 per 100,000. (The magnitude of Tijuana's femicide also dwarfs the numbers in Chicago, one of America's most violent big cities, which in 2015 experienced a rate of 3.5 murders of women per 100,000 inhabitants.) Yet Tijuana and San Diego have roughly the same population and, despite the border wall that separates them, are considered a unified economic metropolis.

That's not all. Fixating on just Tijuana's female murder rate obscures the true scope of the danger women face here. In just one recent year (2013, the last time these statistics were published), more than 1,200 women died in suspicious circumstances in the state of Baja California, where Tijuana is located. Hundreds of women's bodies—often teenagers—have been found bound and mutilated in Tijuana and along the scenic highways that stretch south from the city and down the coast, marking the boundary between the Pacific Ocean and the desert scrub. Most lived in Tijuana or made a living there, even if they died elsewhere. Hundreds more, classified as disappeared, never even make it to the official statistics because their bodies are never found, meaning that the city's official murder rate is likely much lower than the actual number of Tijuanensis women who have been killed. While men are murdered in Tijuana too, the causes are relatively well understood: gun battles and assassinations carried out by the amorphous cartel factions seeking to protect or expand their market share along one of North America's most lucrative drug-trafficking routes. Because women haven't commonly been involved in the drug trade here, their causes of death are murkier. However, epidemiology has a set of tools to parse data like these to find hidden connections. I could be confident that at least one classic marker used by epidemiologists was present here: the pooling of distinct but potentially related harms in one population is an early signal that an epidemic is present, even if its ultimate cause remains hidden.

The epidemiologists' conundrum is that they always arrive too late, only after people have already fallen prey to some new condition. It is a discipline of looking backward to draw patterns connecting the chains of events that we think of as our lives. While we use memories to create coherent identities, epidemiologists use them in aggregate to illuminate how an incipient catastrophe came to happen. Our work follows sorrow like fireweed follows burning forests. We wait until the landscape has been ravaged and then begin to puzzle over how to explain the disaster.

Crafting an epidemic's origin story means moving backward in time, like a cosmologist staring at billion-year-old light from an already dead star. We start with what we can see now: the records of those at risk of infection or those who have died from a common cause, preserved and systematized so that their individual stories, distilled to a few data points and risk factors, become fodder for analysis. It is in some respects inherently unsatisfying work; like the cosmologist, we dream of visiting that star to see its light burning up close. Instead, we settle for a few motes of information on which to base our epidemic's origin story, filling out the details as best we can but knowing that whatever we ultimately end up modeling will pale in comparison to the real thing. Lives become transmuted into statistical models containing a handful of characteristics—a person's age, the fact that they inject heroin into their veins, their home-lessness, their run-ins with police, their deportation from the United States—that allow epidemiologists to make conclusions about entire classes of people and the peculiar host-environment-pathogen knot that has caused them to sicken and die.

Based on the official murder statistics, I was relatively confident that in 1990, Tijuana hadn't yet begun to experience the epidemic of femi-cide that began stalking the women of the Zona and its environs by the mid-2000s. It was a time when both sides of the border were marked by low crime, a casual approach to security, and, consequently, a relation-ship where goods, labor, and people moved easily. Tracing how we got to now—the mass killing of women at a rate four times higher than the epidemic threshold for murder—could only start by going back. And no matter what kind of victim of this femicide I began with   sex worker, drug user, migrant—tracking deaths backward in time always led me to what appeared to be a fundamental environmental shift: the launch of the U.S.-Mexico Mérida Initiative in 2008, which formalized the Mexican war on drugs. It is a war that began as a set of targeted military opera-tions in 2006 when President Calderón came to power, but with the U.S.'s involvement, quickly transformed into a battle with no end in sight.

One of the lesser-known impacts of the grisly national horror unleashed by the Mérida Initiative is the emergence of a scientific cottage industry in Mexico devoted to the quantification of mass murder and violence. Academics from across disciplines—epidemiology, criminology, geog-raphy, and political science—have all taken sides in what has become a defining debate for the country's intelligentsia. At the root is a deceptively simple question: what causes mass violence to spread? One theory put forward by analysts is that Mexican drug traffickers continually push their operations further afield in order to elude the authorities, as if by centrifugal force, thereby setting up violent clashes with other cartels and military actors as they expand. Others see the violence as spreading for exactly the opposite reason: when a cartel becomes powerful in a partic-ular region, the authorities start to harass it, thereby creating a centrip-etal force that pulls smaller entrepreneurial traffickers into the cartel's zone of activity; basically, the smaller players smell the blood of the wounded and come rushing in to carve up the spoils. Others have explained the seemingly endless cycle of violence Mexico has endured since 2008 as a natural outcome of the great quantities of both guns and drugs found in the country; by their reading of the data, the natural product of this statistical function is mass death. It's gotten so sophisticated that Mexican researchers are now the leading scholars on the thresholds beyond which epidemics of violence will expand exponentially and below which they will recede into oblivion. Eduardo Guerrero Gutiérrez, an expert in Mexican public policy and security, describes a "critical mass" of homicides beyond which violence will become self-sustaining. In one of his papers, Gutiérrez graphed spikes in the homicide rate in cities across Mexico over time, each city's murder rate plotted against a fat gray line representing a threshold of murders that, when surpassed, saw violence spiral out of control. Gutiérrez plotted the chaos and bloodletting across Chihuahua, Ciudad Juárez, Culiacán, Tijuana, Monterrey, Acapulco, Guadalajara, and Veracruz, numerating the lives shot down into neat graphs that showed, every time, the violence exceeding the limits of stability and growing into epidemics propelled by their own momentum.

Tijuana holds a special prominence in Gutiérrez's work. In the graph plotting killings in the city, the year 2008 is the axial moment when the murder rate jumps beyond the fat gray line into "contagious homicide"; after that, the rate remains stubbornly resistant to a decline. Gutiérrez's critical mass for contagious homicides was defined as an increase of fifty or more deaths in a short period; Tijuana blew through that threshold

Monthly Killings in Tijuana

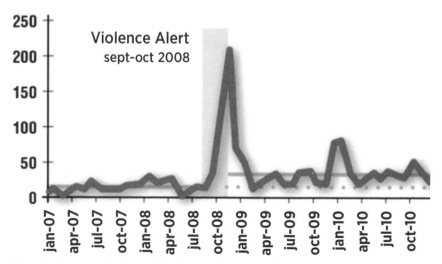

Eduardo Guerrero Gutiérrez, "Epidemias de Violencia," *Nexos*, July 1, 2012.

when the annual homicide rate jumped from an average of 250 in the early 2000s to 844 in 2008, then to 1,257 in 2010, and finally, after a brief lull, to 1,744 dead in 2017.

Though most recorded victims of violence in Mexico are men, women in Tijuana are disproportionately affected by murder compared with women in other cities in the country. Thousands of poor women from southern Mexico and Central America migrate to Tijuana each year in the hopes of landing one of the city's two hundred thousand factory jobs or of finding a way into the United States. Hundreds have been found murdered en route to Tijuana as highways have become the scenes of bloody reprisals by various cartel factions. Other migrant women and children, after leaving homes in Guatemala and El Salvador, have simply disappeared. Since 2006, the annual number of rapes in Baja California has also doubled, which tracks with the uptick in the murder of women across the state; in 2016, over sixteen hundred rapes and sexual crimes were recorded, over half of which were committed in Tijuana.

Most of Tijuana's murdered women are young, ranging from fifteen to thirty-four years old. The bodies, upon examination, reveal multiple causes of death. Many conform neatly to a classification system that has become increasingly refined in Mexico as the drug war has dragged on. Execution: the body presents signs such as bound hands and gunshot wounds to the head (17 percent of murdered women). Assassination: a public murder involving one or more gunmen (1 percent). Levantón: evidence of a forced disappearance prior to being killed (4 percent). Kidnapping: distinguished from levantón by also including a ransom request (1 percent). Robbery: murder as part of a robbery attempt (4 percent). Narco: attack includes heavy weaponry (AK-47s), a narco-manta (warning letter attached to a body) is found, and the victim is connected to organized crime (13 percent). ("This is how all *chapulines* will be left," read a typical narcomanta, which was affixed to a corpse left hanging by a chain from a footbridge over the Tijuana River Canal in 2016. *Chapulines*, the Spanish word for "grasshoppers," is the name drug traffickers give to those who switch loyalties.) Domestic: the aggressor is a romantic partner or family member (19 percent). Sexual: body is found fully or partially naked with evidence of rape, the victim is a sex worker, or the body is found in a hotel associated with sex work (5 percent). Other: alternative causes of death are identified (5 percent). The last grouping— the one that intrigued me the most—is simply labeled as "unclear"; it included 31 percent of the women killed in Baja California in 2016.

Though the information was cobbled together using conflicting governmental reports and online news stories, given the limits of the Mexican state's surveillance systems, there was only one conclusion to make: the rate of femicide here had reached epidemic proportions.

There was another angle to the work of Gutiérrez and others on the killings in Mexico. While their research is focused on a problem with roots in Mexico, it is part of a growing wave illuminating how behaviors, like infectious diseases, can become contagious through social contact. The presence of obese people in a social network, for example, has been shown to increase an individual's risk of being obese; the same applies for behaviors like cigarette smoking. The contagion of violence in Mexico appears to follow the same basic principle. That adds a cruel twist to murder in Tijuana because it implies that its existential horror does not end with the person's killing: once slain, a murder victim increases the risk that those most closely connected to her will have their lives brutally ended as well. La Paloma, La Paniqueada, La Osa, La Lobita, Angie . . . with the deaths of so many of her intimates, I shuddered to think of the risk of dying that Susi had so far eluded.

*

Though Tom Patterson and Steffanie Strathdee started their work in Tijuana in the early 2000s, they had both already been tracking the spread of HIV epidemics for decades. While Steffanie was drawn into the fight against HIV after seeing both her best friend and PhD supervisor die from AIDS, Tom's path was more circuitous. As a behavioral psychologist, he was first interested in animals: the significance of their movement and interactions, what their oblique behaviors implied about a capacity for thinking and social organization. His first stop as an undergraduate was testing the memories of gorillas, orangutans, and chimpanzees, a job he took to support his college education. Eventually he found a scientific home at the University of California, Riverside, where, for the next seven years, he would study—and chase—white-crowned sparrows across San Francisco. Tom would eventually carve out a name for himself investigating how different clusters of sparrows across the Bay Area communicated with one another, with publications in leading scientific journals like *Science* and *Nature*. There is a spare beauty to these early studies, which contain visualizations of sparrow-song dialects across species in the region graphed by a confident hand in ink, the diagonal swipes and short horizontal lines mapping subtle tonal differences in birdsong across clusters.

In practical terms, Tom came away from those early studies with deep expertise in using statistical techniques to analyze behavior, which would prove to be a highly transferable skill. Back in his native San Diego in the 1980s, Tom found fewer job prospects in animal behavior studies compared with work in the growing fight against HIV, which was then spreading primarily among the city's gay men. "At that time, HIV was a death sentence," he told me. "Some people would get infected and they would die in three years; some people would go ten. You never knew what was going to happen." Tom, embracing this new career path, became convinced that without an HIV vaccine, the only way to make a dent in the disease was to start seeing people who had become infected as critical to the fight rather than as victims who had already succumbed to the epidemic.

At around the same time, Tom got an offer from an unlikely player. The Henry M. Jackson Foundation is a quasi-governmental granting agency tasked with managing the U.S. military's medical data, meaning the organization had health records for every HIV-positive recruit in America. In the 1980s, when HIV was still a nascent epidemic, its spread was concentrated enough among military personnel that those in each branch who contracted the virus went to a single location to receive care. The air force and army had sites in Texas to care for their sick; those enrolled in the navy were sent to San Diego, the home port of the entire U.S. Pacific fleet. With thousands of servicemen infected, the foundation needed a first-rate methodologist to manage the reams of data. This was no small feat; the virus's lethality and the military's distaste for controversy meant that it was critical to get the science right beyond a shadow of a doubt. Tom accepted the job, which would set him on the course that would define the rest of his professional life.

From the perspective of Tom's new bosses, the growing HIV pandemic and America's national security apparatus were quickly becoming intertwined. Tom's job was to quantify how the virus might be weakening America's capacity to defend itself by analyzing data from a global survey of all military personnel. The notion that HIV could seriously compromise the U.S. military's readiness wasn't just an idle thought either; as the head of the U.S. Army Medical Research and Development Command put it in 1993, "[HIV] is militarily relevant and will impact on all aspects of the military." In 1996, Tom published a paper using the data from the global survey in *The Lancet*, the world's leading medical journal. In it, Tom concluded that the majority of HIV-positive military personnel were engaging in behaviors that made it more than likely that they would transmit the virus to others. In other words, the data that Tom analyzed confirmed that the threat that HIV posed to national security was real. Not only were thousands of servicemen and women infected, but without a clear strategy an exponentially larger group would soon seroconvert (a term that refers to the moment after HIV infection when antibodies are detected in an individual's bloodstream). The problem, as Tom diagnosed it, was that HIV-positive personnel were using sex to cope with the stresses of being infected within the rigorous confines of military culture. On top of that, the servicemen couldn't gauge how risky their behaviors might be because little was known about viral transmission at the time. Soon after the publication of Tom's work, UNAIDS (the international agency that leads the global response to HIV/AIDS) weighed in, stating that the common practice of posting military personnel far from their families was the single greatest reason for the spread of the disease because it freed soldiers from "traditional social controls," while also causing the flourishing of local sex industries in the countries within which military personnel were stationed.

Tom's greatest insight during his time working with the military was that HIV epidemics could be slowed if HIV-positive people were persuaded to change the behaviors that led to them infecting others. Nowadays this seems obvious, so much so that the global HIV prevention industry is predicated on working with HIV-positive people to retain them in antiretroviral treatment, thereby reducing the amount of HIV in their bloodstream and, consequently, minimizing their likelihood of transmitting the virus further. But in the early 1990s, the notion that people with the disease would have anything to do with its prevention was ludicrous; there was the population of people who had succumbed to the virus and the population at risk, and the focus of HIV prevention was entirely on the latter. "You have to remember that at that time people were afraid that they would get infected if they touched a doorknob that somebody with HIV had touched," Tom told me. "So there was this paranoia—there was a worry that if you identified these folks and focused on them, you'd have a real problem." With stigma about the "gay plague" running rampant, Tom understood that recruiting HIV-positive people into health studies could complicate their lives, or worse. At the time, people who were open about their HIV status were often ostracized from their friends and families and were at serious risk of losing their jobs. Nevertheless, Tom was sure that the trade-off was worth it: bowing to the social mores of the day meant sacrificing lives in favor of the status quo.

Beyond the various moral arguments that surrounded working with HIV-positive people, Tom had practical reasons. Focusing the fight on the at-risk population, he figured, rather than on those who had already become infected meant trying to do the impossible. The sheer number of people who were potentially at risk of HIV infection—mathematically, everyone not yet infected, which is 99.996 percent of the human population—meant that you would be dealing with the whole world. And yet, getting scientists to pay attention to those who already had HIV instead of those at risk of acquiring the virus proved to be an uphill battle. When Tom initially presented his plan to funders at the National Institutes of Health, they balked. It took two years of pressure until Tom and other leaders in the field could convince them to focus their risk reduction efforts on people who were already HIV-positive. Now it's the standard of care.

By the late 1990s, Tom's early predictions about the impact of HIV on military readiness were starting to prove prescient. In sub-Saharan Africa, where HIV prevalence in some countries was cresting at 40 percent of the general population, what was now an AIDS pandemic was leading to the destabilization of governments, a fact not lost on the U.S. intelligence community. In a classified report, the director of U.S. Central Intelligence warned that "African militaries would be severely hampered in multiple ways . . . posing significant security concerns for African states." With multiple American assets in Africa, not to mention American troops stationed on the continent, that call of alarm spurred the U.S. military-industrial complex to enter into HIV prevention in earnest and to recruit the best of the best to carry out the work. "The quote that I was given," Tom said of the military's new research focus on HIV and security, "was, we want senior people who can—I don't know if the word was 'tolerate'—but who can deal with the complexities of international work." Tom fit the bill. But he wasn't prepared to upend his life completely and move to Africa, where the majority of the newly created positions were based.

He was, however, mere steps from an international border. Tijuana, just twenty minutes from downtown San Diego, was the ultimate epidemiologic laboratory: close, convenient, seething with public health problems (made worse by shifting regional economics), and slammed against the world's busiest border crossing. "I grew up in San Diego, and when I was a young person, you went to Tijuana to party," Tom said, chuckling. "It's a bar scene, and you go down there for cheap liquor. There was a lot of tolerance of all kinds of behavior." In Tom's youth, instead of the security perimeter that exists now, the border was essentially invisible, lacking the elaborate fencing (or the distilled paranoia about foreigners that it is meant to radiate). When Tom started making research trips to Tijuana in the early 2000s, he was struck by how lively the city felt. He recalled Tijuana as a bustling place, with street musicians, packed restaurants, and tourists everywhere (including busloads of Japanese visitors who were catered to in specialized bars), many of whom made a beeline for the Zona Norte's red-light district.

Tom's voice was full of affection for the Tijuana that he had grown up with, and it was clear that he still held that earlier image close to his heart. For my part, during our conversation I found myself coming back to Gutiérrez's graph, the red-painted homicide rate spiking in the mid-2000s, rocketing past the threshold of a homicide epidemic. Tom's memories of the city's lively, colorful scenes were difficult to reconcile with news photos of yet another murder victim's body, bearing another narcomanta, illuminated by a camera's stark flash. I would never know the Tijuana of Tom's youth, but his memories attested to the happier, safer city that had existed only a few short years ago, and that might, however improbably, one day exist again.

*

Steffanie had given me access to the Proyecto El Cuete dataset, a collection of numbers that told the story of lives trapped in Tijuana. Blinking on my computer screen like a set of digital blinds, its systematic layout concealed the fact that each row of numbers was another Susi, injecting drugs with used veterinary needles, or another Rosa, trapped in a hotel room as a teenager wielding a broken glass bottle at a much larger man. Perhaps that was for the best; if I could see the face of every study participant, I wouldn't even be able to get past the first row. Better to be a pointillist, making landscapes from scraps of color until the image comes into focus.

In the blinking dataset, women's paths through risk emerged, their lives broken into columns representing six-month increments. The more columns filled in in any given row, the longer the participant had been in Tijuana, unable to leave. Some, of course, did manage to get out or were disappeared; these events, profound changes in trajectory, were represented on the screen as nothing more than a blank cell, inconspicuous in a field of integers bound within identical rectangular boxes. It was the same for those participants who had died. Their trajectories ceased altogether, their deaths recorded as an absence of data.

While Susi and Rosa had given me hints of a social pathogen moving through Tijuana's female population, there was not much I could do with just their two accounts. As compelling as they are, stories are only useful to epidemiologists in aggregate. Journalists use narratives as trail markers, leading them down a path. In epidemiology, individual narratives act like boundary posts, fastened together to create a fence demarcating specific territory. Though the spreadsheets appeared to offer little insight compared with the stories, the accumulation of quantitative data was more valuable to me: it made up the raw material with which to launch an epidemiologic investigation. The data made it clear that there was a hidden force in Tijuana drawing women in and pinioning them within a femicide epidemic's event horizon. That much was evident from the statistics on the last decade's killings.

I wanted to begin in the way that I was trained: with an examination of the pathogen itself. With most epidemiologic investigations, that's the simplest place to start. We see symptoms and can immediately tell what infectious agent we're dealing with: sneezing, coughing, and fever means it's flu season, the virus newly mutated and arriving in our homes just in time for the holidays; shivers, muscle pain, and weakness mean cholera has returned once again with the rainy season. If the relationship between pathogen and symptoms was always that clear-cut, we wouldn't need the sophisticated statistical techniques that power epidemiology. But as humanity interacts across greater distances in increasingly complex ways, we need a science that can meet that complexity and reflect back only the important connections, like an X-ray cutting through superfluous membrane to show the bones holding the body together.

The analysis of hundreds or thousands of cases is how, in the 1980s, when patients flooded emergency rooms with an array of strange illnesses—spontaneous blindness, pneumonia, white tongue, and sudden weight loss—epidemiologists were able to confirm that these vastly different conditions were all related to a common source: AIDS. The game is to find signals amid the noise, like faraway beacons blinking in the night, their shared rhythm hinting at a greater purpose. Once the statistical signals flare up, the next step is to make sure that what you're seeing isn't just coincidence. To do that, epidemiologists construct statistical models that isolate and weigh how different factors impact the spread of the epidemic they're trying to control. When you test the effectiveness of a new drug in a lab, you can account for everything that might corrupt your findings by totally controlling the space in which that research is being done. But trying to account for everything that might influence how an epidemic spreads in the real world is a fool's errand. Real life is just too messy.

So when statistical associations in epidemiologic data appear, you need an intimate knowledge of the environment from whence they came in order to spot irrelevant connections and focus only on those that matter. This key facet of the discipline is part of how modern epidemiology came into its own. In the early nineteenth century, English physician John Snow began investigating a cholera outbreak in London's Soho neighborhood. The prevailing thinking at the time was that cholera was caused by miasma—some sort of invisible gas—inhaled by those unlucky enough to be near it. Snow was skeptical of that explanation because only half of the households on specific city blocks were affected by the outbreak. If miasmic clouds really caused cholera, Snow pondered, why wasn't the whole neighborhood succumbing to the illness? By mapping the pipes of London's two private water suppliers and analyzing the clusters of cholera in households along their paths, Snow realized that the spread of the disease was occurring almost entirely among families supplied by the Southwark and Vauxhall Waterworks Company, meaning that a waterborne agent was to blame. The beauty of Snow's epidemiologic investigation was that he never needed to identify the actual pathogen responsible for the cholera epidemic. All he had to do was identify the risk factor—drinking from the Southwark and Vauxhall water supply—to end it. After this revelation, Snow famously broke the handle off of a public pump on Broad Street, which had been supplying choleric water from a poisoned well, and thereupon ended the epidemic.

The upshot of Snow's story is that to understand an epidemic, we first need to know as much as possible about the place and the people upon which these unexpected outcomes are being visited, even if we don't exactly know what's propelling the epidemic in the first place. And while that might seem straightforward in a lab, epidemiology is inherently an applied science, meaning that protocols and guiding principles can only take you so far. It's when the cardinal rules of the science crash into the real world that things have a way of taking on a life of their own. All epidemiologists, at the end of the day, grapple with the same questions that drove John Snow: Where is the hidden well? And how can we break the handle?

The process is prone to error, of course, and one of the most common that epidemiologists contend with is confusing symptoms with causes. All of us have ideas about the order in which the components of our world fit together; without realizing it we end up moving the puzzle pieces around to suit stories that we've so painstakingly constructed. Did the criminalization of drugs across North America cause the proliferation of picaderos, addiction, and HIV in Tijuana? Or are those drug laws, backed by force, the only thing keeping those epidemics from spreading even further? So far, I was aware of two epidemics pooling together in Tijuana: HIV and homicide. Both were affecting women, with those involved in the sex trade at greatest risk. But beyond that, Tijuana was a blank canvas, the association between the factors I was uncovering still unknown. I needed to learn more.

*

In one fabulist version of the hagiography of Saint George, set during the days of the Roman emperor Diocletian (A.D. 284–305), the soon-to-be-martyred Christian soldier happens upon a lakeside village called Silene that is being tormented by a dragon. The monster has been burning the countryside and slowly killing the villagers by spreading a plague residing deep within its guts. To appease the diseased dragon and stop the plague, the villagers offered it sheep to feed on. When they ran out of sheep, they resorted to sacrificing the village's girls, who were chosen by lottery. Upon arriving, Saint George spies the king's daughter dressed in bridal white; her number has come up and she's heading out into the waters to meet the dragon and her fate. Saint George intervenes, asking for her stockings. She acquiesces and the saint rides out to meet the dragon in her stead, bravely lancing it with his spear before encircling its neck with the princess's undergarment. All of a sudden, the plague-spewing beast becomes meek, contained by the intimate fabric wrapped around its neck, the ends of which the princess holds in her delicate hand, the woman now its master. She and Saint George lead the now docile dragon back to Silene, where it is summarily killed. On that spot, the Silenese king—ecstatic at having his daughter brought back alive—constructs a church to the

Virgin Mary and to Saint George, the dragon killer and plague eradicator. From the church's altar, so the story goes, springs holy water said to cure any disease.

The Hotel San Jorge in Tijuana, named after the saint, is less conspicuous than its heroic namesake. Located on Avenida Constitución on the outskirts of the red-light district, the hotel is one narrow strip of a yellow-painted three-story concrete building spanning half a block, real estate the San Jorge shares with a twenty-four-hour pharmacy, internet café, hair salon, and one of the ubiquitous Oxxo convenience stores that dot the Mexican landscape. Across the street, an abandoned department store, El Águila (The Eagle), sits fallow.

In the San Jorge, as with many of the nondescript hotels in the Zona Norte, scenes of explosive energy play out in a container mostly invisible to passersby. People come and go, often for just an hour or two, sometimes for a night. The second and third stories contain sixty rooms in all, modest and dirty, and free of amenities—no TV, no lamps, just fluorescent bulbs flickering overhead and thick blackout curtains hanging above the windows—and it's a given that like in most of Tijuana, the tap water from the small bathroom unit will make you sick.

But these are not the things most of the Hotel San Jorge's guests remember about their time in those rooms. They remember, instead, the feeling that comes with negotiations of power and submission when the stakes—One hour? One night? A life?—are unknown. Or the peculiar way in which agreeing to a contract—money for flesh—becomes the precondition for violent lust.

"In the San Jorge hotel," Susi told me, "La Paniqueada was killed, suffocated with her own stocking." We were in the El Cuete offices, a five-minute walk away, steps from the red-light district's main drag. La Paniqueada was Susi's friend from her days as a hit doctor, her nickname translating roughly as "The Panicked One." "She used a lot of *criko* [meth]," Susi explained when I asked how she got the nickname. "She would lose it sometimes and pull her hair, her eyebrows out . . ." Like so many of Susi's friends, she went on a bad date and never came back.

I made a kind of noise of disbelief; Patty, sitting with us, nodded sympathetically. I'd seen her give the same look to anyone—be they homeless, dopesick, or just plain confused like me—who could use a bit of compassion. "The sex workers that don't use drugs, they have like a protector or a pimp," she explained, "and they work only in a few motels—"

"—El Caché, El Valentinas—" Susi interjected, naming a couple of Tijuana's high-end brothels.

"—but like, for sex workers who do drugs, they usually go with whoever; so it's like they make themselves more vulnerable," Patty continued. "And if sex workers don't use drugs, they don't go with just anybody. If they see a john that is under the influence or something, they won't go. Others will go to anybody." Patty wasn't being judgmental: these were just the facts as she understood them. As the El Cuete study's field director, it was her job to understand from the ground up what makes some women vulnerable and others able to successfully walk the line. In Tijuana, like in so many other places, having a pimp lends a modicum of protection from the ferocity of male sexual desire.

Susi shook her head. "But it was also the case that many times they were trying to rob the clients, and if they found out, well, that's why they died. Some inside a hotel, others just thrown away." Using my rudimentary Spanish, I asked Susi to show me where they were "thrown away," but she didn't say, and I couldn't tell whether she didn't understand or just chose to ignore me. Maybe her point was that, in a world where women are so often treated like trash, nobody really cares where the garbage is scattered.

One thing that I still couldn't piece together, as we sat in the midst of the red-light district, was how the massive level of police enforcement figured into the femicide's schema. Everywhere you looked there were police eyeing you suspiciously. They watched from cars rolling by slowly or stood around pickups truck awkwardly parked in the middle of intersections with sirens flashing, automatic weapons in their hands as they lazily scanned the crowd. La Paniqueada's client was never found. How was that possible with this much police presence?

With the local plaza system having broken down, street warfare and tit for tat killings were the norm here, bringing an increase in police patrols. Earlier that day as we toured the Zona Norte, we had come upon a couple of angry-looking beat cops yelling forcefully at an American teenager who seemed desperately far from home and, near tears, was trying to explain himself in English; the cops just yelled and yelled and let him sweat. I followed Patty and Susi's lead and kept walking briskly, my head down. It may be counterintuitive, but the red-light district should have been one of the safest places in the city given the virtual panopticon of police surveillance. In our conversations, Susi and Patty made it plain that these types of shakedowns were part of the problem.

"Nowadays, nobody remembers the old-school Zona Norte," Susi complained, laughing. "Before this time, it was a no-man's-land. The police officers didn't have any formal presence here, they would just pass by, but it was never permanent." Before the Mérida Initiative, she explained, the police were here to party too, just like everybody else. Now, everyone came to get rich or go to war.

*

The next chance I got, I asked Steffanie and Tom about how the violence and the buildup of police presence in the Zona Norte had affected their HIV prevention research in Tijuana. "We've each had project coordinators that have been touched by violence," said Steffanie, as we sat in her comfortable office on campus. "One of our project coordinators' father was kidnapped for ransom—and they paid. They didn't go to the police. They said, 'No, that's the worst thing that you could do. Hey, there's heads rolling in the canal of people who have been beheaded, this is the last thing I wanna do; I love my father.' Tom had a project coordinator whose husband was shot—allegedly by the Ciudad Juárez police—when he answered the door in the morning; they just shot him in the head."

"It wasn't just random," Tom interjected quickly. "He was a lawyer and he was defending someone who was in the cartel, so it was thought to be in retribution."

Steffanie nodded. "Yeah, but it casts a pall over every bit of work that you do."

"Everything that we've done in Mexico has been affected by this violence," Tom said slowly. "But so many people have benefited from this work and have gone out of their way to help us be successful."

It was clear that Steffanie and Tom believed deeply that their HIV prevention work served a greater good, even if it meant that some people might be placed at risk of the other epidemics that Tijuana was facing. Again, just like so much in epidemiology, their decision-making was a fine-tuned study in probability. If there was a statistically significant chance that they would be able to prevent someone from acquiring HIV, and if the competing risk of death to those involved in that work was kept sufficiently low, then the research had integrity. Listening to their theory of the case, which they made forcefully, it was hard to disagree, but a nagging thought kept buzzing around. What was the price worth paying to reduce the spread of HIV? If the parameters shifted even slightly—say, one staff member killed—would that end the whole enterprise? Or would the probability of preventing an HIV epidemic still be worth it? I could only assume that Steffanie and Tom had figured that one out; they knew the risks better than most, and Tijuana wasn't their first experiment in the field.

I think Steffanie sensed where my head was at. "These aren't the kinds of things that you think about when you're working on HIV prevention in Vancouver or Baltimore or Toronto," she said. "But we've had to reorient the way we do science."

"People often ask us, 'What do you do? Aren't you afraid?'" Tom continued. "Well, when we go to Tijuana, we don't dress up, we don't wander the streets, we don't go at night. There's a safety protocol for everyone, so we know when someone from our group is in Mexico, where they are, and what's happening." This was the price of working in the laboratory they had chosen.

PART II

The Environment

CHAPTER 4

The Canyons and the Mesa

I sat in the back of Oscar Romo's pickup truck and listened to him banter with his assistant, Jennifer. It was 8:30 on a Friday morning in July 2014 and we were driving west along the Vía Internacional. I watched as the border wall undulated to the right of us as it crested the hills and sudden drops of the Tijuana River Valley. The expanse of brown and green on the American side was a vast watershed largely untouched because of political necessity; the U.S. government protected its open fields from development in order to keep border agents' views unhindered as they focused their binoculars south on various threats. Not so on the side we drove, which had squat houses and industrial outbuildings layered haphazardly on the unforgiving terrain. I was getting used to this road by now and knew where it ended: at Playas de Tijuana, where you could spy the rusty and abrupt edge of the border fence sinking into the waves fifty feet from the beach, the Pacific Ocean lapping at the fence's ruddy iron columns. In the midst of the traffic, which had barely moved since we had crossed over from the U.S. a few hundred yards back, all we could see was the desert scrub, no water in sight.

I was heading into the canyons of Tijuana with Oscar to better understand why women at risk of the femicide epidemic were drawn to this city. My work has always focused on the interplay between HIV and addiction among people dependent on illegal drug markets. Dealers, sex workers, street kids, and people who use drugs; these were my populations of interest. The hidden industries that sustain them also bind them to often inescapable fates. But despite the fact that Tijuana's reputation for paid prurience takes center stage, Tijuana's moneymaking industries don't end at the boundary of the Zona Norte. The reality is that factory work is the main economic engine here, drawing hundreds of thousands of women to the city each year for a spot in this precarious labor force. The factories are a magnet, and though I knew little about how they fit into the epidemic model I was building, they no doubt played a role. It would be foolish to ignore their pull.

Fit and handsome, Oscar looked to be in his fifties, but his tanned face revealed youthful dimples when he smiled, which he did frequently. I'd tracked him down on campus, where he was a professor of urban studies and an expert on Tijuana's maquiladoras—assembly plants— and the slums that ring them. I also knew he led environmental renewal projects in Tijuana, and eventually he invited me to join him on a visit to one of his field sites. I jumped at the chance.

"This is peak time for people going shopping," Oscar explained, his hands on the wheel as he guided the truck along a bumpy stretch of road. "Earlier, around four A.M. to seven A.M., the first shift of people going to work makes it pretty difficult to cross, then it gets bad again around now, and then again in the afternoon. And it's Friday," he added, a day when the cross-border traffic was always worse. Many Tijuanenses who had made it across the border still had family who could not enter the United States. Fridays were a day when thousands would stream home for a weekend reunion. For Americans heading south for cheap liquor or off-label pharmaceuticals, Fridays were also a good time to get ahead of the weekend shopping rush.

We passed some workmen and pylons on the road, and with some exasperation Oscar explained that this was another in a seemingly endless series of road improvements. "This time," he said, "they're elevating the road because it's the lowest point on the watershed and it's always flooded, whether because there's rains or whether because there's a water main broken . . . whatever. They're thinking that this is the final fix, but the design has lots of flaws."

While Patty had mentioned Tijuana's periodic rains, it still struck me as odd that this desert landscape was prone to flooding, and I said as much to Oscar. He waved his arm out the window and pointed south at the canal down below us, where I had gone on my first day in Tijuana. The Tijuana River Watershed, the area we were driving on, he explained, extended as far as we could see and beyond to the other side of the border wall. While nowadays it's dusty and brown, it had all once been a giant floodplain. That changed in 1966, when the U.S. and Mexico jointly decided to start building the canal to manage the periodic water flows that were as unpredictable as they were destructive. By 1979, the project was complete, and while it looks like a scar severing Tijuana in two, the surgery was necessary to bring a modicum of stability to the growing city.

I looked down at the thin trickle of polluted water that ran along the bottom of the canal, four feet across and no more than a few inches deep. "I guess I'm a bit confused," I said. "It's supposed to be for flood control, but the canal is always empty."

"I've seen it completely filled twice in my life," Oscar said. "It's designed for what they call a 'thousand-year flood event,' which if it ever happens, the entire city of Tijuana would be impacted. So it serves its purpose." Though the area's original marshes and tributaries made up a self-regulating ecosystem, they weren't fit to build a city on. The canal reduced the flows and destroyed the watershed, allowing the Mexican government to claw back formerly unusable land from the floodplain's massive footprint. Destructive though it was, it brought investment to the city: shortly after the canal was completed, developers erected a string of hotels and a shopping mall just beyond its concrete walls. Though there weren't any customers at first, the government gave land away to banks, which in turn leased the land to investors for pennies. It was a low-risk proposition that spurred continued development.

I had been so focused on what was happening among the people living inside the canal that I hadn't thought of it as an investment scheme. And looking out from the pickup as we slowly plodded forward on the highway, I saw for the first time a handful of dark glass skyscrapers set haphazardly off of the canal walls to the south. They rose precipitously, architectural oddities isolated from the city. I had never noticed them from within the canal itself.

The traffic started to quicken and we continued west along the route to Playas de Tijuana. Oscar took a turnoff early and steered the truck down the side of a steep hill and then back up another, canyons to our left and right. I became disoriented without the border wall in sight, and Oscar explained that we were now driving roughly due south through San Antonio de los Buenos, one of Tijuana's nine *delegaciónes*, or boroughs, along the Periférico y o Libramiento Sur, the city's main north-south thoroughfare. Much of the borough is made up of one large

MAP OF TIJUANA'S DELEGACIONES (2011)

geographic feature: Los Laureles Canyon, a four-mile gorge starting at about Tijuana's latitudinal midpoint and stretching north past the border fence and into the United States. The road we drove along was hemmed in on both sides by steep desert ravines covered in dusty scrub. The forbidding topography of the canyon meant that San Antonio de los Buenos could only be zoned for industrial parks set amid vast stretches of land, which were otherwise too jagged and shaky to safely build homes upon.

In the distance, mesas atop other hills were dotted with long buildings set low against the horizon. These were the maquiladoras, the manufacturing and assembly plants that have done more to define Tijuana's modern age than anything else. Oscar gestured for me to look and slowed the truck as we passed a small settlement to our left. "This is the typical neighborhood here. This place is about twenty years old, and it's called Colonia Obrera. It started as a place for squatters, and they moved from building with garage doors to solid walls to nice houses. That's the type of evolution and transition that will happen in these canyons we're passing as well." I craned my neck to study the neighborhood. It didn't look so different from other parts of Tijuana I had visited: poured concrete roads connecting low-hanging two-story homes, some of which overflowed with palms and cacti, the whole scene baking in the heat. If this place had started as a squatters' camp built out of recycled industrial waste, the relics of that time had long been covered over.

*

Tijuana is home to over six hundred maquiladoras, the largest conglomeration of these plants in Mexico, employing approximately two hundred thousand people in this city of roughly 1.7 million. The maquiladoras are here precisely because of Tijuana's liminal status as a kind of American appendage, half in and half out of the United States. Regardless of the volume of people crossing the border, which contracts and relaxes at a rhythm set by the U.S. government, Tijuana's deeper economic relationship with America is one in which the border basically does not exist.

Picture it falling away, the imposing border fence one day crumbling to the ground, its dust mingling with that of the desert. What you are left with is the meeting place of two Californias—the one America claimed, once called Alta California (High California), and Baja California (Low California), its sibling, the twin states severed after the Spanish-American War. Since then it has become the place where rich and poor are held within each other's gaze. Tijuana sees opportunity and wealth to its north and is seen, in turn, as a cheap place to do business, located conveniently just down the road. Unlike the city's sex trade, drug trafficking, and tourism industries, all of which are affected by the border's tightening, Tijuana's booming manufacturing sector operates with largely unencumbered access to the United States. That's a result of a long-standing economic free trade agreement that has, along with the city's proximity to the world's richest economy and its large supply of low-paid workers, created a seductive set of financial terms.

The maquila program kicked off in 1965 at a time when Mexico's economy was languishing under the presidency of Gustavo Díaz Ordaz. Díaz Ordaz's presidency is best known for the Tlatelolco Massacre of 1968—during which he ordered the Mexican military to shoot at hundreds of unarmed students occupying the Universidad Nacional Autónoma de México in Mexico City—as well as his decision to dispatch troops to quell peasant uprisings in poor rural areas. Despite his willingness to kill his own people, Díaz Ordaz's longest-lasting legacy is the reorientation of the Mexican economy toward big business, beginning with the maquila program. This flagship project established a system of deep tax breaks for local companies while at the same time bolstering international investment in Mexico's moribund manufacturing sector. It did so by allowing 100 percent foreign ownership of local businesses and by "temporarily" waiving Mexico's value-added tax on foreign imports. The only conditions were that the company doing the importing had to be a manufacturer and the goods being imported had to be quickly exported (hence the "temporary" status of the tax exemption). This meant that international corporations could set up wholly owned subsidiary manufacturing firms in Mexico, ship components into the country tax-free, then have products assembled and shipped right back out for wealthy consumers in other countries. While these incentives set the stage for greater international investment, it wasn't until the signing of the North American Free Trade Agreement (NAFTA) in the early 1990s that what had been an enticing set of terms became irresistible. Suddenly, trade barriers between Mexico and the United States melted away. With the fluid movement of capital and goods across the border, the maquila program blasted off. With NAFTA, not only could international companies manufacture products in Mexico tax-free, but they could ship goods to millions of wealthy Americans without onerous import taxes, thereby satisfying the world's most powerful democracy's demand for the latest dishwashers and televisions. The tax incentives and access to an American market more than made up for the brief Mexican detour products had to take before they were assembled and shipped to market.

Tijuana, given its location on the Pacific coast and access to international shipping routes, is the greatest recipient of the maquila program's incentive structure. Nowadays, the companies doing business here are overwhelmingly Asian corporations. Since the signing of NAFTA, Samsung, Foxconn (a major Apple product manufacturer), Panasonic, Toyota, and a host of medical device manufacturers have all invested in building maquiladoras in the city. Of the forty million or so flat-screen televisions bought by Americans each year, three quarters are assembled in Tijuana. In 2016, the city's maquiladora industry was worth an estimated $5.6 billion, with roughly one hundred thousand women, many of whom are migrants from Central America or other parts of Mexico, making up over half of the labor force. The rise of this manufacturing industry has also spawned a curious interdependency between the United States and Mexico. For instance, almost every single pacemaker sewn into the hearts of Americans is assembled in the plants lining the mesas along which Oscar drove me that day. Without the interlocking trade mechanisms that maintain Tijuana's status as a source of cheap labor for Asian conglomerates while also turning it into a sort of live-in relative with access to the United States market, the price of pacemakers would skyrocket, potentially dooming some Americans to death.

*

In the front seat, Oscar and Jennifer continued to chat unguardedly as we moved off the Periférico and onto a wide dirt road leading into a shantytown laid out in a broad horseshoe pattern around a canyon. "They tend to cluster together," said Oscar, as he pointed to a group of buildings along the ridges of the canyon. "Like, all the aerospace maquiladoras are congregated in one single industrial park, and all the Korean factories are in one place." He paused. "Let me retract what I just said," he laughed, "because there's so many nowadays it's almost impossible to create a cluster for one sector for each industry." Just as in Colonia Obrera, the walls of the homes here had begun as garage doors and washing machines. By two or three years in, Oscar explained, they had been replaced by concrete bricks; windows were probably added in years four or five, the shifting architecture a reliable barometer of a neighborhood's age that Oscar likened to reading tree rings. The slum had been expanding and evolving as waves of migrants arrived from Oaxaca, Guatemala, Honduras, El Salvador, and elsewhere in the Americas. The process was destined to continue, with the maquiladoras attracting newcomers who left their homes because of violence, environmental calamities, and poverty.

While Tijuana's maquiladora industry has expanded since the 1990s, the number of migrants coming to the city far exceeds the number of jobs: over half of Tijuana's population is born in another state or country. Across Baja California, the proportion of residents born abroad increased fivefold between 1990 and 2010; in that same span, the number of Baja Californians who had lived elsewhere five years earlier rose from 15,000 to 58,000. It's worth noting that those are the official figures captured on the Mexican census, meaning that the actual number of migrants in the city and the state could be twice or three times as high.

Jennifer chimed in: "Sometimes the maquiladoras even buy up the surrounding land to rent and sell the lots to their workers, because they're easier to control that way, right?" She looked to Oscar, who was looking for a place to park on the side of the road.

"Right," he replied. "That's the case here. There's a Korean cluster; they don't make the same products, but they're all Korean. And the same guy who owns the land," he gestured to the slum ringing the bowl-shaped canyon, "also owns the school, owns the church, and owns . . . everything. So you see that cluster up there—" I looked to the crest of the canyon before us, "to the left, that orange building, that's a school. And to the right, those white buildings, those are factories. And at the bottom, these colorful houses, they're owned by this Korean consortium. And there's the church, and the church is sponsored by the Korean investors. And most of the people that go to that church actually work for them in these factories. And they exercise huge control over that community."

"So the maquiladora companies take care of their education—" I said.

"—and their spiritual needs," Oscar continued, "their housing, the outlets selling food and other goods, they're also owned by these Koreans . . . the beer outlet. Everything is owned by them."

"So do you work with—"

"—the Koreans? I tried in the past, but no, it's pretty difficult." We were both silent for a moment as we gazed at this space, entirely owned by a single company. It amounted to a fiefdom set amid this network of desert canyons. "They don't need my help." The arrangement was akin to the labor colonies established across empires, designed to maximize both natural resource extraction and the docility of workers. One such enterprise, Fordlândia, was founded by the Ford Motor Company in 1928 as a prefabricated town on four thousand square miles of remote Brazilian rain forest. Intended as a rubber plantation, Fordlândia was meant to house ten thousand workers in a community entirely controlled by the company. The industrial utopia ended only six years in, though, after workers revolted over the food (American hamburgers and canned goods) and the rubber crops failed. The foreign conglomerates running the communities in Los Laureles had, presumably, learned from the errors of past colonizers.

Oscar hollered warmly to some men standing idly on the road. They moved aside so he could park the pickup, and we all stepped out into San Bernardo, this small community in Los Laureles Canyon. The sky was a uniform gray. On the opposing hillside, the squat white concrete mass of the factory pierced the horizon like a sentinel. The high mesa ended at a sheer forty-foot drop just beyond the maquiladora's edge, where the gray rock, scarred by erosion, was too steep even for the hardy desert shrubs to gain a foothold. Underneath was a zigzag of short dirt roads intersecting in a jumble, the canyon crudely terraced like a Chinese rice paddy with low-rise buildings set at strange angles and awkward distances from each other, as if each dwelling site had been hurled there randomly by some force up above.

The dwellings—people's homes—looked to be mostly made of concrete bricks, some of which had been painted a deep red. Other houses were missing walls. I could see a few pickups parked along the canyon's clipped roads, and yet it was eerily quiet compared to the constant thrum of downtown Tijuana—loudspeakers, traffic, sirens, and gregarious salespeople—that I had come to expect when I crossed the border. Despite the city's expanding sprawl, Los Laureles Canyon is still isolated, and the community that exists here remains officially off the books. There was hardly anyone around at all when we visited. Almost everyone living in this Korean-owned community would also have been employees of the Korean-owned maquiladora, and would have been busily assembling products on a twelve- to fourteen-hour shift, most likely making an average salary of about five dollars a day.

Oscar started to move toward a railing, below which the ground seemed to have been carved away. I followed him to the edge and a wide flat amphitheater opened up below us. Some children were languidly playing soccer on its surface, kicking up clouds of thick dust that obscured their movements with each sharp turn. Next to us stood towers capped by colorful bent metal sheets painted glossy reds, whites, and greens; they loomed over the scene and struck me as impossibly gaudy against the canyon's deep poverty. Oscar, a rueful smirk on his face, gestured toward the white-painted wrought iron railing. I looked down and saw that in its center, the metal had been soldered into two words painted in black and red: OSCAR ROMO. And then I realized that not only was this dusty expanse below us manmade, but every part of it was highly intentional: this was Oscar Romo's latest—and greatest—art project.

"We built the park," he said triumphantly as we looked over the edge of the viewing platform and down at the kids playing soccer below. "It was a dump site, so we removed all the trash; we turned that trash into the park, and parts of the infrastructure came from the trash itself. And the slope—" here he pointed toward the scarred cliff across from us, "below that, it was also all a dump site and we removed all that trash." His voice quickened. "We also created a little restoration project with the plants—you see they're all native plants—by trying to extend a linear park from here all the way to the bottom of the canyon that would also feature this type of infrastructure made out of trash." With a smile, he gestured for me to lean over the fence and look down at the slope directly under the viewing platform. Instead of the smooth concrete retaining wall I had expected to see, there were instead thousands of black cylinders filled with dirt and piled neatly on top of one another in three terraced sections about twenty feet high. Oscar explained that the cylinders were made out of the inner linings of discarded tires, which had been carefully separated from waste-tire shells, rolled up, filled with dirt and seeds, and stacked one upon the other. The United States Environmental Protection Agency (EPA) had funded the whole enterprise after sending out a request for proposals to clean up some of the millions of discarded tires dumped in these canyons. It was Oscar who came up with the idea of using the old tires themselves to create the infrastructure to hold them in place.

The EPA hadn't funded this project, impressive as it was, out of a concern for the people that lived here in Los Laureles Canyon. The agency's priority was, instead, the quality of the beaches north of the border. Over the years, the number of discarded tires washing up on the shores of American beachfront communities had grown, and citizens of San Diego suburbs like Imperial Beach, which was located close to the border and populated mostly by retirees, had become increasingly exasperated by the endless stream of industrial waste and sewage seeping north from Tijuana. The cleanup was complicated by a simple topographical fact: Tijuana's canyons—where the industrial waste was dumped, where the maquiladoras built goods for the American market, and where their dependent slums had sprung into being as migrants congregated here to work—were all on higher ground than San Diego. The tires only had one way to go: down.

It is cheaper for American companies to dispose of industrial waste in Tijuana than it is to dump it at home. So Los Laureles Canyon and many other sections of Tijuana have become the final resting place for America's junk—broken dishwashers, out-of-date stereos, old mattresses, and, most ubiquitous, discarded tires. You can see the black rubber everywhere, crowding the slums, millions of worn American tires lying across this arid landscape, semistable and clotted with dust. Car-obsessed California drivers burn through forty-two million tires a year, more than any other state, and they all need to be discarded somewhere. Tijuana, true to form, turned what is an unpleasant by-product of the American Dream into a lucrative industry. Nowadays, the cross-border used-tire trade is worth about $180 million a year for Tijuana, and unwanted tires are either resold in Mexico or disposed of for a fee, no questions asked.

Here and in countless other canyons in Tijuana they end up forming hills and paths of their own or filling deep crags; sometimes they're used as flowerpots or planters, sometimes as building materials. They are fixtures of the land but only until the hard rain comes, which it does a handful of times a year. Then, the water runs steeply off the edge of the mesas, flooding the canyon slums and turning the dust into a slick mud. When it rains in downtown Tijuana, the water is directed into the canal's hollow walls, safely out of sight (except for those living and using drugs inside, who must flee or be drowned). But when it hits the high mesas of Los Laureles Canyon, the rain runs straight down, dislodging the mud and raising tires into the air, thousands at once, great black masses shuttling down the steep cliffs and into the ocean below. The water follows the ancient path of the Tijuana River Estuary, and jettisoned tires spool north, landing on the pristine banks of Imperial Beach and San Diego Harbor across the border, spoiling the waves. On the way, tires float past the rusting security fence where pelican squadrons skim the ocean's foam, along the same open waves that conceal undocumented migrants seeking the United States. In just one recent year, beaches in San Diego County had eighty thousand pounds of waste tires removed, almost all of which came from south of the border. Mexican pollution made of American trash, flowing unstoppably back.

One curious quirk of this cycle is that the sale of every tire in California includes a $1.75 levy called the California Tire Fee, which is paid directly to CalRecycle, the state government's recycling agency. The fee, of course, is supposed to cover the disposal of millions of waste tires produced by California's drivers. But through some bureaucratic wrinkle, CalRecycle doesn't actually recycle tires. The California Tire Fee only covers a small number of expenses: temporary tire storage, for instance, and contracts for private companies to haul and dispose of tires. CalRecycle can only act as a middleman, subcontracting private companies to do the actual disposal. And while there are some regulations on how the private hauling companies with which the agency does business can get rid of waste, the system is loose and many of California's tires—as many as four million every year, by some estimates—end up being resold or dumped in Mexico, mostly in and around Tijuana. It boils down to profit: if you're a private company, why go through the expensive and highly regulated process of tire disposal in California if you can actually make money getting rid of the junk in Tijuana? Over time, that economic incentive has turned tires into a fixture of this city.

As it happens, CalRecycle is not only one of the progenitors of this highly profitable cross-border tire-disposal trade but also the agency mandated to clean up the waste tires that end up hurtling down Tijuana's canyons, into the ocean, and back onto American beaches. Ironically, the cleanup is required only because the agency isn't authorized to recycle tires itself. The northern flow of tires, like the regular path of returning migrant birds, is the final coda on a process that maintains an entire financial ecosystem. The tires keep getting made, getting used, getting shipped, and returning back home to America.

Here in Los Laureles Canyon, Oscar's job had been to find a way to secure tires to stop them from dislodging with the rains. He had taken that simple task and created something elegant: a civic space, built out of the tires themselves, that also secured the entire canyon against flooding by absorbing rainfall through an ingenious irrigation system built into the plaza. And so, beyond the thousands of tires that the structure itself holds in place, when loose tires start to slide they now end up pressed against the amphitheater's bulk instead of tumbling into the creek below. Because the rain is absorbed into the plaza's interlocking cylinders, the water pressure is also reduced, tempering the force that would have otherwise dislodged the black rubber.

I looked up at the towers that lined the viewing platform, the ones that were capped by glossy metal squares. "What are those sheets on top?" I asked.

"Car hoods," Oscar replied. He gazed up at his handiwork, lost in the moment. "I purposefully asked the welder to get recycled metal. It didn't cost me less, but I wanted to make a point."

*

Oscar had set up an open-air workshop next to one of the dirt roads subdividing the canyon, where a local employee was dutifully removing the inner rubber linings from waste tires, rolling them into cylinders, and stacking them neatly against a freestanding concrete wall. As he and Oscar chatted, I wandered down the road; Oscar had told me that it was perfectly safe here, and in any case, nobody seemed to be around. I needed some space.

I crouched down at the intersection of two short dirt roads and considered the small community living here in the canyon. My head was level with the plaza and I could see the rows upon rows of neatly stacked tire linings, each stitched in a figure eight and sewn together in bundles, which peeked out from the retaining wall upon which the kids were playing soccer. What Oscar was doing made sense: he had found a problem and he was solving it. That clarity of purpose was one of the main reasons I was drawn to him and had followed him to this poor enclosed community. As for me, what was I doing, exactly?

On the one hand, my research was about women like Susi who had skirted death or succumbed to it as they were left to their addictions in the canal and in Tijuana's many picaderos. And then there was Rosa and the other women with whom she worked, carving out a piece of the Zona Norte's sex trade to eke out a livelihood, keeping their heads down to avoid the blows, sometimes unsuccessfully. Drugs and the sex trade. Where did Los Laureles Canyon fit in: how were the lives of the women here connected with those others, if at all? I crouched in my quiet place below the plaza, breathing in the stillness, interrupted every so often by a sharp noise above, only to glimpse the edge of a boy twisting at the corner of the field to keep a ball in play, a silhouette momentarily softening the sun's light as it kicked up dust into the sky. And then, as I sat there, the sudden smell of toxic runoff burned my nose: a miasmic cloud was passing over from somewhere up above, off-gassing from the maquiladora. It smelled to me like slow death, the stench of burning plastic and concentrated cleaning agents.

Later, while reading more about Los Laureles Canyon, I discovered that researchers had studied the pollution's effect on local communities. They had interviewed hundreds of people across this canyon, asking them questions about their ailments and the way in which living and working amid industrial waste had changed their lives. The accounts were uniform: people had developed rashes, extreme fatigue, stomach discomforts, eye irritation, and sudden tears, along with bouts of confusion and difficulty concentrating. The researchers mapped the ailments across different parts of the canyon and found that the particular community where Oscar's project was located, San Bernardo, marked the epicenter of a toxic zone stretching across Tijuana and into the United States. Compared to the informal settlements in the rest of Los Laureles Canyon, people in San Bernardo were two to three times more likely to experience all of the symptoms. They were also more likely to be women.

We are so reticent to admit when we are witnessing something truly new. It's one of the ways novel pathogens elude us: they often conceal themselves behind those we already know, the way a tropical frog's patterned skin mimics a larger predator's eyes, when the real danger is the amphibian's poison. When we fail to recognize an emergent epidemic, the symptoms it produces will be chalked up to known causes. Too often, it's only when a population has been decimated that we can finally admit that we are witness to a menace we have never seen before.

The wind carried the sound of Oscar's laid-back voice from up the hill. There were two points of connection linking San Bernardo, with its factories spewing toxic runoff, to the women of the Zona: The first was the pollution itself, which ran down the canyons and into the canal, where it trickled past the encampments of deportees and others injecting drugs. The second was the population of migrant women who lived here and became sick from their work, just like the sex workers of La Coahuila. Were the women who migrated to Tijuana for maquiladora work the same population that ended up in the Zona's sex trade? Was death by toxic poisoning another aspect of this multifaceted pathogen I was seeking, alongside HIV, murder, and overdose? If these causes of death were indeed all connected, then I would need to design a framework to understand how they all fit together.

I could only do that by clearly defining who was at risk. In the language of epidemiology, the sampling frame is made up of the vulnerable population—the people, or hosts at risk of being infected by the pathogen—from which participants are recruited into a study. I always pictured the sampling frame as a bucket on a beach filled with sand: the contents of the bucket are, for all intents and purposes, a good representation of what's lying across the entirety of the beach. Similarly, epidemiologists strive for a sample that is representative of the population they are investigating. What the pathways of the women who ended up in Los Laureles Canyon suggested was that the beach stretched further than I thought, though the same ocean pounded the coast.

As I considered how to construct a sampling frame to identify a pathogen that was affecting women in so many different ways, I was brought back to a study I had once undertaken on another mysterious pathogen: the hepatitis C virus.

If a patient develops fatigue, nausea, or bloating, doctors will often attribute it to stress or an unhealthy lifestyle that can be remedied by better diet or more exercise. If a patient develops jaundice, which is a relatively serious condition in adults, the diagnosis is often a poor diet or gallstones. And if a patient presents with cirrhosis of the liver or liver cancer, both of which can lead to death, there are a number of potential causes a physician might use to explain their emergence: in the case of cirrhosis, drinking too much alcohol, and in the case of liver cancer, simply bad luck.

And yet, all of these symptoms can be caused by the hepatitis C virus, which is among the most protean and unpredictable pathogens with which humanity contends. In most people with hepatitis C, infection results in no symptoms at all, but for an unlucky minority, infection can mean death. And because the wide range of health conditions produced by the virus can be attributed to other causes, for many years they were. It was only in 1989 that the virus was identified, providing a unified explanation for why clinicians were seeing different symptoms cluster in certain individuals. Though identifying the virus was a herculean task that spanned decades, it was just the start of the fits that hepatitis C would cause scientists. The virus's inconsistent disease progression within its hosts makes predicting how it might spread through a human population arduous, probabilistic work. Once infected, about a quarter of people spontaneously clear the virus, though foretelling who will have that built-in immunity is impossible. Among the rest that don't, some bodies have a built-in aptitude to limit the virus's damage, though the length of the reprieve varies wildly, from weeks to years. And then there are those within whom the virus ranges freely after infection, replicating and destroying as it goes, aggressively attacking the liver and ultimately killing its host. To complicate things further, disease progression sometimes includes "reverse transitions": for some reason, after running rampant, the virus may retreat and lie dormant, the body getting the upper hand and forcing the pathogen back into a defensive position, at least temporarily. And the reasons why still remain largely unknown.

In the early 1980s, thousands of Canadians became infected after receiving transfusions from a government blood supply that had been tainted with hepatitis C. Despite the virus not yet having been definitively identified, the Canadian government nevertheless agreed to a payout to those who had been infected. The problem for the government, given the unpredictability of the virus's impact on a human body, was twofold: First, how do you calculate the number of people who had likely been infected by blood transfusions versus other potential sources of transmission? Second, how do you assess the likely severity of their infections? It was an exceptionally complicated task, with financial implications in the billions of dollars. The government's solution was to develop a probabilistic model to predict the various ways in which people who had acquired the virus during the period of the tainted blood scandal might have become infected. Doing that would distinguish those who likely deserved a payout for being infected with tainted blood from those who had been infected by other means. Put in those terms, the choice of who to design the government's model was simple: who better than life insurance actuaries, trained in projecting profit, loss, and liability in exceedingly complex ways?

While I'm not an actuarial scientist, a collaborator of mine gave me access to the model that the Canadian government had commissioned. The results it generated were based on the behaviors and sociodemographic backgrounds of thousands of infected Canadians, which took a massive amount of computing power (the model was so complex and data heavy that it ran on its own servers). I was interested in getting my hands on the data because it struck me as an ideal way to predict how hepatitis C had spread through Canadians who injected drugs. For the government, this group was an afterthought: they almost certainly didn't warrant compensation in the tainted blood scandal because they had likely become infected from sharing syringes contaminated with the virus rather than through the Canadian blood supply. But for me, theirs was the more interesting story to tell. I could use the actuarial model to show the economic cost of Canada's failure to provide care for this forgotten group. More to the point, I could demonstrate that billions of dollars in treating hepatitis C could still be saved by providing people who injected drugs with clean injecting equipment, which could stop them from being infected in the first place.

The modern epidemiologist's go-to approach to risk is the logistic regression model, which is the statistical workhorse of the discipline. Logistic regression models track how one factor (the predictor) influences the trajectory of another (the outcome), while taking into account the contribution of other pertinent variables. These others are described as "confounders," because they influence both the predictor and the outcome, and for that reason they might be responsible for the observed relationship between the predictor and outcome (for example, coffee was believed to strongly predict lung cancer; however, people who drank coffee were more likely to also smoke cigarettes, and when cigarette smoking was added to models, it "confounded" the relationship between coffee and lung cancer, rendering it largely insignificant). At its most basic, the outcome is graphed as a sloping line, and the model assesses how much of the slope is influenced by a predictor. The models I usually build use numerical data aggregated from people's experiences of drug use: someone reports injecting drugs in the past six months, and all of the thrill, pleasure, and anguish that accompanied that act is boiled down to a 1 (or a 0 if they haven't injected in that period). The 1 or the 0 is added to a dataset, and once that dataset is big enough, I enter the data into a logistic regression model to identify connections between particular behaviors and a person's subsequent experiences. Regression modeling is the most common approach that epidemiologists take to understand how two variables are related because it balances simplicity and insight. To pull this feat off, though, regression models make one major assumption: that the relationship between the variables being modeled will hold indefinitely. It's not that epidemiologists think that this is necessarily the case; it's more that we're generally focused on understanding what's driving an epidemic in the here and now rather than projecting how the epidemic might look in some distant future. Statisticians label that approach "deterministic" because it confidently claims that a future situation can be determined based on the current evidence. It's reductive, yes, but there's no sense in complicating matters if it gets the job done. Attempting to model the complexities of hepatitis C, this mercurial force of nature, using a deterministic approach is foolish, though. The virus is just too sneaky and itinerant to assume that its current trajectory through a person or population will hold indefinitely, so you need to instead model the risks and probabilities that influence both its present and future trajectory.

Actuaries, because they are obsessed with risk and uncertainty, do just that kind of modeling. Their models include additional layers of computation outlining how confident the model builders are that the results reflect both a present and future truth. Actuarial models are stochastic (meaning that they assume that variables will act randomly in the future), so rather than just trying to draw associations between events that have occurred, they are meant to portend the many possibilities to come. The actuarial model I was given access to compressed the trickiness of the hepatitis C virus into elegant pathways that tracked the risk that people, once infected, would move from symptom to symptom, from disease state to disease state, taking into account the uncertainty with which all paths unfold in the real world.

Like the best models of disease transitions, it presented numerous routes and accounted for all manner of probabilities. It also followed every single pathway to its ultimate end: death. It was jarring, at first glance, to wrap my head around what amounted to a closed loop. Though people might become infected, and though they might move from a severe disease stage like liver cancer only to see their condition improve to a less severe stage, the lines and the curves of the model inevitably brought everyone to that final stage, no matter what path they took to get there. The model I was given included a diagram outlining this unavoidable truth. I stared at it for weeks as I worked on my calculations, sometimes tracing my finger along the various connector lines and disease state bubbles to try to tease out the variety of ways a person might move through this illness. There were a multitude of intricate transitions that people could make in a life marked by disease, but they all ended at that final bubble marked with a capital *D*.

The model mapped out the potential futures of thousands of people who had no connection to each other except that they had somehow acquired a virus. Though there were profoundly different subpopulations captured within the model moving in what amounted to random paths through life—accident victims who needed blood transfusions, cancer patients reliant on public blood banks, people who shared needles, others who acquired the virus by having sex with an infected person—the model implied that there was a method to link them all together. The discovery of the hepatitis C virus confirmed that they all had been touched by the same elusive pathogen, at which point work towards a cure could begin. But even before the virus was identified, epidemiologists were able to chart these disparate paths toward a common ending.

Crouching in Los Laureles Canyon, this all made some kind of sense to me. All of these causes of death, seemingly disconnected at first glance, were bound together in some way. The maquiladoras attracted hundreds of thousands of migrant women to Tijuana each year, with others like Rosa and Susi coming to the city to make money in the sex trade and its dependent industries. Drawn in, these women either found a job in a factory, quasi-legal sex work in the Zona, or, for the unlucky, an even more precarious future in a darker part of the city's vice economies. Meanwhile, the burning tires and toxic runoff from the maquiladoras on the mesas were slowly killing the women that worked and lived here. Elsewhere in the city women like La Paniqueada, strangled with her own stocking on a bad date, succumbed to the perils of the sex trade, while others numbed pain, sometimes fatally, with black tar heroin. And then there were the police, those uniformed perpetrators, sometimes protecting, sometimes needing comfort, and sometimes exacting violence.

These deaths read like various pathways of a disease, just like hepatitis C. They were all linked to a greater stochastic trajectory sweeping up an underclass of women here at the border. And just as the discovery of the hepatitis C virus revealed that a range of symptoms were actually related to just one infectious agent, identifying a shared pathogen was a critical step to understand the femicide epidemic. Its composition still eluded me, but in Los Laureles Canyon, with my nose burning from toxic runoff, I was beginning to understand how far it might spread.

*

We drove back in midafternoon, trying to beat the border traffic. Oscar and Jennifer were heading to some kind of Tijuana block party so I jumped out and found my way to the end of the pedestrian line waiting to cross over. Since it was a Friday, the throng snaked along the fence, through a cul de sac, and out into the intersection of two steep highway off-ramps, set against each other at an angle, crumbling concrete blocks spilling off their shoulders and into a small triangular park that still contained some tufts of grass.

Thousands of us mingled in an unruly mass as we waited to advance north. The summer heat beat down as I stood, hardly moving, waiting for my turn at the distant gate far up ahead. The smell of cinnamon and frying oil from a mobile churro stand wafted over the crowd; I turned my tape recorder on as I passed the legless man who sang and played chords on an old synthesizer accompanied by a canned beat, the sound coming out of a blown out speaker set at the base of his chair. Later, a couple of young hipster-looking Tijuanenses played acoustic guitar and flute to the listless crowd. My mind eventually went blank and I just stood there, flanked by two *abuelas*, grandmothers, standing stoically as sweat dripped down their brows. I wondered how many years these old women had been crossing back and forth, and how many thousands of hours they had spent waiting to be let into the United States to work.

I stood in line for four hours, eventually reaching the gate as the sun began its slow descent. I flashed my Canadian passport to the border guard; he looked at it quizzically then quickly waved me through. I stepped back into the U.S., the slow bustle of San Ysidro disorientingly calm.

I jumped on a trolley and started moving north. Behind me, on the other side of the high wall, Tijuana was growing, the maquiladoras multiplying. Plasma TVs were being assembled, the canyon slums expanding. Millions of old tires settled into the city's crevices like wasted blood cells, a disease of the land spread from the United States and destined to infect it once again. And down below it all, the deported were arriving in Tijuana—hundreds each day, at the foot of the canal, waiting for the police to arrive.

CHAPTER 5
The Beat

Tom Patterson once told me a story about his first research study in Tijuana. Knowing practically no one in the city and needing to hire a coordinator, he ended up being introduced to a Tijuanensis medical doctor looking to propel his career forward and move up the social scale. It seemed like a perfect match. Tom was desperate for someone who could both navigate Tijuana's byzantine health bureaucracy and manage police interference, while the doctor hoped to burnish his reputation by collaborating with an impressive American scientist. Tom set up some meetings to negotiate a position for the doctor, who mentioned that he was also a professor at a local university. Later, Tom was surprised to find that the doctor also ran a couple of karate dojos in his spare time, and he began to worry that this busy man would have little capacity for the arduous task of doing research in the Zona Norte. As Tom described the specifics of the job—recruiting poor and drug-dependent sex workers, interviewing them about their injecting habits, and managing the inevitable interference by the police—the doctor balked. The problem, Tom said, wasn't so much that he was overly busy but that he "wasn't anxious to rub shoulders with people on the street who were down and out, including sex workers." The doctor wanted to be one of Tijuana's elite, not spend his days being hassled by the police while interviewing women about whether they were enrolled in methadone treatment or not.

The story stuck with Tom because it was quintessentially Tijuana: dig past the first impression and everyone has another job or two, another identity, an alternate path to achieve a scrappy version of the American Dream. As I would learn, this duality pops up like a fractal across Tijuana's many strata, mostly benignly. It's only among those with power that these hidden identities, so necessary for survival here, have the potential to unleash horror.

*

The headquarters of the Tijuana Municipal Police Department has well-washed concrete walls and circular pillars holding its squat structure in place. The day I visited in November 2014, the mood was relaxed and casual—once I'd passed through the security checkpoints—with officers standing around and chatting at brightly lit cubicles, offering friendly nods and smiles as I was ushered by. I was there to meet Victor Alaniz—the head statistician of the department and a thirty-one-year veteran of the force, fifteen of which were spent on the street—and his colleague, Arnulfo Bañuelos, a senior police commander who everyone called "Contador," or "Accountant." Through an interpreter, I ended up telling him Tom's story of the dojo-owning doctor, and he smiled wanly. To Alaniz, the story of someone playing more than one role was familiar: it was just a thing that living in Tijuana did to your soul. In the world that Alaniz and Bañuelos inhabit, though, the slide into duality is a whole lot more menacing than holding karate classes at night. "It's a local problem, one that everyone knows about," Alaniz said. "When you live in a city where you have cousins, uncles, grandmothers, mothers-in-law, brothers-in-law, more than one of them is going to be involved in some bad stuff. When the police are friends with the thugs, when the thugs work within the police, that becomes very common, until it explodes."

Alaniz said something under his breath and Bañuelos opened up a small laptop, preloaded with a PowerPoint presentation titled "Tijuana: Ciudad con Orden" (Tijuana: city with order). The title struck me as more an aspiration than a reality given the spasms of violence that had rocked the city over the past few years and the thousands of people who regularly injected drugs in the canal and other semipublic places. Bañuelos gestured for me to pull my chair up and he swiveled the laptop around on his big oak desk, both of us hunched over as he delivered a rote presentation while tracing the words on the small screen with his thick fingers. I looked up for a moment to take in my surroundings. Bañuelos's office was big and tidy, with a large thick-backed laminated poster of Tijuana on the far wall with fat red arrows drawn on top and the names of some of the city's delegaciónes scrawled in marker with an impatient hand—Playas (the beaches), La Mesa (flats), Centro (downtown; where the Zona Norte and the canal/El Bordo are located), Otay (east Tijuana), Presa and Presa Rural (two delegaciónes on the eastern fringes of the city), and San Antonio de los Buenos (the canyon-filled borough where I had traveled to visit Oscar's art piece).

Like Alaniz, who had pulled up a chair beside me, Bañuelos was a longtime member of the police force. They were both on the ground when Tijuana's cozy relationship with the cartels exploded in the mid-2000s after the PRI was ousted from power and the final collapse of the plaza system took place. Bañuelos gestured for me to look at the computer again, where he had pulled up a slide with a graph of violent crimes in Tijuana. The number rose dramatically after 2008, when President Calderón had launched the Mérida Initiative, which formalized and expanded the drug war that he had begun waging upon taking office in 2006. Eight years later, its main objective—to weaken the country's drug cartels by military force—had been an abject failure. Tijuana, in particular, had seen no measurable decrease in drug-related activity, while violence had skyrocketed as the initiative transformed into a brutal drug war. I had assumed that police officers like Bañuelos and Alaniz would agree with that assessment, given that they were on the beat when the war was at its bloodiest. To my surprise, they saw things differently. When I politely interrupted Contador Bañuelos's presentation to ask him what Tijuana was like during those days, he didn't hesitate. "How was the city doing? In 2006, in Tijuana, kidnappings exceeded one hundred sixty. Now, in a bad year it doesn't reach thirty. For example, this is going to be a bad year, and we are going to have around thirty or thirty-two kidnappings." Later, I checked Baja California's statistics, which contradicted Bañuelos's claim. That didn't mean he was lying or incorrect; government statistics in Mexico are notoriously unreliable. For what it's worth, though, in 2014, the year I met him and Alaniz, 32 kidnappings were officially recorded in Tijuana. In 2006, the year President Calderón took power, the number was about the same: 30 kidnappings. In the interim, though, the annual number had seesawed: in 2007, it dropped to 14. But the year after that—2008, when the Mérida Initiative was launched—kidnappings spiked to 92.

Bañuelos returned to the PowerPoint and a slide of mug shots materialized. "This is what you saw back then: organized crime, common crime, criminals acting with impunity," he told me. He flipped to a new slide. This time, the slide showed rows upon rows of clean-cut faces interspersed with press shots of men being led away in handcuffs by heavily armored police, many hiding their faces from the camera. I asked the contador who the faces in the rows were. He paused, pursing his lips, then looked at me sternly: "The main commanders of this institution."

Beginning in 2000, Bañuelos explained, the usual corruption of the Tijuana Municipal Police Department became so extreme that the department was twisted beyond recognition. "You used to watch the director as he brought ten people into the police academy one day, and then the next day they would be in uniform and armed," Bañuelos said. Some— the faces he showed me—had even been placed in positions overseeing the police department's command structures. At that time, Bañuelos and Alaniz could only quietly bear witness as the corruption turned their department into a platoon of cartel-controlled mercenaries.

The infiltration of the department by corrupt recruits reached its peak during the 2004–7 mayoralty of Jorge Hank Rhon, Tijuana's flamboyant casino magnate and a longtime shady political operator. "In Hank's administration, that's when the collision begins, cops killing cops," Alaniz explained. "Because they were no longer even cops—that is, you had bad cops killing good cops, sí?" While this bubbling intrapolice violence was a sign that the old order afforded by the PRI had crumbled for good, in hindsight it also represented a tipping point. It wasn't that average Tijuanenses suddenly believed it possible to eradicate the graft that had long ago become inseparable from the city's basic functions. But even here, on the very furthest fringes of the Mexican state, at the border of two poorly matched empires, there was a limit to what the city would tolerate. This was a monumental shift, because for decades there had only been a few lonely voices challenging the status quo.

The most notable dissenter was *Zeta*, a fierce and sensational weekly magazine that made its bread and butter by publishing biographical information about gang members in an effort to publicly shame them. The magazine sometimes even included photos of suspected narcos, which was very risky given the climate of fear the Mexican cartels had created to silence journalists. In 2017, for instance, Mexico was ranked the most dangerous country in the world for journalists, edging out Syria and Iraq.

Zeta's favorite target was Jorge Hank Rhon. Aside from his tenure as mayor, Hank is also the owner of Grupo Caliente, Mexico's biggest sports-betting company, along with the Agua Caliente greyhound racetrack (the last remnant of the famed Agua Caliente casino grounds in Tijuana), and the Club Tijuana Xoloitzcuintles de Caliente, Tijuana's soccer club. The Xoloitzcuintles, or Xolos, are named after a type of Mexican dog; after buying the team, Hank had a vest made out of Xolo skin. This was not out of character. He regularly boasted about having a menagerie of twenty thousand exotic animals and claimed to have had a bespoke jacket made from the skin of donkey penises. Since the 1980s, Hank has been pursued by allegations of criminal behavior. True to form, one of his charges came when he tried to traffic a Siberian white tiger cub across the border from San Diego in the back seat of a car.

In 2009, confidential diplomatic cables from the U.S. consulate in Tijuana (later released by Wikileaks) stated, "Hank is widely believed to have been a corrupt mayor and to be still involved in narco-trafficking." The cable, with the subject heading "Law Enforcement High Jinks in TJ," was sent after consular officials watched helplessly as a drug trafficker exiting the consulate evaded a planned capture by local police and was instead taken away by men in uniforms driving a black Ford Crown Victoria, the usual vehicle for undercover law enforcement operations in Tijuana. The local police gave chase but refused to follow once the car entered the parking lot of Hank's Agua Caliente racetrack. When asked why, the police told consul officials that they simply "could not enter" Hank's compound.

The police had their reasons: in 1988, journalist and *Zeta* co-founder Héctor Félix Miranda, an unrelenting critic of Hank, was shot and killed while waiting in traffic on his way to work. Two security guards from the Agua Caliente racetrack, one of whom was Hank's personal bodyguard, confessed to the killings, though one of them would later recant, saying that he had been tortured into a false confession. For more than twenty-five years, *Zeta* has run the same full-page ad each week, personally addressed to Hank. It features a photo of Héctor Félix Miranda locking eyes with the reader, his finger pointing accusingly. Around the photo, the following text appears: "Jorge Hank Rhon: Why did your bodyguard Antonio Vera Palestina kill me?"

By 2006, two years into Hank's mayoralty, the cartels had so deeply infiltrated Tijuana's echelons of power that nobody quite knew how far their influence extended. When President Calderón announced the following year that the military fight against the cartels was to be scaled up, the first mission for Bañuelos, Alaniz, and the other "good cops" was to figure out who among their ranks had been compromised. To do so, the department was put under the command of a well-known human rights advocate named Jesús Alberto Capella Ibarra, along with a hard-nosed military officer named Julián Leyzaola. While Capella Ibarra had no policing experience, he was one of the few civic leaders brave enough to organize public rallies in Tijuana to denounce the cartels. Leyzaola, for his part, had a reputation as a dispassionate and ruthless military commander. Under their joint leadership, the newly empowered police department quietly went to work. By digging into officers' files and cross-referencing what they found with information provided by captured cartel members, the police department began to get an idea of how deep the infiltration of their organization went. "Before, policemen were bought. Now, the bad guys were inside of the police force," Alaniz remembered. "But it wasn't an open war. It wasn't public."

It soon would be. On November 12, 2008, the Tijuana Municipal Police Department announced the arrest of twenty-one of their own officers for suspicion of involvement with the Tijuana Cartel. Another one hundred officers were fired. Later that year, five hundred more officers were sent back to the police academy for training and background checks. All in all, this totaled more than a quarter of the entire twenty-two-hundred-member force. It was an unprecedented move in Tijuana, where collusion with the cartels was so long-standing that it seemed impossible for the cycle of corruption to ever be broken.

The mission was hailed as a success. But the day that the initial wave of arrests was announced on Mexican television, the Tijuana Cartel sent a simple message. Bañuelos remembered it well: "Kill every cop you run into." By the end of that first night, seven police officers had been murdered. Over the next few weeks, forty-six officers would be killed by the cartel in retribution for the internal investigation—more than double the number of corrupt cops that had been arrested in the first place. After a high-ranking officer was shot dead as he slept, along with his wife and their eleven-year-old daughter, officers began hiding their faces behind balaclavas during press conferences in fear of reprisals against their own families. On December 1, 2008, less than three weeks after the initial arrests, Capella Ibarra was fired, ostensibly for failing to rein in violence, and Leyzaola took over his duties.

Bañuelos claims that the deaths and dismissals were worth it, and that in the space of a few short years, the police were able to seriously weaken the Tijuana Cartel, mostly by arresting its senior leadership. But doing so meant pushing the city into what amounted to civil war, with Tijuana becoming a prime example of what those Mexican criminologists were talking about when they described the ballooning of violence through centripetal force. As the Arellano Félix Organization (named for the five brothers that ran it, who are also the nephews of the founder of the Guadalajara Cartel, Miguel Angel Félix Gallardo) took over the remnants of the Tijuana Cartel, it attracted the Sinaloa Cartel (run by Joaquín "El Chapo" Guzmán), which subsequently moved north to challenge for the Tijuana plaza just as the old order was dissolving. The Sinaloans weren't alone, though: tempted by the chaos, the ascendant Cartel Jalisco Nueva Generación (another cartel originally based in Mexico's southwest) also tried their luck, probing for weaknesses and bringing even more chaos to the city, which was already becoming numb to military-grade firefights happening within the downtown core. The drug war years amplified the intensity of the cartels' jostling for power, but a consolidation of the drug market—the only thing that would have brought peace to the city—remained elusive.

By 2009, the original Tijuana Cartel was definitively destroyed, split between the Arellano Félix Organization and a group run by Teodoro García Simental, aka El Teo, a high-ranking capo. Perhaps sensing the end was near, El Teo and his lieutenants eventually aligned with the Sinaloa Cartel (one of those lieutenants, El Pozolero [the Soup Maker], confessed to prosecutors that he had personally dissolved hundreds of bodies in vats of acid). Meanwhile, smaller factions and outside syndicates emerged, aligned, and split apart again, always violently. Narcos hung corpses from a bridge near Tijuana's airport in a display designed for maximum terror. Police found a severed head under a pedestrian walkway near the Zona Norte; they later retrieved the corresponding body on a placid stretch of highway linking Tijuana to Ensenada. Bodies with narcomantas (warning letters) became the medium of choice to deliver messages and set ground rules between cartels, with some threatening violence and others exhorting rivals to avoid killing minors. When a lull in the violence began in 2010, some experts speculated that the Arellano Félix and Sinaloa Cartels had brokered a truce and that the city would finally see a lasting peace. But then, narcomantas signed with a new moniker began to appear: that of the Cartel Tijuana Nueva Generación. The name was a mash-up of the old guard from Tijuana and the upstarts from Jalisco, suggesting a reshuffling of the deck yet again. The game was far from over, and Tijuana would need to brace itself for more years of terror.

Despite Bañuelos's optimism, observers estimate that, in the ten years after the drug war was launched, over one hundred thousand Mexicans were killed and thirty thousand went missing because of drug-related violence that became, as the years dragged on, increasingly gruesome. The situation got so bad that, in 2008, Mexico's federal government briefly stopped releasing annual statistics on drug-related homicides, which is a strange way of trying to make the problem disappear.

*

During the drug war, decapitations, hangings, and kidnappings fed the news cycle, but the murder of the women in the border areas barely caused a ripple of outrage. When I met Rosa, she had been working in the Zona Norte for over twenty years, and she had experienced up close the ebbs and flows of the violence that Bañuelos and Alaniz described. She concurred with their description of the daily chaos the city faced in the years leading up to the war. But unlike the officers, who spoke broadly of "corruption," Rosa told me exactly who the perpetrators were and how institutionalized the violation of women had become. "I do feel it was more violent back then," she said, "because they would do whatever they wanted with you: they would threaten you, take you away to an isolated place—not only clients but also the police. They would take you and make you have sex with them or make you give them a blowjob. Or when the police took us to La Veinte [The Twenty; Tijuana's municipal jail] we would have to give a blowjob to the judge to be let out."

For Rosa, undeniably, the greatest danger came from the police. "They would take us to isolated places and do whatever they wanted to us," she repeated. "The policemen were real assholes to us, and you could see that they were high." In the years before the Mérida Initiative, officers would regularly search the rooms of the Hotel Michoacán, where Rosa and other sex workers lived and worked. "Policemen would get there hooded and would take you out of the hotel room and do whatever they wanted to you," she said. "One time I was able to hide in one room, but a policeman went to my friend's room and raped her. That was really scary—they just did whatever they wanted." Thinking back to Bañuelos and Alaniz's descriptions of the success of the counterintelligence operation, I asked her if there was less corruption now, and she contemplated the question, clearly torn. "Maybe it's the same *chingadera* [the same old shit] now, but it used to be more *descarado* [shameless]." She offered, though, that the hardest edges of the day-to-day violence and terror enacted by the narcos had lessened after 2006. Before then, "they would arrive to the brothel with guns and no one, not even the police, would do anything, and they would do whatever they wanted to us," she said. "Before, you used to hear shooting and see a lot of killings. You would see the violence everywhere. I feel that has decreased a lot."

*

Later, I walked with Susi and Patty through the Zona Norte toward the El Cuete field offices. It was late afternoon, the sun tilting low along the two-story buildings of the red-light district, illuminating the dust that hung heavily in the air. The wind blowing in from the Pacific Ocean had been unseasonably strong that day, and I thought back to the kids playing soccer and kicking up clouds in Los Laureles, high above us in the canyons to the south. The wastewater and pollution pumping from the maquiladoras there would be finding its way through the canal, just a few blocks to the east of the red-light district, and then into the sea. We approached the unmarked front door of the El Cuete offices, white paint peeling around the edges of the wired glass frame. The office was on a narrow street in the middle of the Zona's action, and I kept having to move aside as people—sex workers, laborers, men living rough—jostled past me. As Patty fumbled with her keys, two uniformed police officers walked by, giving her and Susi a polite nod. The two of them smiled back with what looked to me like typical Tijuanensis warmth, though the officers never slowed their pace. As we climbed the stairs, Susi and Patty looked at each other and laughed mirthlessly. The officers, they explained, were particularly vicious extortionists who preyed primarily on the city's drug injectors, the same population that Patty and Susi were trying to care for.

Alaniz and Bañuelos had been confident that the crooked cops had been removed from the Tijuana Municipal Police Department in 2008. But here, in the midst of the Zona in 2014, the graft continued. At the very least, there were officers everywhere you looked: from Patty's second-floor office window I could see that the closest intersection was rammed with police vehicles. A couple of cars and a pickup truck—just like the one they had used to haul Chango away during my very first day in Tijuana—were parked at severe angles, officers milling around the scene with machine guns, set expressions under their crisp short-billed caps. It looked chaotic, as if the vehicles had been driven up in great haste to respond to some violent threat. But they had been there for years, and the intersection now had the feel of a permanent checkpoint.

The show of force was impressive. That said, it was there largely as a symbol, and as I would learn, policing affected the lives of the Zona's women in more insidious ways. Chief among these was by inadvertently denying drug-using women access to addiction treatment. Susi had been telling me about trying to stop using heroin during the same years that Bañuelos and Alaniz were chasing down bad cops and Rosa was fending them off in hotel rooms. "Around 2000," Susi told me, "methadone clinics started opening; there's one around here on La Sexta and they charge eighty pesos for the dose, I think." La Sexta—Sixth Street—was a five-minute walk away. "Now they implement methadone in various rehab centers, or there are even methadone clinics, but before there was nothing of the sort around here, nothing." Susi sighed. "We would try to break away by ourselves or with pills, Roches or Valiums or Darvons, and so on, but that simply meant that you would get even higher because you wouldn't stop taking the pills. It was self-deceit, that you could quit on your own. But it can't happen: you can't quit on your own."

Opioid addiction is exceedingly difficult to overcome even with vast resources at your disposal. When there are barriers to accessing treatment facilities—like the threat of police violence—the addiction can be insurmountable. Nowadays, as the opioid overdose death rate climbs in the United States, jumping past motor vehicle accidents as the leading cause of unintentional injury, it's contributing to a decline in the life expectancy of Americans for the first time since the early 1960s. This seismic shift, driven largely by the disproportionate deaths of young people by overdose, is finally waking people up to how complex drug addiction is and how colossally bad our approach to preventing it has been. One of the main reasons for that is lingering suspicion about the effectiveness of drugs like methadone in helping people manage their opioid dependence, especially among the police, who in places like the Zona have a massive amount of control over what services people can access.

It can be a hard case to make: methadone is an opioid, just like heroin or OxyContin. So why should we be prescribing it to people who are already hooked? If anything, wouldn't that just prolong their addiction? In Susi's words, isn't that just another form of self-deceit? Making matters worse is that methadone and other opioid-based medications like buprenorphine aren't silver bullets. On average, people who enroll in these types of treatment stay on medication for five years and might relapse three times, though the numbers vary widely. That's an incredibly messy process, and from the outside it can often look like the treatment is no better than the disease, especially if you're the beat cop whose job it is to reduce the impact of addiction on public order. From the inside, it can feel like you're simply not making any forward progress at all. That's at odds with the abstinence model that has been at the heart of American culture since at least the mid-1800s, when the Christian-tinged temperance movement claimed that alcohol use was a moral failing requiring eradication. While the drugs have gotten more addictive since those days, when smoking opium was the only opioid on offer, the effectiveness of abstinence programs has remained basically the same (to sum up: not great). Methadone, despite its limits, despite its inherent messiness, and despite the fact that it doesn't fit neatly into ideas about whether someone is "clean" or a "junkie" (incidentally, two words that most people who work in addiction really loathe), is the most effective tool we have to treat addiction. That's why it was added to the World Health Organization's List of Essential Medicines in 2005. And yet, nearly fifteen years later, it's almost nowhere to be found: in the midst of the continent's worst epidemic of opioid overdose death, with tens of thousands of Americans dying each year, only about 8 percent of people eligible for methadone in the United States have access to it. In Mexico, the situation is even more dire; across a country of 126 million people, with tens of thousands of people injecting opioids along the country's northern border, less than four thousand people are officially enrolled in treatment, equal to 0.00003 percent of the population. That sad state of affairs is what happens when the prevailing opinion about addiction is that it's best solved by the state's security apparatus.

As Susi talked to me about her experiences of trying and failing to quit using, the sounds of the cops milling around their jumbled encampment floated up from the intersection, while the flashing red and blue of their vehicle lights played an erratic rhythm against the window. When I was down on the street, I was scared to even look in the direction of that checkpoint lest I be shaken down and forced to pay a bribe, which I had witnessed happening to people all the time. The way that I had found to avoid that kind of scenario was to get off the street and out of the neighborhood before police could start wondering what I was doing there. For women like Rosa who injected drugs in the Zona, the best way to avoid confrontations with cops would be to enroll in a methadone program. By doing so, she'd be able to stop injecting in alleys or picaderos and thereby avoid making herself an easy mark. That meant, however, scraping pesos together to buy methadone instead of street heroin, which was a leap of faith for someone with few means and who was physically dependent on the drug. It also meant staying on methadone treatment for long enough for its benefits to kick in, which could take anywhere from one to six months.

Susi knew of at least one methadone clinic operating in the Zona Norte. But if the Zona was full of cops, and if at least some of them were extorting people who were using drugs, then how would the Susis and the Rosas of the world—those scarred women walking El Bordo at night—ever have enough money to free themselves from the neighborhood's dangers? I was scared of staring too long at the checkpoint, but there was nothing stopping me from walking in a different direction until I was far, far away. Women who were bound to this neighborhood because of addiction, sex work, or both simply couldn't avoid the cops patrolling their beat, which meant that they would continue to have to pay the uniformed masters—using money, drugs, or their bodies—to avoid becoming another victim. As I stared at the red and blue lights dancing in the window, I began to think about how I might model this relationship between police extortion and access to treatment. I had a hunch that it might just get me closer to understanding the femicide epidemic.

"Susi," I said, "I guess one more question I have is around how the sex trade operates: like, what is the relationship between the bar owners and the cartels here?" I felt a little naïve asking the question, but it suddenly seemed important to fully understand the system of control here. "Are the bar owners also involved with the drug cartels, and are they in charge of drug trafficking?"

"Yes," Susi replied, "but only brothels like El Caché, like El Valentinas, like those that are more renowned—the ones that have the pretty girls. They'll look at the girls and say, 'You are a dancer, you are a *fichera*,'" a *ficha* being a token purchased by clients at certain brothels, and ficheras being sex workers that the men spend their fichas on (usually by buying them exorbitantly priced drinks). "The good ones have them under control because the girls live upstairs; they bring them their breakfast up there. They can't go and work at another bar—unless they are going out with a federal police officer."

I made a mental note. "Right," I said. "And are the big bar owners also the cartels, like is that all the same?"

"Yes, of course!" Susi replied, clapping. "Of course, of course, like the one that was on the corner, the one called the Río Rosas. The owner died already, but it was something special. They would sometimes ask me for girls like, 'Hey, don't you know girls that can come and work here?'" Susi looked visibly pleased at having been useful to the cartels running the neighborhood. "Now the cartel ones are El Kun Kun, El Chavelas; basically, the best brothels in Zona Norte."

Cartel involvement in the sex trade was perhaps unsurprising. But if the narcos ran the neighborhood's best brothels, what were all the police in the neighborhood doing there? Earlier, when I had met with Alaniz and Bañuelos at the Tijuana police headquarters, I had asked them about the Zona Norte, about the women living and working here and the dangers they faced. Well, I had tried to at least. Perhaps Bañuelos was too focused on his presentation and didn't want to be led off topic; the slide show, after all, cast him and his allies in the force as heroes for having ousted the narcos who had infiltrated the department. For whatever reason, they didn't really care to talk about the Zona's women. Eventually, I tried a different tack: could they tell me about the different police forces that were operating in the red light district?

In Tijuana, like other Mexican cities, it can be difficult to get a handle on all of the multiple law enforcement agencies working the same beat. The city has its own municipal force, made up of roughly two thousand officers, including Alaniz and Bañuelos. But there is also the Baja California State Police, whose officers sometimes make incursions into the city depending on the severity of the situation or the specifics of the crime being responded to. Then there are the *federales*, the federal police force, who became increasingly ubiquitous across violence-prone areas of Mexico as the war against the cartels became bloodier and the loyalty of local law enforcement eroded in frontier outposts like Tijuana. There's also the Federal Ministerial Police, an internal security organization akin to the FBI, only the latest name for a long line of agencies that had (like the Dirección Federal de Seguridad, the agency that created the Guadalajara Cartel) been formed, dismantled, and repackaged as corruption turned it from a counternarcotics tool into an indispensable ally to traffickers. And finally, there are the police units that I had been seeing all across the Zona Norte.

According to Alaniz, these last were by and large "commercial" police—officers hired directly by the brothels and strip clubs in the red-light district for protection. Rent-a-cops. "It is not protection for illegal actions, obviously," he explained somewhat apologetically. "It is precisely to provide security and control within the Zona." The rationale was sound: the red light district was a raucous neighborhood that required extra security. During the worst years of the war on drugs in Tijuana, the assassinations and running gun battles (between cartels and police, and among the cartels themselves) also largely took place in the Zona Norte. There was a simple reason why: the Zona was the most lucrative district in the city, not only for the quasi-legal sex work that happened here, but because of the drug trafficking that went along with it. It made sense, then, that the cartels would seek to protect their assets. And who better than police officers themselves to provide that protection?

I let my mind slow down and watched Susi and Patty talking boisterously and laughing, I suppose, at how crazy all these stories must sound to an outsider like me. I half-listened to Susi name-drop her old haunts and I watched the easy smile that creased her face rise and recede as she recounted memories good and bad. And as I sat there, the statistical frame, like a latticework of woven strips, came together in my mind, a way to model all this new information, to make it hold water.

Up to this point, I had assumed that here in Tijuana, the police and the cartels represented the twin poles of power. They were, basically, good guys and bad guys, morally opposed forces that were inevitably in conflict. Yes, there were some bad cops—and at one time, hundreds and hundreds of them—and who knows, maybe even some good-hearted cartel members. In any event, my read had always been that the two factions acted in binary opposition. I had heard it in Bañuelos's story and read it in countless news articles showing the haggard faces of police as they responded to yet another assassination of one of their own. I had watched footage, aghast, of a helicopter gunship hovering over a city skyscraper and launching missiles into an apartment to take out cartel leaders. The war was real.

In the Zona, though, this liminal space, the moral fabric of society was stretched so thin that it had disintegrated like a cheap blanket. Here the cartels operated quasi-legitimate business through the de facto legal sex trade, which is believed to generate hundreds of millions of dollars each year (though reliable statistics are lacking). And perversely, as Alaniz had explained, the people making sure that the whole enterprise ran smoothly were the police themselves. While the scope of the cartel's stake in the sex trade is unclear, it's evident that the major players—the clubs, the cartels, and the police—all benefited economically from the arrangement. Susi, at least, having spent almost three decades here, was convinced that the cartels and the owners of the district's major brothels were one and the same. That meant that my conception of how the Zona functioned was wrong. The police and the cartels weren't just in violent opposition. They were also tethered in a hierarchical financial relationship, with the criminals controlling the trade and the police being paid to protect their investments. These two situations occurring simultaneously was another example, like Tom's dojo-running doctor, of the schizophrenic duality of this border town.

It seemed like a tidy arrangement, but on the ground it was a different story. Those two friendly officers who had walked past us earlier pointed to a whole other set of realities for women like Susi and Rosa. Women who used drugs, who operated on the margins of the sex trade and weren't valuable to the major players, were seen as pests. Susi had gone straight, but there were many women who occupied her former role as a hit doctor for sex workers; neither those women nor women like Rosa who worked at the lower rungs of the trade were protected by the arrangement between the commercial police, the bar owners, and their cartel masters. The two of them, and the constellation of women in their orbit, were considered parasites that the commercial cops were free to squash. As Susi said, the only way out was to date a federal police officer.

That raised an impossible dilemma. What was worse, being trapped in the violent clashes between the police and the cartels or being oppressed under the weight of the two of them working in concert? Perhaps in La Coahuila it didn't translate as neatly as that. Rosa and Susi both agreed that for the women working the margins of the neighborhood, the death's-head was more than likely to wear a uniform.

During my scientific training in Vancouver, a medically supervised injection facility called Insite opened right in the middle of the Downtown Eastside, near the neighborhood's large open-air drug market. Opening the facility had been a rallying cry for a decade among the various advocacy groups and scientists trying to improve the lives of the thousands of people who injected drugs there who were dying at alarming rates of HIV/AIDS and overdose from having to inject in alleys and in Vancouver's countless shooting galleries. And yet, when the supervised injection facility finally opened, nobody showed up to use it.

The reason was simple. The Vancouver Police Department, ideologically opposed to what they perceived as the normalization of illegal drug use, decided to demonstrate their dissatisfaction with the new facility. And so, on the day that Insite was slated to open, before anyone could access the space, a police car quietly pulled up and parked outside its entrance. No officers got out; they didn't have to. They just sat in the car, steps from the site's front door. Waiting.

Despite the community's desperation for a clean and safe place to inject drugs, and the fact that choosing to inject in a facility that provided clean equipment and overdose response meant literally choosing life over death, the mere presence of a cop car was enough to make Insite inaccessible. It was a useful lesson in competing risks: in the hierarchy of dangers faced by people who use drugs, police rank number one, before dying of overdose alone in an alley or becoming infected with HIV from shared needles. All the police had to do was show up.

I suspected the same thing could be happening in Tijuana. And if it was, I assumed the threat of interacting with the police here would be a lot scarier. After all, the police could act with greater impunity given that they were being paid by the cartels running the Zona's sex trade. "Just out of curiosity," I asked Susi, "do the police target methadone clinics or treatment centers to try to round up drug users?"

"No."

"No?"

"Methadone, no; *conectas* [drug-dealing spots], yes. Or around the project too . . ."

"Yeah, like our office for the El Cuete project," Patty said. "They target that."

"Yes, to take study participants' money . . ." Susi added.

"But not support groups, groups like AA. Cops don't hang out around there," Patty said.

"But if they happen to go by," Susi said, "the cops target the users that are outside. Many go to AA to ask for coffee or cookies, or others just go inside for a bit and take what they see—cookies, candy, or coffee—and then they leave. So it does happen that the cops come to hassle them, sometimes when their shift is changing or if they need to fill their quota. Then they take them away."

The scramble of cops on the streets of the Zona below Patty's window, the endless police raids into the canal and into Tijuana's conectas—if these were the daily rituals of life that you came to expect, how would your days be shaped? It was just like the cop car parked outside of Insite: even if the police in Tijuana weren't specifically targeting treatment centers, their mere presence was likely enough to keep people who were seeking help with their addictions from engaging with care. My next step was to quantify that complicated phenomenon using epidemiologic tools.

Building a statistical model is kind of like writing a news story. You want a solid argument backing the whole enterprise up, and you never want to bury the lede. In epidemiologic terms, that means developing the most important outcome possible and matching it with the most relevant coefficient of interest—that is, the part of the model that you think is influencing the outcome. Nobody could deny that Tijuana was a corrupt place, and I wanted to know how those at the lowest rung of the social order here were affected by that, so zeroing in on the transactional corruption that happened on the beat made sense. With that in mind, the coefficient of interest was easy to define: the near-ritual extortion by police of people who inject drugs.

A model's outcome can sometimes be trickier to define. If your model is sound, the outcome will at the very least represent a fundamental aspect of how the epidemic spreads, like whether someone becomes infected with HIV or not. But sometimes an epidemic is so complex and the ways that people find themselves engulfed by a pathogen so multifaceted that you have to break it down into component parts. Think of the outcome as a nail driving through a piece of wood, the sharp metal point splitting and recombining the material. The coefficient of interest is the hammer: that instrument without which the nail remains inert. When there's only one nail, one hammer, and one piece of wood, the process is simple. But the mercurial epidemic I was tracking was big, as big as the city of Tijuana itself. That meant choosing a specific starting point—one hammer and one nail from among thousands—that might not explain everything but that would set me along a path to uncover some kind of truth.

All of the data I was working with came from people injecting drugs enrolled in Proyecto El Cuete. I had to find an outcome that was equally important for them as it was for the larger scientific community working on issues around substance use and HIV transmission. Talking to Susi had made that easier. While the police weren't necessarily targeting addiction treatment centers in Tijuana, Susi said that a certain kind of cop looking to fill a quota or make some extra pesos would cruise by those centers to fill his or her coffers. There was enough epidemiologic precedent to know that the mere presence of police near frontline health services could cause epidemics related to drug injecting to spread. The police didn't necessarily have to interact with people who were desperate to use the facility to cause them to stay away. The threat of violence was enough of a deterrent. The question was, could I prove it? Now that would be a story, I figured: a city on America's border inundated with drugs, buckling under the weight of an epidemic of femicide experienced by sex workers and women who injected drugs in the city's hidden spaces. The kicker? Even though methadone was available in the city, those who needed it the most couldn't access it because of endemic police corruption carried out in and around the treatment centers themselves. That, in turn, meant that women couldn't escape the dangers of a neighborhood in which a disproportionate number of them were dying. What better way to show that the whole justification for drug law enforcement— that it would somehow make streets safer for everyone—had been perverted by the hyperempowerment of the city's police force? With that, I had my outcome (access to methadone), and I had my coefficient of interest (being extorted by police). I had the foundation for my model.

The next step was to begin populating the model with data. I reviewed the El Cuete survey and found two questions that I could use to begin my model building: *In the past six months, were you arrested or stopped by police? [Y/N] If yes, what happened? (forced to pay a bribe vs. all other responses)* As a participant in the El Cuete study, Rosa had sat down in a small white room and been asked hundreds of standardized questions spanning her drug use, experiences of violence, her sex life, where she lived, how she made rent, and myriad other factors that shaped her life. I pictured her there, most likely in the very same room where we occasionally met, trying to run through the endless array as quickly as possible, desperate to outpace her *malilla*—the "little pain," or opioid withdrawal—and get to the modest honorarium that she was promised by the research staff, some pesos to support her for a few days more. Did the images of hooded police cross her mind? Or did she, after years of answering the same questions every six months, simply respond automatically? Were the scars she was left with after decades in the Zona coarse enough to protect her from the traumas the interrogations raised?

Even if I had wanted to, there was no way to find Rosa's responses amid the dataset. I understood that ensuring the anonymity of subjects was done to protect them from potential reprisals, and that was of course as it should be. But as I began to manipulate the data—identifying the columns that would serve as the coefficient of interest and the outcome, my hammer and my nail—I realized that perhaps there was another reason why anonymity was so highly prized by epidemiologists. With just a massive sheet of numbers to work with, it's easy to forget that the information comes from real people, and perhaps that is the point. Epidemiologists are supposed to be coldly objective when investigating even the most sinister of circumstances. It is our only weapon and the single greatest source of our credibility: the professional responsibility to look past the individual case, past the story of a sex worker hiding in a single hotel room, listening to the sound of a friend being raped across a narrow hallway. To construct a functioning model, to run the analysis without error, and to interpret the findings appropriately, I would have to put these scenes out of mind. Otherwise, the horror of the epidemic would obscure my vision.

*

For Bañuelos and Alaniz, the drug war never really ended. The year 2013 saw 492 homicides, a spike of 54 percent over the previous year, as well as increasingly audacious messages from new cartel factions, who were once again threatening police who interfered with cartel business. Some measure of calm returned in 2014, when homicides dropped back down by 40 percent, though officers like Bañuelos and Alaniz were too cautious at that point to celebrate. They were right to trust those instincts: 2017 was the bloodiest year in Tijuana's history, with over 1,700 murders in the city, the homicide rate spiking to 101 homicides per 100,000 (or 105 per 100,000, depending on which dataset you trust), making Tijuana the most dangerous big city in the world. Meanwhile, a decade after its counterintelligence *operativo*, the police department was still recovering from the purge of corrupt officers and the stricter enrollment procedures that were subsequently put in place to ensure that it never happened again. Those new rules meant that fewer cadets were enrolling in the police academy and the department was having trouble keeping its ranks filled with high-quality officers. Despite it all, Bañuelos clung to an unyielding optimism when we met. "Even though we are fewer," he said, leaning back in his chair and looking me in the eye, "we are now more dependable, more effective." He seemed to me like a good man, and I took him at his word.

Before wrapping up, Alaniz wanted to make one thing clear: "Tijuana is not an isolated phenomenon." When I asked him what he meant, he waved his arm in the air dismissively; I noticed that the fingers on one hand had been partially sliced off, an old wound that had evidently healed years ago, perhaps from early in his career on the force. "Americans are always afraid of everything. They are phobic. And it's not me who says that: everybody knows it. And through their own fears they see a different perspective than the one we've got having lived through those years in Tijuana. Those weren't pretty times, but Americans magnify it even more. I've been to New York, Tennessee, New Jersey—they all have their areas just like the Zona Norte."

I asked Alaniz if he was ever scared, given Tijuana's ongoing corruption and the ebb and flow of violence, which was likely to remain a threat for the foreseeable future. He shook his head firmly. "You know your area, you know the past, so with that you can do satisfying work." When state institutions are strong, he explained, "you can work with the bosses that are there, because of the trust that exists. When there's no trust, well . . . you pull yourself back and work on the more practical day-to-day stuff, no? You remain in your post. You don't talk too much." He paused. "That's why I am able to tell you the story that I'm telling." It was as cogent an argument for survival and perseverance as I had heard down here.

I rose to leave, but Bañuelos, with a smile, gestured to me one last time. I looked down at the small computer screen, to the final PowerPoint slide that he was clearly anxious for me to see. After the billowing corruption of Hank's mayoralty, after the insidious cartel infiltration, after the counterintelligence operativo, after the campaign of mass murder of police officers, and after the loss of over five hundred corrupt cops, Bañuelos was sure it was all worth it. He traced the last few lines of text on the slide with his finger and recited them out loud: "Resultado: Paz, Tranquilidad, Armonía Social, y Seguridad Pública." Peace, Tranquility, Social Harmony, and Public Safety.

CHAPTER 6

Shore Leave

By January 2015, the Southern California winter had come again, leaving me feeling restless and at loose ends. It was less a season than a subtle retreat: most days, the sun continued to rise unobstructed in a cloudless sky, its light shimmering off the blue waves of San Diego Harbor and becoming absorbed by the camouflage paint of the battleships, impossibly large against the sailboats and sea lions. The city looked the same as ever, as far as I could tell, but the days and nights grew colder. I was freezing all the time.

I spent weeks in my cinder-block office in Hillcrest, the El Cuete dataset blinking at me from my laptop screen. The sheer scope of the problem was daunting. With a city as chaotic as Tijuana, where the population we were studying was getting sick and dying from so many different causes, the needs far outweighed the response. As an epidemiologist, it didn't matter how I defined the starting point to track the epidemic: all roads led to the same pernicious mass of problems. Here was a city with such obvious public health issues handcuffed by an interlocking set of circumstances that appeared beyond anyone's ability to change.

That made it hard to focus my mind on just one single aspect of the plague befalling the city, but that is what I had to do. And so I stared at the screen, 1,825 rows of data capturing the movement of Tijuana's drug-using underclass staring back at me. Though I could not know them, I nevertheless followed their trajectories over time and caught glimpses through the data of how people were living. One participant had been dutifully returning every six months for the last three years to report back on her life, which had been marked intermittently by arrest and police extortion (*Have you been forced to pay a bribe to police in the last six months? Response: YES.*). I followed the variables along the woman's multiple rows (one for each visit), the ones and zeros turning the complexities of her life into simple binary signals. It wasn't just that she had been arrested and assaulted; she also hadn't been accessing addiction treatment even though she also reported believing that doing so would reduce her risk of getting arrested. It was a perilous feedback loop, and at the end of her progress—visit six—she seemed to be exactly where she had started, except a little older and perhaps a little more worn out. And then she was gone; no more rows. Officially, she was "lost to follow-up," a euphemistic term used by epidemiologists to cover all the many reasons, often dire, that someone stops coming to interviews.

I collapsed the dataset down, removing the rows showing participant follow-up data. I needed all the follow-up data points for my analysis, but I sometimes found the sheer volume of numbers overwhelming; or maybe it was that seeing the progress of someone's life turned into a series of static cells was discomfiting. When I stripped the superfluous rows away, I was left with one row for each individual participant, 637 in all. About half of them were women, many of whom reported that they worked in the sex trade. Considering that there were somewhere between five and ten thousand people who injected drugs in Tijuana, it was a pretty good snapshot—between 6 and 12 percent—of that population.

I had my coefficient of interest (being forced to pay bribes to police) and my outcome (accessing methadone treatment). The next step in my model-building process was to settle on the various factors that I thought might influence the relationship between the two. It's that last step that transforms a rudimentary investigation into a robust statistical model.

Choosing the right variables for a model is where the science of epidemiology starts to shift into a kind of art form. Though there are many approaches, there is no one accepted method to construct statistical models, so the variables that are ultimately chosen for inclusion reflect deeply on the skills, wisdom, and experience of the model builder. And like any art form, epidemiologic models are susceptible to cultural trends and sweeping social change. Nowhere are those trends more evident than in the history of epidemiologic models seeking to explain addiction.

*

In 1971, in the midst of the Vietnam War and the presidency of Richard Nixon, news began to emerge that roughly one in five American servicemen sent to fight against the Vietcong had become addicted to heroin. Amid a brutalizing war in a country that had become a leading international heroin producer, the addicted GIs—about thirty thousand in all—presented a conundrum for the president. If he brought them home, their easy access to Vietnam's cheap heroin supply would be cut off, but doing so, Nixon surmised, would spread the cancer of addiction across the soldiers' home communities, seeding a generalized American addiction epidemic. Should he let tens of thousands of soldiers linger in a war zone, at risk of succumbing even further to their addictions, or bring them home to the United States, where they might spread the social ill to others?

While Nixon's decision would mark the beginning of the modern American war on drugs, this episode is also noteworthy for how it influenced scientific thinking on the relationship between an individual's environment and their drug use. Before 1971, scientific work on addiction that would now fall under the discipline of epidemiology was mostly conducted by psychiatrists who observed substance use disorders among individual patients. Instead of a population-level issue, substance use was instead largely understood as a personal weakness, the result of a certain "psychopathology" that doomed an unlucky few who were simply not strong enough to handle the rigors of daily life.

Individual psychopathology was a handy theory to explain addiction, largely because it reinforced the structural sexism and racism of the time that assumed that women and people who weren't white were simply inferior to white men. For instance, psychiatrists studying addiction in the 1950s observed that African-American populations living in urban centers marked by poverty were disproportionately impacted by addiction. Nevertheless, these doctors refused to interpret drug use within a social context. To them, it was simply the result of frustration among classes of people incapable of meeting the responsibilities of living in a civilized (read: white Christian male) world, and the reasons were just too hardwired to warrant real scientific investigation.

Even when basic epidemiologic tools like logistic regression models became more widely used and population-level analyses became the norm, the theory of individual psychopathology wasn't abandoned by the scientific class. Rather, scientists just mapped it over these new methods to further confirm that addiction was caused by nothing more than basic human weakness among specific human subgroups. So, when clinicians started to consider which variables to put into their statistical models to explain why some people became addicted to drugs and others didn't, the focus was almost entirely on group personality traits, which essentially can't be changed. As one seminal study from 1962 put it, "The addicts seen in American treatment facilities are predominantly young, male, psychopathic, immature individuals drawn from foci spotted about certain big city slums . . . The relationship to the so-called psychopathic personality is close and several epidemiologic characteristics of psychopathology and addiction coincide fairly well." The reference to "big city slums" here was, of course, racist dog-whistling dressed up as scientific jargon. And what about that throwaway line about psychopathology and addiction being often indistinguishable? For the authors, drug-addicted people were "suffering from strongly passive-dependent needs . . . Their personality is also called immature and pseudo-aggressive since the aggression when it does occur is self-defeating and ineffectual . . . the self-destructive effect of the behavior of the addict is similar to that of the classic psychopath." The takeaway is that "addicts"—like psychopaths—are born and not made. Sure, you could treat the symptoms, but the inherent weakness of the person was beyond medical care. This psychopath argument about addiction was the kind of scientific theory that we should always distrust: one that somehow manages to explain away a societal ill while exonerating the society itself. And perhaps it would have remained the prevailing view if it hadn't been for one little problem: the behaviors of the doctors themselves.

While up until the 1960s the medical and scientific establishments were united in the view that addiction arose almost solely from an immutable personality defect, interest in the emerging scientific field of epidemiology had motivated investment in all manner of large and long-term observational cohort studies. The best known—and still active seventy years later—is the Framingham Heart Study, which recruited five thousand residents of the town of Framingham, Massachusetts, in 1948 and followed them, their children, their children's children, and so on, throughout their entire lives. We have the Framingham Heart Study to thank for seminal research linking heart disease to risk factors such as cigarette smoking, cholesterol, and obesity, and for correctly estimating the lifetime risk of heart attack of American men and women. Though this kind of study is incredibly useful in showing that specific lifestyle factors cause certain health outcomes, recruiting participants into studies of this sort can prove challenging. To get around that, many early epidemiologic investigations (including the Framingham Heart Study) originally relied on physicians as volunteer participants, given that they were easy to follow and generally willing to participate.

So, in the 1950s and 1960s, just as modern epidemiology was coming into its own, a glut of studies following physicians were launched in the United States. At the time, the main concern among epidemiologists was that these studies' findings were likely biased because physicians generally exhibited higher than average levels of overall health and wealth, making them poor representatives of the overall population. What nobody counted on was that in the area of drugs and drug addiction, physician-powered observational studies would reveal an uncomfortable truth: beyond their high economic capital and good health, it turned out that doctors were disproportionately more likely to become addicted to drugs and alcohol. This finding—repeated across medical disciplines and geographic settings—was the tip of the spear that forced the scientific community to lurch beyond its origin story of addiction as personal weakness or insanity.

With physicians more likely to become addicted to drugs, compared with the general population, it became a lot more difficult to argue that a drug-dependent person was a "classic psychopath," or inherently "immature and pseudo-aggressive." The situation was particularly untenable given that during the fifties and sixties, physicians were the people running most epidemiologic studies and authoring the scientific manuscripts about drug use. They were, unsurprisingly, loath to suggest that the high prevalence of drug addiction among members of their own vocation was caused by the fact that doctors are all psychopaths. And so, instead of blaming that same collective form of psychopathology that they had diagnosed as innate to African Americans, Latinos, and women, epidemiologic papers about addicted doctors quietly gravitated toward different language to talk about drug use and its effects.

In one study from 1966 ("Narcotic Addiction Among Physicians: A Ten-Year Follow-Up") that compared one hundred physicians treated for addiction with one hundred matched controls, the authors—physicians themselves, of course—wrote, with a level of subtlety absent in studies of drug use among black Americans, that they found "no correlation between psychiatric diagnosis and drug used" among the study's participants. Gone was the psychopath theory. As far as the researchers were concerned, doctors couldn't be crazy, even the ones that overindulged. In a lingering sign of the times, though, the factors that the authors deemed most likely to increase the risk of drug use reflected myopic ideas about the root causes of addiction. These included whether participants were married, whether they were Protestant, and whether they came from the American South (on the assumption, I suppose, that Southerners were less well bred). Another study, published in the *New England Journal of Medicine* in 1970, again written by a physician, reported that after twenty years of following a group of sophomore college students, half of whom had gone into medicine, twice as many of the then-physicians had used drugs compared to the group of people that, one assumes, found less respectable careers. Here, the authors again sought to include variables in the model they assumed would be most likely to influence their vulnerability for addiction: having had a feeding problem in infancy, having had a private school education, scoring badly on a math test, and being "psychologically sound" (which wasn't ever defined). Today, this kind of paper wouldn't even make it to a scientific journal editor's desk, let alone get published. But these early efforts to explain addiction not by some immutable group-level inferiority but through individual circumstances represented an early trend in addiction research that has continued to evolve until the present day. What these midcentury epidemiologists overlooked about substance use among doctors were the high levels of stress, anxiety, and lack of sleep that characterize the medical profession. Coupled with ready knowledge of and access to highly addictive pharmaceutical drugs and a culture of intense competition, doctors were primed to self-medicate.

Having pragmatically turned themselves into their own guinea pigs, doctors had inadvertently revealed their own heightened susceptibility to use drugs and, with it, the fatal flaw behind the racist and sexist addiction science that they had popularized. This led to only one conclusion: if morally upstanding, intellectually sophisticated white men with great careers were succumbing to addiction in droves, then it could not be a disease of the mind. The upshot for epidemiologists was that the kinds of variables included in models of addiction had to expand to include factors beyond an individual's personality or upbringing. While this was a welcome step forward in our understanding of addiction, it came on the back of the unsettling cultural truth that when it happens to wealthy white guys, it isn't their fault.

Meanwhile, the Vietnam War raged and Nixon found himself with thirty thousand opioid-dependent GIs waiting overseas. Like the drug-dependent physicians, the situation of the GIs—traumatized by war in a country with ready access to drugs—upended the psychopathology theory of addiction. In its place, and reflecting the growing power of epidemiology to explain a vast array of health and social phenomena, an increasing number of thinkers began to describe addiction using language cribbed directly from this emergent discipline. In 1971, the same year that Nixon would make his decision about the fate of the GIs, the American Medical Association published a report describing drug dependence as arising from the interplay of three factors: the agent (or pathogen), the host, and the environment, otherwise known as the epidemiologic triangle. Whereas before the physicians running addiction studies had focused exclusively on the host—that is, those "weak" groups in America inherently susceptible to drugs (and who ostensibly deserved what came to them)—this new approach better explained how drug use spread across all manner of populations in many different settings.

It was no accident that epidemiology provided the exact type of language that the burgeoning field of addiction studies needed. Beginning in at least 1965, the U.S. experienced a textbook epidemic of drug use that would last fifteen years before subsiding. In 1965, between 100,000 and 200,000 Americans had started using opioids, tranquilizers, stimulants, or sedatives in the past year. By 1971, close to 500,000 people had started using opioids or sedatives in the past year, while over 600,000 Americans had started using stimulants. "In the epidemiologic model, the infectious agent is heroin, the host and reservoir are both man, and the vector is the drug-using peer," read a paper from the time, which went so far as to describe heroin use as a communicable disease.

Nixon's personal views toward drug use were cut and dry. "Dope? Do you think the Russians allow dope? Hell no," he is recorded as saying in the White House in May 1971. "Not if they can allow, not if they can catch it, they send them up. You see, homosexuality, dope, immorality in general: these are the enemies of strong societies. That's why the Communists and the left-wingers are pushing the stuff. They're trying to destroy us." Despite the intensity of his antidrug feelings, Nixon was at a loss to find a solution to the addicted GI issue consistent with his own thinking.

Eventually, the president relented in the face of the inevitable. With scientific studies increasingly touting the benefits of using methadone—an opioid itself—to treat heroin addiction, he was left with little choice but to base policy on evidence. The risk of following his heart was just too high. So, despite launching a "war on drugs" in June 1971, Nixon also agreed to provide all thirty thousand opioid-addicted GIs in Vietnam with methadone-assisted treatment, instructing military personnel to only allow soldiers to board planes for the United States if they were no longer exhibiting symptoms of addiction. This quarantining of "infectious" cases is an old strategy to contain outbreaks—and it worked. While levels of substance use disorders among U.S. military veterans remain higher than the national average, Nixon's approach with the Vietnam GIs averted what the White House had feared would be a catastrophic expansion of heroin addiction across the United States. At the highest levels, the epidemiologic triangle—agent, host, and environment—had managed to convince a president hell-bent on punishing drug users to treat them instead.

Nowadays, the statistical models epidemiologists build to explain health outcomes do more than account for feeding problems in infancy. Like good art, good statistical models reflect the world as we know it and illuminate it further. The tenets of personal responsibility, prosperity, and an obligation to avoid harm that make up the prevailing American ethos have been eclipsed by the reality that systemic racism, a self-protecting oligarchy, and political structures resistant to change (and willing to punish those advocating for it) limit the capacity of some groups of Americans to avoid injury or ruin. Our models have shifted with the times to reflect this understanding. It matters less whether someone could take the nipple as a baby than whether they were born into poverty. And so, we choose to model one and not the other.

*

I had the entire El Cuete survey at my fingertips, but I was facing a familiar issue for epidemiologists. As I constructed a model to assess whether police bribery affected treatment access, I was less worried about identifying which variables mattered, but I was having trouble figuring out which ones I could reasonably exclude. Did age matter? Did gender? Did the type of drugs that people used make them more or less susceptible to police predation in Tijuana? Building my model required a conceptual understanding of how people operated when living under the multiple pressures of a city that existed by its own set of rules.

As I looked at the data, though, a troubling thought came to mind. What if the crucial factor dictating patterns of police extortion wasn't captured in the El Cuete survey at all? What if it was so deeply ingrained among the population as to be invisible? One of the reasons why proving a link between smoking cigarettes and lung cancer was so difficult was that the research started at a time when pretty much everybody smoked. The basis of epidemiology is the parsing of groups to see how they differ; if everyone is smoking, its health risks, statistically speaking, recede into the background like yellowed wallpaper. Was police extortion in the Zona like cigarette smoke, so ubiquitous and hazy that it was impossible to really see?

I pictured Rosa moving through the neighborhood during her daily routine: leaving her run-down hotel room to find her regular clients, her regular dealer, her regular dose. I pictured Susi, in the days before she got clean, leaving the club at four A.M. to walk to La Línea (the border fence east of the canal), drawn back along the way to the canal, lingering on the pedestrian bridge in the middle of the night, the only sound the trickle of polluted water below as she scanned for movement. Within the Zona, like clockwork, police would start their shifts just as the women would start theirs, everyone allotted a space within the larger wheels of industry and graft, the *paraditas*, "standing women," pressing their backs against the wall as officers passed. I could add variables to my model all day, important ones, but if there was a risk factor that hung like a collective curse on every single member of the El Cuete study, I wouldn't ever be able to measure it using the data they provided.

It was the tension that I had felt as a scientist from the beginning: trying to understand how the whole edifice hangs together while only ever being able to hammer away at a single nail. I closed the dataset and pulled up a map of the city. The Zona Norte, a crude rectangle no longer than a mile and no wider than fifteen hundred feet was bounded by the border to the north and the canal to the west. Despite being nestled in the heart of Centro, Tijuana's downtown delegación, the neighborhood felt like an island. It reminded me of something I had experienced in Vancouver. Growing up there, I had always assumed that the rough Downtown Eastside neighborhood was somehow disconnected from the majority of us that lived elsewhere in the city. The difference was just so stark; in the

Downtown Eastside, the usual social boundaries that proscribed "disorderly" behavior elsewhere evaporated. Strangers would talk to you. People would smoke crack out on the street or inject heroin in alleys in full view of passersby. It felt, always, like a wholly other place, self-contained and distinct. But then, working at a hospital in a tonier part of downtown, I was asked to investigate where street kids in the city were transitioning into drug injecting. I assumed that the answer would be the Downtown Eastside, but I was wrong. The kids, by and large, had started injecting within the very same neighborhood where I worked; it was only after they started to inject that their lives slowly shifted toward the Downtown Eastside and into the heart of the injecting scene. It wasn't that the neighborhood spontaneously produced addiction; it was more like a beacon for those who had become addicted elsewhere. This is your home now, your people, a place where you will be welcome.

The Zona Norte's near-mythic reputation as a cauldron of iniquity dwarfs that of any other district in North America. As far back as 1926, American newspapers were running headlines with claims like "Tia Juana Is a Disgrace to Mexico, a Menace to America" to explain away criminal behavior on the part of American tourists. In one such case, a family in San Diego was found dead in a murder-suicide a few days after a trip across the border to the Zona. Shortly after, crowds of angry Americans declared that Tijuana itself was to blame and called for San Diego's local government to burn its offending sister city to the ground. Hollywood played its part as well, with films like Orson Welles's *Touch of Evil*, based on a fictionalized version of Tijuana, depicting the city's red-light district as a lawless labyrinth that turns women into drug addicts and men into alcoholic thugs. As the protagonist Inspector Mike Vargas, a native of Mexico City, explains to his wife early on, "This isn't the real Mexico, you know that. All border towns bring out the worst in a country." The neighborhood, in these conceptions, has an uncanny ability to unfasten the moral bindings of anyone that visits, with a specialty in seducing Americans. The Zona, it is believed, can unmask and unleash sexual perversions, malice, and even murderous drives that are hidden even from the would-be murderers themselves. It's no accident, then, that the Zona slams into the border wall, as if the neighborhood were breathing down the neck of America, on the cusp of entering. The wall isn't just state security; it is a barrier to prevent Tijuana's madness from entering American minds.

As with the Downtown Eastside, it was easy to believe that the Zona was an island, unmoored from its surroundings. After all, it's enclosed on three sides by a border, a highway, and canyons. But it's a neighbor-hood like any other, coexisting with the world that surrounds it. The power of the border to separate America from the Zona is a fiction; it is the border that has, after all, allowed the Zona to thrive for over a century, giving it just enough exoticism to attract lusty Americans.

For a select few facing the wall from the south, the border is an opportunity as much as it is a burden, its impenetrability a mirage that they routinely puncture. *Pollero*, or "chicken farmer," is the less predatory term used here for the man known elsewhere as *coyote*, or human traf-ficker. In reality, the pollero is a loose network of people—taxi drivers, lookouts, safe house operators, corrupt border guards, and whoever else might be needed—who work the border's broken seams to get their clients across. Tijuana has been a destination for those seeking to pass covertly into the United States for decades, though as the border has hardened, the logistics have become more complicated. That has meant that the cost of the pollero's service, which in the mid-1980s was $250 per trip, has now skyrocketed as it meets the evolving obstacles presented by the U.S. Department of Homeland Security. The cheapest option is a guided trek through the southern Sierras to the east of the city, which will cost the *pollo* (literally the "chicken," or the person being crossed) about $4,000; it also involves a three-day hike through an unforgiving mountain range where people regularly die of thirst. The area is also often used by drug traffickers for smuggling, and coming across a narco convoy means being maimed or executed. With $5,000, the pollero will direct his pollos as they try to run and vault over the border near Playas de Tijuana. Using a system of safe houses and sentries, poll-eros will study the U.S. Border Patrol's shift changes for days, then run alongside the pollos to the fence and boost them over; the first fence is often doable, but the second, which is higher and surrounded by ditches, is much harder to scale. Once in the U.S., the pollos are picked up in cars and stored in safe houses in San Diego before being sent along the last leg of their journey (which generally ends in Los Angeles). Those with $8,000 to spare can try by Jet Ski: in the dead of night, crashing through the waves, the pollero will shuttle the pollo out fifty miles from the coast, zigzagging north through the Pacific Ocean in the hopes of eluding the U.S. Coast Guard. If the client is moneyed, though, things get easier. With $13,000, the pollo can ride in luxury straight through the San Ysidro border crossing, the pollero having struck a deal with a border agent to let them pass without question.

In the 1990s, the punishment for being caught crossing the border was usually a trip back to Mexico. The wall here had not yet transformed from a symbolic obstacle into the hard barrier it is today. In those days, according to the stories polleros tell, it wasn't uncommon to lead hundreds of pollos at a time through holes in the fence in a place nicknamed "the Canyon of Death," located in the northern limits of Los Laureles, and still used today as a crossing point. The day I toured Los Laureles' shantytowns and the maquiladoras that stood sentry above them, Oscar had told me about the tires becoming uprooted with the rains and flowing into the Pacific Ocean and back into California. For the polleros working that route, the rains brought more immediate danger. Walking the canyon floor with their clients, they were at risk of being swept up in flash floods, pinned down, and drowned. In 1993, in just the first two months of the year, 175 migrants were saved from the rising water by U.S. authorities; twenty were killed. The bloated bodies of the dead washed up on the same beaches as the waste tires. "For every body that we have found," a lifeguard from San Diego told the *Los Angeles Times*, "there's a lot more people that have drowned."

I had been tracking some kind of social pathogen and the epidemic of femicide that it caused, and I had done so assuming that everything I needed to uncover would be located here, in Tijuana itself. But my reliance on a dataset of people in the city had caused me to ignore one of the most dynamic aspects of the environment: that Tijuana made up half of a metropolitan region that was spread across both sides of the border, and that while the relationship between those sides had changed dramatically over the years, they had been linked for centuries. That was important, because as an epidemiologist I knew that shifts in the environment often preceded the emergence of epidemics. So, if I was ever going to really understand the femicide, I would need to track how Tijuana and the border had changed, and what had caused those changes. I had only been here a short time, but I knew someone whose memory stretched back decades and who had experienced the environmental shift up close.

*

"The *baquetonas* that hung out in El Gusano—they were the ones assaulting the paradillas of Calle Primera back in those days." Susi was in full-on manic mode, talking a mile a minute as we walked slowly through the Zona with Patty.

"They weren't sex workers, right?" Patty asked, referring to the *baquetonas*, a term that translates as "female thugs.'"

"No. They were addicts. They would steal from the Americans who went there."

"To El Gusano?" I asked, trying to piece together what I could from Susi's wild recollections. I had been asking her and Patty about how changes in Tijuana and the flow of human traffic over the border affected the rhythm of the Zona. Susi had responded with half-remembered stories of bars and people that had vanished after the fortunes of the red-light district dwindled in recent years. There was El Molino Rojo, now closed—named after Paris's famous Moulin Rouge. El Redacción— The Edit—was the newspaperman's brothel, where ficheras had to meet a nightly quota of drinks, bought by clients, using whatever means possible; it too had come and gone.

"Bar names like that are very common in Mexico," Patty said as we ambled along Avenida Constitución, Tijuana's main tourist strip, passing stores selling knockoff NFL jerseys and novelty sombreros. "They name bars like 'The Office' or 'The Edit' because then a client is like, 'Honey, I'm going to my office.'" Patty laughed at the silliness and I did too. She had a funny way of making jokes that made you laugh and wince at the same time.

El Gusano—The Worm—was one of the most popular spots for military personnel from both sides of the border. "Mexican soldiers always went there," Susi said, as did Americans. If they wanted drugs, her gang of sex worker friends would go buy them. "Then we would get paid ten or twenty dollars. It used to be the place where all the *bajadores* gathered. A lot of Americans used to come from the naval base down here to the Zona Norte."

"It was basically the spot for people that, you know, stole things; that's what the 'bajadores' are," Patty explained.

"Thieves?" I asked.

"Yes, thieves. It was their major headquarters," Patty said, laughing again.

"So it was a club?"

"It was like a . . ." Patty tried to find the right word.

"Like a building?" I offered.

"No, it was like a place where they sell . . ." She turned to Susi. "What did they sell there, beer . . . ?"

"And drugs." Susi said.

"Drugs and beer." Patty shrugged. "It was the contact spot for visitors or people who wanted to have drugs."

"But they used to sell other things too," Susi said. "Passports, *micas*,"—a slang term for an American green card—"*pollos* . . ."

"In that same bar?" asked Patty.

"There and elsewhere," Susi replied. "But not so much now. It still exists but not as much as before. The American soldiers that came down here; I don't know what happened. They don't come anymore. Police officers don't come either. Only when they are working do you see them, but not in the bars anymore. There was a big brawl and the Mexican military stopped coming." Susi looked glum.

We peeled off the main tourist drag and started walking toward the red-light district. There were women everywhere during the day, though there was also a feeling of forced idleness and desperation undercut with the threat of violence. On some nights, mostly weekends, the main clubs were still full of men looking for sex, but Tijuana's sex trade was clearly an industry in decline. From its glory days, when thieving was easy and clients were plentiful, the place had lost its sheen. Women like Rosa—too old or too independent to work in the clubs and requiring the spillover from a large clientele base to make money—felt the effects of the downturn first. The money having dried up, the streets becoming emptier and more dangerous, Rosa was no longer able to set the terms of her encounters.

In her heyday as a hit doctor, Susi had also found a strong market for her skill set. "The women used to pay me to inject them," Susi said, "and not just drugs but penicillin. I used to buy antibiotics and apply the injections for the women." In those days, the going rate was one dollar per injection. And while Susi spent the money on drugs, there was enough work between the women in the clubs and those on the street that she could make a living. "A lot of Americans came to the Zona Norte, to the Avenida Revolución. They used to come and we would go buy drugs for them, in the pharmacies, things they couldn't buy over there [in the U.S.]. And they would give us money." She laughed. "I would do *travesuras*,"—mischiefs—"especially when I went out with Americans, to shoot up and get high. But years ago," she continued, "tourists stopped coming." There were no more Americans with whom Susi could play mischief. Where had they gone?

With Susi it was always hard to piece the whole story together. Memories came in fragments, and between my feeble Spanish and her

Tijuanensis slang I often struggled to make sense of what she was telling me. As much as it pained me to admit, sometimes I wasn't even sure that she knew who I was from one day to the next. We would meet for lunch and she would embrace me; once she gripped my hand hard while tears rolled down her face. Then, the next time I saw her in the El Cuete offices, she stared blankly at me as if I were a stranger. I only knew a little about her background, all of which came from stories that she freely shared. But when she was unwilling to talk there was no point in trying to pull information out of her. When pressed on a subject she didn't like, she would narrow her eyes and stare out fixedly into the distance, her mouth clenched shut. At first I thought it was cultural, some social cue I hadn't followed or understood. Later, I started to understand it as a kind of defense mechanism that protected her from particularly traumatic recollections.

Susi, like Steffanie, overwhelmed you with her exuberance and the immediacy of her knowledge. Talking to Steffanie about HIV research, no matter how arcane the topic, felt like listening to someone's cherished memories. While my scientific knowledge always felt like it lived outside of me, set apart somehow, there was no disconnect between Steffanie's formal expertise and her personality: they were fused, as if the statistics she quoted were an indelible part of her. With Susi, every dusty corner of the Zona held some significance. She would be overwhelmed and start crying while talking about a friend she had not seen in twenty years as if they had just parted, or laugh uproariously as she described the tricks she used to play on unsuspecting tourists a decade earlier. I often got the sense that the intensity of the past had overwhelmed her present life and that I, and everyone else, would always be on her periphery, barely registering. Once, she spied a man about to inject drugs behind a parked car half a block up and sped toward him, yelling at us to catch up. "See, see," she called out loudly as she stood directly over him and pointed down at his arm, "you wanted to see injecting, right?" I blanched and tried to call her back; the man didn't seem to care. The awkwardness and humiliation of the moment didn't register for Susi, as if her life in the city had pushed her beyond the edge of feeling.

What I did get from her stories, though, was a vision of Tijuana's sex trade that resembled an ecosystem rather than a monolithic unit. Behind the phalanx of commercial police guarding the large clubs dominating La Coahuila, a whole web of players was operating. This being Tijuana, it would be wrong to call them out of sight. It seemed instead that you just needed to hang out long enough and somebody like Susi would usher you behind the curtain. There were the big clubs—Hong Kong, Adelita's, El Chavelas—that enjoyed the protection of the commercial police and which, Susi claimed, were affiliated with cartels. Then there were the smaller, less reputable brothels, spartan places, where women and rooms were bought as a package, devoid of a glitzy façade. Another step down and you encountered places like the Hotel San Jorge, where La Paniqueada was killed, and which relied on the paraditas outside and women who lived on the premises to bring clients in and keep the lights on. Below that, the ecology of sex work in Tijuana gets more complicated. Women do house calls to johns, sometimes living with them for a spell. Others, more desperate for money or drugs, will work the network of picaderos that stretch from the Zona across the city, these outposts at the edge of the border fence and along the canal that extend like sentinels into neighborhoods otherwise untouched by Tijuana's vice economies.

Las Palmitas, the picadero at the edge of Zona Norte overseen by the ancient manager, is just twenty feet from the border. From its crumbling edifice women run toward the wall to evade police. Other picaderos are scattered across the city: Las Bombas (The Bombs), El Azteca, Vecindad Del Loco (Crazy Neighborhood) southwest of the Zona, La Conchita (The Little Cunt or Little Seashell) in the canyons near Oscar Romo's symbolic plaza. The list goes on and on, a picadero for every neighborhood, as conveniently located as subway stops. Yes, they were quiet, hidden places to do drugs. But they were also unofficial outposts of the city's sex trade, often the last stop for women who had tumbled down the tiers and then kept tumbling. They spread the monetization of women's bodies from its epicenter in the Zona and across the entire city.

Buried in the El Cuete dataset were stories of these women and of picaderos, hundreds of stories transmuted into data. The numbers described scenes of hidden favors exchanged for drugs behind dusty crumbling half walls. The sex trade lay across Tijuana like a probability distribution, its center looming over the Zona with the big clubs and hotels, its tails extending to the picaderos, the outliers of activity. In statistics, an outlier is a data point that resembles no other, lost in the margins of probability, often ignored lest it corrupt your analysis. But in this strange epidemic, those hidden spaces, ignored and isolated, were exactly where I needed to be looking.

At each level of the sex trade, there is a balance between danger and freedom. The women chained to the big clubs were surveilled and protected; those on lower rungs could roam with greater freedom but faced mounting threats the further they fell. It isn't a static system: women move across strata as they become too old or addicted, as clients come and go, or as the industry contracts. Women tumble down the tiers, fanning out from the Zona into a rough patchwork of sites across the city. And in this way the sex trade creeps past the formal boundary of the Zona and out into the city beyond. As I learned more about Tijuana, I also discovered that this ecosystem didn't even end at the wall. Like the goods assembled and shipped from the maquiladoras, like the waste tires, like the clients of polleros, and like Tijuana itself, the sex trade presses up against the border and spreads across it.

Until a couple of years ago, a turnstile was all that separated the United States from Tijuana. The border's daily rhythm, the push and pull of people, over one hundred thousand every day, kept the mechanism well worn, and tourists sweating in the desert heat slowly worked the paint off of the steel bars. Susi and Rosa both talked frequently about the good old days, when the Zona was overwhelmed by Americans and their fortunes were buoyed by a surfeit of willing johns and easy marks. Their "good old days" were the late 1990s and early 2000s. But as I dug into the history of the city, the era of good fortune they were talking about extended far back into the past century, with only a few interruptions. That's because one particular visitor has been nurturing the red-light district throughout Tijuana's history, and has done more than any other to sustain the sex workers and the industries they serve. That visitor is the U.S. military. What's more, I discovered that the long relationship between the military and the Zona better explained the dangers women now face in Tijuana than any risk factor I had encountered to date.

*

America's skittish relationships with power and substance use were the twin catalysts that caused Tijuana—and its reputation—to grow exponentially. In 1921, the city's population was just 1,028, but the sleepy village at the border swelled throughout the ensuing decades as U.S. policies made Tijuana an increasingly indispensable place to service the needs of Americans. The first of these lucky policy changes came in the 1920s as Americans sought refuge from Prohibition. By 1931, Tijuana had expanded to 8,328 permanent residents, and that year the townspeople were overwhelmed by more than five million Americans who crossed the border seeking alcohol, prostitution, and horse races, all of which were illegal in California during that time. While Prohibition made Tijuana a haven for booze, American moral authorities nevertheless tried vainly to stop the flow south. During the Prohibition era, Christian volunteers stationed themselves at the border and pleaded with American revelers to turn back in order to save themselves. In 1926, a director of San Diego's Methodist Episcopal Church sounded the alarm in no uncertain terms: "Tijuana is not so much a place as a condition which extends for some eighteen hundred miles along our Mexican border . . . It represents a step over the line which means to many the temporary breaking from accepted standards and the letting down of moral conduct." Unfortunately for the church, this is the kind of publicity money just can't buy.

With the buildup of the U.S. Navy's presence in San Diego during the Second World War, a steady supply of young men on furlough were placed mere steps from this moral danger. This placement was another lucky policy change that helped Tijuana's growth continue unchecked even after Prohibition ended in 1933 and Americans didn't have to leave their country to legally drink. Shore leave in the Mexican outpost became a rite of passage for the thousands of military personnel up the road. By 1940, Tijuana's population had once again doubled, this time to 16,486 residents.

Two years later, in support of the war effort, the U.S. Office of Price Administration imposed mandatory rationing across the United States. All at once, the purchase of tires, cars, typewriters, bicycles, stoves, and rubber-soled shoes was limited to people who demonstrated a special need, in an effort to divert rubber and metals to the production of military equipment. Butter, coffee, sugar, cooking fat, and gasoline were all closely rationed. The result was a run on the border to purchase goods in Tijuana, to the benefit of both the city and American households. By 1950, the city had expanded again, this time nearly quadrupling its size from just a decade earlier to 59,952.

Tijuana's continual growth during this period, fueled largely by the naval presence across the border, concealed a critical shift that would set it on a path up to the present day. The illegality of alcohol, gambling, and prostitution in California in the first part of the twentieth century was the pillar that made Tijuana an indispensable part of American border life. But the end of Prohibition in 1933, the opening of the Santa Anita racetrack in Los Angeles County in 1934, and the banning of casino gambling in 1935 by Mexican president Lázaro Cárdenas abruptly transformed the economy of the city. This triple shot crippled Tijuana's market share of American vice. In 1936, after President Cárdenas forced the closure of the luminous Agua Caliente casino, the crown jewel of Tijuana, the *New York Times* declared the city a "ghost town." With its decades-long monopoly on two of the three vice industries gone, the city had no choice but to invest heavily in the only one that still remained exclusively under its purview: prostitution. At a time when Americans saw sex as dangerous, that made Tijuana something like the gates of hell.

Articles from those days paint a picture of a city with a fully realized power to undo the American psyche. A "border hell town" as *Coronet* magazine described it in a lurid front-page story in 1956, where American teenagers "step in to a saloon and buy drinks, then stroll back to the washroom and buy marijuana, then wander into a book store and study pornographic books and pictures, then walk along the main street and pick up a prostitute, and top off the evening by stopping at an all-night pharmacy." The American Board of Temperance, Prohibition, and Public Morals of the Methodist Church, called Tijuana "a mecca of prostitutes, booze sellers, gamblers and other American vermin." This vitriol did nothing to slow Tijuana's ascent: by 1960 the city had more than doubled in size yet again, its growth fueled by yet another buildup of naval power in San Diego during and after the Korean War (1950–53). It seemed there would be enough American vermin (in uniform) to keep the city afloat for decades to come.

Field trips to Tijuana continued to be an ingrained ritual for naval servicemen stationed in San Diego on liberty from their duties. The city played an essential function in maintaining the mental health of young men whose freedom had been usurped in exchange for some kind of patriotic glory. In Tijuana, though, the collusion between the all-American conservatism of the military and the boundless fantasies of the sex trade was abnormally intricate; it's no accident that the Zona Norte is by some estimates the largest red-light district in the Americas, while San Diego boasts the largest naval base on the West Coast of the United States.

The U.S. Navy, it turns out, after decades of informally financing Tijuana's sex trade, readily understood both the risks and the need for a conveniently located playground for its servicemen, to the point that it saw the trade as falling under its protection. And so, in 1988, as the AIDS epidemic spread across North America, the navy began covertly testing Tijuana's sex workers for HIV. "Its sailors visit Tijuana every weekend," argued one of the program's directors at the time. "It was beneficial to both sides to see how extensive the problem was along the border." The

HIV testing campaign wasn't the end of it: the navy also took the unusual and logistically challenging step of shipping eight hundred thousand condoms a month to Mexico, reflecting the scope of the problem it believed its personnel were facing in Tijuana. Despite these steps, though, there were warnings even back then that the epidemic could spread out of control. "Many of those women were intravenous drug users," added the program director, "so we can't be sure that sexual intercourse was a significant factor" in the spread of HIV.

*

Tijuana transformed itself from a village into a thriving metropolis by following the simple logic of supply and demand and providing Americans what they wanted—gambling, alcohol, and sex. Throughout its history, the "border hell town," a place of American vermin and vice, saw its fortunes rise and flag. But it was always able to rely on the energetic lust of the American military, as reliable a force of good fortune for the denizens of the Zona Norte as it aspired to be on the battlefield. With the navy's backing, Tijuana's vice economy could be confident in its future, and with good reason. Where else were those young men going to go when their regimented daily routine—and the boredom that inevitably set in—became intolerable?

But as Tijuana became overwhelmed by drug war violence, its biggest customer got cold feet. In December 2008, at the close of a year in which 843 people were murdered in the city, Lt. Gen. Samuel Helland, commanding officer of the First Marine Expeditionary Force based at Camp Pendleton, San Diego, declared Tijuana off-limits for its servicemen. "The situation in Mexico is now more dangerous than usual," he said at the time. "The intent is just to look out for the Marines' safety and well-being." The order, enforceable under the Uniform Code of Military Justice, meant that violators could face a court-martial.

Suddenly, forty-four thousand active marines were no longer able to make the trip south, a huge hit to Tijuana's target demographic. A few weeks later, in January 2009, similar restrictions were placed on the approximately seventy-five thousand active duty naval sailors also stationed near the border. The twin bans cast a chilling effect on the sex trade. For the first time in almost a century, Tijuana could no longer rely on a steady supply of clientele to support the roughly ten thousand women there who sell their bodies and who in turn provide the fulcrum for a set of ancillary businesses—bars, drug dealing, hotels, restaurants—that rely on those same bodies to keep the dollars flowing.

This is what Rosa and Susi meant when they happily reminisced about life in the Zona in the early 2000s. This was the period when the Zona was still the U.S. Navy's entertainment annex. By the time I arrived in 2013, the city had become used to its abandonment, and hope seemed by and large to have disappeared as American dollars dwindled and the horrors of the drug war escalated. It wasn't just the drug war's violence that had changed life in the Zona. Listening to the stories, it had always been a place riven by conflict; the city could handle that. The most consequential part of the drug war, arguably, was that it caused that most august American institution—the military—to pull out of the city, decimating the last of the vice markets that Tijuana still had cornered. Without that market, the Zona became an empty landscape. Here was the perfect environment to force women into survival mode, a place where the social pathogen could thrive and a femicide could take root.

The Zona nowadays is like a bruise on the body of the border, an unwanted reminder of love or violence. But the history of the place demonstrates that this epidemic is not just Tijuana's, and the border is no separator; a mere physical barrier cannot achieve that aim. Instead, it is a complicator of relationships. If anything, the imposition of the border along the edge of the Zona has revealed one important truth: the higher the wall, the deeper the secret.

PART III

The Pathogen

CHAPTER 7

Mythmaking

The medieval Spanish fantasy novel *Las Sergas de Esplandián* (The Adventures of Esplandián) follows the titular Spanish knight as he embarks on picaresque adventures through mythic lands. One of his stops is an island called California, peopled by female warriors, the Black Amazons, who fight with gold weapons from encampments atop high cliffs and who only leave their homeland to steal loot from sailors. The island teems with griffins, beasts with the head and wings of an eagle and the body of a lion, to which the women feed baby boys and male prisoners captured in battle. In the novel, the Amazon queen of California is tempted into joining a Muslim Turkish army readying to sack a Christian town for its gold. Esplandián, good Christian knight, is on hand to stop their villainous piracy.

Upon arriving for battle at the head of a great Amazonian armada, the queen releases her troop of griffins, which promptly set about destroying the Christian army. The monsters catch soldiers in their claws, fly high into the air, and drop their bodies onto the rocks and waves below. It's a rout. But no sooner do the Turks and Amazons start celebrating than the griffins set about destroying them too. Once released into battle, the creatures are too wild to tame; their violence has crossed a threshold and cannot be contained. The accidental massacre of the Turks creates an opening for Esplandián and his Christian forces. As the monsters attack their masters, the Christians take advantage of the chaos to capture the

Amazon queen and her female warriors. The women are put in chains and enslaved.

Despite herself, during her captivity, the Amazon queen falls in love with Esplandián. Instead of consummating their romance, though, Esplandián offers the queen a deal: repent, convert to Christianity, and marry a lesser knight, and she and her warriors will be freed. She assents and the prisoners, Amazons when they left, are led back to California as broken women under the ownership of minor Christian knights in command of their bodies and their home.

The earliest known edition of *Las Sergas* dates to 1496. In 1533, Hernán Cortés's army landed at the southern tip of what is now known as the Baja California Peninsula. A rival to Cortés first referred to the place as "California," in 1540, a name that was meant as an insult. The peninsula's terrain was so inhospitable that it reminded him of the island of California, the home of the Black Amazons and their queen. The name stuck, creating a strange legacy for this novel-turned-landmass. The U.S. state of California—known as Alta California prior to the Spanish-American War—has, fittingly, long been the place where fiction comes to life, where Disneyland and Hollywood spin stories into myth, and where identities are as interchangeable as cheap T-shirts. Meanwhile, across the border in Baja California, the basic plot of *Las Sergas* echoes on today in Tijuana. Women seek gold and their right to govern their own bodies in a patriarchal world, and both of these goals can end up leaving them in chains. In the Zona, men just like Esplandián and his knights set the rules, demanding women submit and then calling it freedom. Those dangerous women who cannot or will not yield are held captive until they do, their bodies turned into a new kind of currency.

*

Every epidemiologic model requires a comparison group. It's a straightforward concept: the only way to measure the effect of a risk factor driving an epidemic is to find a subset of the population that has not been exposed. When that risk factor is the city itself—the stage upon which the entire phenomenon plays itself out—the epidemiologist finds herself in a predicament. Just as with cigarettes and lung cancer, if absolutely everyone is affected by a certain risk factor, you're patently unable to account for it in a model. It just disappears into the background. That leaves the epidemiologist with two options for constructing comparison groups. One approach is to search across geographic space for a setting similar enough to the one under study and then compare the health of populations in both places. While those populations might be separated spatially, they should be similar enough to allow for meaningful conclusions to be drawn about what makes people in one setting susceptible to an epidemic compared to the other.

The second approach is to move back and forth through time. If the epidemiologist is convinced that there was some kind of disruption in the environment that let the pathogen loose, she can compare data from the same people before and after that disruption. It's a sneaky way of creating a comparison group out of a single damaged population, the assumption being that one can go back far enough to a time before the epidemic began, when the victims were still ignorant of what was to come. The epidemiologist then observes the passage of time as the population succumbs to something that feels to them like fate. To the epidemiologist, though, it is the predictable conclusion of variables working in concert to sicken and kill.

No other town across the U.S.-Mexico border rivals Tijuana in the richness of the available data on drugs, sex, and disease. It was unlikely, then, that a spatial comparison of the circumstances of women's deaths would yield meaningful results. But Tijuana has history, both a well-documented official version and the secret stories of the women who live in the Zona and its environs. Worming my way back to a time before the femicide flared could reveal important clues about how it had been unleashed. I already had a sense of when that might have occurred: the U.S. Navy's abandonment of the city in 2009 appeared to be a key environmental shift that unlocked the full virulence of some kind of social pathogen stalking women. That abandonment had been undertaken after the city's cartels had already grown too powerful and too reckless, leading the Mexican government to initiate a military campaign against them, which had, in turn, quickly transformed into a civil war.

Cartel power enveloped Tijuana in a pervasive and corrupt system of rule that acted in tandem with the city's formal system of government. As I learned about how that looked from the perspective of people living in the city, I was reminded of Tom's first attempt at hiring a research coordinator—the medical doctor who also happened to run a few dojos—whose story seemed to epitomize a core survival strategy for Tijuanenses. It struck me as zany when I first heard about it, this tale of the karate master/doctor, but this duality exemplifies border life. In the way that everyone in Los Angeles has a film script in their back pocket, everyone in Tijuana appears to have another personality, another life riding along with them. It amounts to side hustles metastasizing into full-blown identities, and it comes, in part, from the basic demands of being poor: in the Mexican states bordering the U.S., where between 30 and 40 percent of the population lives under the poverty line, there's a need to find more than one source of income to survive. But that isn't the only reason. People in Tijuana and other border cities are tantalizingly close to vast wealth. It's there across the wall in America, but it's closer still in the graft that bubbles up from the beat cop on the street to the opulent narco ranches, touching everyone along the way. Participating in a system of corruption that far-reaching means always being willing to become another person if the situation demands it.

When everyone is in on the game, the cartels and their allies in Mexico can use tools other than violence (which can backfire, after all, and lead to infighting between warring factions, weakening the market as a whole) to maintain power. They are also able to convince ordinary people that there are only two options: nihilism or complicity. That every system of control they are led through in their daily lives has a basement where the bodies and the money are kept, that everyone knows about it, and that resistance means death.

*

If I was going to map the femicide, I would need to better understand how this system of control had transformed over time. Underneath the schematic I was building to analyze the multifaceted epidemic, I was starting to glimpse a common element. Cartel forces infiltrated the Tijuana Municipal Police Department because they knew that they wouldn't be stopped. La Paniqueada was murdered in a room at the Hotel San Jorge, where she was surrounded by sixty thin-walled rooms in the middle of Tijuana's busiest district, and nobody intervened. The cartels came brazenly, alongside the hooded policemen, to violate Rosa and her friends; they did so because there was no higher power to whom their victims could appeal. In their wake were left the bodies, found dead and dismembered across the city and its coastal arteries.

Narcos will do whatever is required to cling to their market share. It's the line that they have trumpeted for years, and they've backed up their words through the thousands of atrocities they've committed in Mexico. At last count, the country's drug war has claimed over 170,000 victims, with over 280,000 people internally displaced. Mass graves have been found all over the country, the victims often migrant laborers or students who have found themselves at the wrong place at the wrong time.

The terror enacted in Mexico makes it difficult to think of cartels as anything but one-note actors, trigger happy and reveling in the explosion of violence. That may make a good headline, but the economics behind the drug trade make it clear that that's simply not the case. The formalization of the plaza system kept the peace in Mexico for almost four decades while the cartels expanded their power, everyone involved in the system making money while violence was kept to a low boil. It was the state under President Felipe Calderón—not the cartels—that finally launched the initial attack in 2006, which signaled the end of an accord that had been decaying since the 1990s and set the stage for the Mérida Initiative–funded drug war of 2008 and beyond. This is obviously not to absolve the narcos of guilt. But it's important to remember that while violence can be a powerful political tool, it's terrible for the bottom line, and the one aim of the cartels is to maximize profit. They are businessmen, after all, and like most businessmen they want the kind of market predictability that comes in times of peace. The chaos of war allows control to slip away. The challenge for me was to understand what the Zona was like during this earlier time period in order to turn it into a comparison group of sorts. If done correctly, that approach would then lead me to the root causes of the femicide.

*

There is a way to describe the interactions between a woman and her predators—the sale of her body, her arrest by police and subsequent blackmail for sex, drug use forced upon her by a client—in terms of human lust and the excesses of power. In a place without rules, everyone is susceptible to being so overcome by desire that moral boundaries recede past the horizon. And, the story goes, if the women are pretty and they inhabit a role—as a sex worker—that practically begs a man to give into his basest wants, how can he resist?

Epidemiology tells the story another way. Multiply that interaction thousands of times, across hundreds of men in power and thousands of women day after day within the Zona Norte, and the specifics of a single man's relationship with a sex worker blurs into a larger pattern. The abuse of women was endemic, a systematic consequence of working in the Zona. Endemic in its truest sense—meaning "within the people"—a condition as predictable as the winter flu.

When a system of violation against women's bodies is that deeply ingrained, it can spread in unlikely ways, even colonizing those who believe they are there to prevent its damage. The core mission of epidemiology—to stop people from getting sick and dying—may be noble, but the track record of the science isn't spotless. Epidemiologists have engaged in ethically dubious practices that, far from empowering their subjects, have risked amplifying the conditions that cause them to get sick and die in the first place. Unsurprisingly, this most often arises when research is being done in lower-income settings (like Tijuana), where scientists have to thread the needle between producing rigorous research, optimizing public health, and working with local actors and institutions. Take HIV test results: while it might seem obvious that people who participate in HIV research studies should be given the option of learning whether they are HIV-positive or not, doing so isn't actually the standard of care. In fact, some scientists engaging in research in sub-Saharan Africa have argued that there's an ethical imperative not to share HIV test results with study participants. Providing test results, their argument goes, would artificially skew the study's findings because participants might change their behavior after they learn their status, thereby making it harder for scientists to craft a disease prevention strategy that can respond effectively to the true local conditions driving the epidemic. That amounts, of course, to sacrificing the health (and potentially the lives) of current participants to the promise of an effective scientific solution to the epidemic. In HIV research, women who work in the sex trade or who inject drugs—marginalized and poor women—often make up a study's sample. In this cold scientific calculus, their lives are worth far less than those people in the (perhaps distant) future that might be saved. That's quite a cost to weigh, especially when there's no guarantee that the promise will be fulfilled.

This willingness to subordinate the well-being of study participants in favor of a supposed greater good can lead scientists to troubling choices. In the early 2000s, as the era of highly effective antiretroviral treatment for HIV was transforming the disease into a manageable chronic condition, scientists began to explore a new strategy to stop the global pandemic. Treatment for HIV had become so effective at preventing viral replication that providing it to people who weren't yet infected but who were at high risk of seroconverting might, they posited, prevent HIV from establishing reservoirs in new hosts even if the virus entered their bloodstream. This approach, known as pre-exposure prophylaxis, or PrEP, is now a central plank of global HIV prevention, but it almost never got off the ground. That's because some of the earliest PrEP clinical trials, carried out in Cambodia and Cameroon, were halted after activist groups discovered that the trial scientists and their funders had engaged in major ethical lapses.

It's common practice to provide HIV research participants with HIV prevention counseling during their time enrolled in a study. In fact, access to these types of services is one the most basic reasons why people agree to be enrolled in trials of this kind because it provides them with a modicum of protection from disease. But in the case of the Cambodian trial, which was restricted to female sex workers, none of these basic preventive benefits were offered. Beyond a small honorarium, the sex workers were getting nothing while risking their bodies testing experimental medicines—drugs that would potentially make pharmaceutical companies billions of dollars.

That situation arose precisely because scientists wanted to isolate the impact of PrEP on preventing HIV. Perversely, the higher the number of participants in the non-PrEP arm that acquired HIV, the better the results looked for the PrEP arm. That meant there was an implicit incentive on the part of the scientists to skimp on providing basic forms of disease prevention. That's a situation that's not unique to PrEP: with practically any intervention being tested, scientists generally prefer to see as many positive results as possible among participants exposed to the intervention they're testing and as few as possible in the placebo arm to justify the work they're doing. Normally, though, this desire is tempered by an obligation to ensure that participants receive substantive benefits from their enrollment.

Similar concerns ended up halting the PrEP trial in Cameroon. Worse, unsubstantiated rumors began to spread that not only were the scientists failing to provide basic HIV prevention services but they were also intentionally infecting participants with HIV. That latter claim was untrue, but it reflected suspicions about the low value the scientists placed on the lives of participants—suspicions that weren't entirely unfounded. The prime example of this lack of concern about participants' well-being was the fact that both the Cambodian and Cameroonian trial sponsors refused to provide PrEP to participants after the trial ended. Anyone who wanted the drug—including the women who had been paid a pittance to test its effects on their bodies—would have to buy it. This being a novel, first-generation pharmaceutical, the price was far beyond their means. When the news got out, both trials were halted.

The failure of the PrEP trials reveals the power imbalance that can emerge when scientists—often from wealthy foreign countries and backed by well-heeled funders—embark on research in settings in which they wield power. That's not to say that scientists will artificially ratchet up the dangers faced by some study participants. Institutional research ethics boards oversee all credible scientific research involving even the slightest risk, and they make sure that any study that moves ahead includes basic provisions to protect everyone involved (since the PrEP trials, post-trial access to HIV treatment for participants has become the norm). Nevertheless, the PrEP saga makes plain that scientists sometimes end up skirting or even crossing ethical lines. Take away the specifics of the situation and that can look remarkably like that familiar phenomenon: the powerful enacting injustice on the vulnerable.

Health and social dangers have a tendency to pool among poor people. That's why we see higher rates of smoking, diabetes, overdose, poor nutrition, untreated drug addiction, and a slew of other preventable health harms among poorer cross sections of the population. It's also why we often see higher rates in poorer countries versus wealthier ones. These are structural issues, meaning that when you swap in new power players—even when they are scientists—they are still beholden to an old system of control.

Just like anyone else, scientists are at risk of carrying their unconscious biases and cultural norms into new situations. The main difference between scientists and everyone else, one could argue, is that the former have had their sense of empathy systematically eroded through their training in the scientific method, which replaces natural human instinct with rigorous protocols of action. Add to that the hubris of the scientific class—supreme confidence in the power of our good intentions and our methods to overcome any obstacle, ethical or otherwise—and the possibility of ethical lapses is always present.

Each PrEP study participant given a placebo who subsequently acquired HIV bolstered the results of the study in favor of PrEP. That is an unavoidable yet troubling scientific fact. It lays bare the truth that people's bodies are the basic currency of epidemiologic work. The Cambodian PrEP trial was undertaken among women who worked in the sex trade; this made sense given that these were the women at highest risk of acquiring the virus. But they were also women whose bodies were regularly traded for money. It isn't coincidence that these same women, experienced in this type of exchange, were asked by scientists to repeat it again, this time in the name of a potential HIV cure. Science is a system of power, liable to be corrupted just like any other. Spend even a little time in places like Tijuana, and it becomes clear that it will take more than a scientific protocol to undo the systems of control that run ragged over the people living in its margins.

*

I thought back to Rosa's accounts of the impunity that she had witnessed, stories of rape and violation. The only difference was which side of the law the perpetrators operated on. In my office I listened back to the tapes of our interviews. "It's more *descarado* now," you can hear her saying calmly amid the din of the daytime noise of the Zona Norte on one recording, a good day when *la malilla* wasn't holding her hostage as badly and she was able to relax a little. *Descarado* means "shameless," and Rosa's implication was that life had gotten more hazardous lately for women like her. Her word choice stuck out to me because she'd used it more than once during our interviews. I scrolled through some of the audio and listened again to an earlier conversation, rewinding to a line that had stuck with me: "Maybe it's the same *chingadera* [the same old shit] now," you can hear her say, a throttled tension in her throat, "but it used to be more *descarado*."

Upon listening to it a second time, I was stumped. The "chingadera" interview had been recorded in 2015, and Rosa was adamant that life in the Zona had gotten safer (less descarado now); the second interview was conducted about eighteen months later, in 2017 (more descarado). Even though you can tell from her voice that she's less afflicted by her heroin addiction, she speaks of the shamelessness almost as if it were a plague that had returned to the Zona. As far as I knew, there had been no radical change during that time, at least not on the order of the drug war violence that had come crashing down on Tijuana in 2008 and which had largely receded by 2013. And yet, some essential quality in Rosa's life had been altered. The shamelessness of those years of extreme corruption that she had lived through back in the 1990s had returned. She was quieter, more cautious, and while she seemed more focused, some essential energy had been sapped from her. I let the audio play.

"I'm fifty-two years old," you can hear her say on the later tape, "and I've been here over twenty years. When I moved here the police were responsible for the violence. I used to sleep with a big lock on the door of my room to keep them out."

"Where did you live?"

"Really close to here, close to El Bordo [the canal]. When I moved there it was really dangerous, but it's different than what you see today."

"And before, when you moved here, that didn't happen?"

"Well kind of, but it was more that we were abused by police officers and *malandros*"—rascals—"the abuse came from both sides."

"So let's say twenty years ago, the violence was between the bad guys and the police?"

"Yes, and now it's different—now anyone who wants to get rid of someone and has *feria* [money]; just like that, in the middle of the day, they can stab you."

Rosa arrived in the 1990s into a place and time that Susi once referred to laughingly as "that old-school Zona Norte," where women's lives were bounced between cops and narcos, and the paraditas got by using their bodies as distractions while they emptied out the wallets of passed-out johns in nondescript hotel rooms. A time when people were descarado. I was seeking my comparison group—whether through space or in time—to further understand what made women succumb to the femicide. Rosa's memories of the waxing and waning of the Zona's shamelessness were a perfect lens to divide up the Zona's most important time periods.

The early 1990s was a "pre-femicide" period when the murder rates in Tijuana and San Diego were still relatively low, averaging about 10 per 100,000 inhabitants in both cities, before whatever rip in Tijuana's fabric exposed women to the virulent social pathogen and its consequences. The period of shamelessness reached a nadir with Jorge Hank Rhon's corrupt mayoralty in the mid-2000s and the infiltration of the Tijuana Municipal Police Department by the cartel shortly thereafter. These were incremental shifts, marked by the ascension of the Tijuana Cartel; these were Rosa's malandros, her rascals. But then came the crash: the counterintelligence operation undertaken by Arnulfo Bañuelos, Victor Alaniz, and other "good cops," ending with forty-six officers killed in two weeks, and then the spasms of drug war violence flaring in 2008, with narcomantas pinned on desecrated bodies, daytime executions, and dismembered female corpses. The shamelessness returning, now as a frenzy of horror and mass murder. The worst extremes of violence began to recede from Tijuana in 2011; still, the city's homicide rates for both men and women stayed high enough above the epidemic threshold to be self-sustaining. It was a period of charged pause, everyone aware that the respite was temporary.

Now, in 2015, only a few years later, it wasn't just the homicide rate that marked how bad things had gotten; it was also the rate of solved versus unsolved murders. The seventy-person Baja California homicide investigations unit, which does far and away the bulk of its business in Tijuana, has a clearance rate of 12 percent, meaning that about nine out of ten murders in Tijuana and across the state remain forever unsolved. It was another telltale marker of how deeply the impunity of violence had been absorbed into the system.

The most dangerous epidemics are those driven by pathogens that become more virulent over time. The 1918 Spanish flu infected 500 million people and killed between 20 and 50 million. When evolutionary biologists studied the virus, they found that it was made up of eight separate genetic segments common to previous avian, human, swine, and equine flu strains. Genetic mutations occur at predictable rates over time, and animal-specific flu viruses each mutate at different rate, set to a distinct "molecular clock." That allowed the researchers to follow the patterns of the molecular clocks back in time. When they did, they found that the ancestors of the eight strains that make up the Spanish flu first appeared together in a virus that showed up sometime between 1866 and 1878, at least forty years prior to the epidemic. What's more, one of the Spanish flu's ancestors almost certainly caused an 1872 horse flu epidemic that originated in Toronto and spread across North America that year, wreaking havoc on the continental transportation network, which at the time was almost wholly dependent on horses to move goods and people. Tens of thousands of horses either died or were killed to prevent further infection, and the economies of major cities ground to a halt. In a sense, the virus was even responsible for the Great Boston Fire of 1872; the city's firefighters were tragically late to the scene of the blaze because, without horses, they had to pull their own water wagons. All of that, though, was just a prelude, an initial feint. When the virus reemerged in 1918, unbowed and with newfound brutality, its virulence was no match for a nascent globalizing world left weakened by total war.

A similar phenomenon occurred in Tijuana. There, some kind of pathogen—which emerged during periods of impunity or shamelessness— lurked for decades. Occasionally, it led to the death of women, though others, like Rosa and Susi, continued to live, work, and use without succumbing. Then, somehow it mutated. A new form of the pathogen arose in the aftermath of Mexico's 2008 drug war, more brutal than before, when the shamelessness suffused the Zona like a gas. The silent protector and client of the city's sex trade, the U.S. Navy, pulled up stakes and returned to its base on the other side of the wall. A month later, two rogue sailors killed a sex worker in a hotel, in a sign of the upending of the old order. As the local market for drugs expanded into Tijuana's extended network of picaderos, that centripetal force pulled rivals like the Sinaloa Cartel into the city with the promise of new profits. The result was more violence. In the wake of increased competition for the drug trade, the police became just another faction for the narcos to deal with through violence or graft. And while most people, myself included, saw a city that was returning to calm, hoping that this cycle had finally ended, Rosa—who lived in the epicenter of the epidemic—saw something else. Shamelessness was on the rise again. I had no reason to disbelieve her.

The Tijuana we were in now was a different environment altogether than it was twenty or even ten years before. Rosa's accounting of the changes she had witnessed within the Zona suggested a way to compare past versions of this place to the period after an environmental shift had allowed the femicide to expand. I would have to pinpoint when the pathogen became more virulent, unleashing a true epidemic. Like the Spanish flu, it had mutated from some earlier threat. Like hepatitis C, it was, for a brief moment, just lurking. The descarado, Rosa knew, was returning.

CHAPTER 8

Modes of Control

The novelized fiction of the Black Amazons and the island of California isn't the region's first origin story. The Kumeyaay, indigenous to lands spanning present-day San Diego and Tijuana dating back twelve thousand years, have a creation myth—the Story of the Shooting Star—that begins with the incestuous coupling of the Sun and his sister the Moon. The product of their union, a girl, bathes in a pond every day and soon becomes pregnant with twin boys. From the start, the sons are willful and dangerous, disobeying their mother and at times coming close to killing her. As they come of age, the two pugilists leave home, marry two sisters, and are eventually killed by the father of their brides; their flesh is eaten by villagers and their bones used for a ball game. One of their wives bears a child who is then hunted by his grandfather, the same man who killed his father and uncle.

This boy survives the hunt and systematically takes his revenge on the people that killed his ancestors. In some versions of the myth, he kills everyone responsible for the murders, including his grandfather, his grandfather's wife, his own mother, his aunt, and the entire community of villagers who supported them. He then flees the village, setting out with another uncle who takes pity on him.

Calamity soon meets them once again. The boy and his uncle are pursued by the elements of Fire and Wind, and flames start to lick at their house. Fire itself tells the boy to become icy and to hide in the dirt. Once the flames have died down, the boy searches for his uncle and eventually digs up the charred body from the piles of dust and ash that have buried it. The dead uncle speaks to him: "You ought not to have done this," the uncle says, "as you will make a great deal of trouble, sorrow, and sickness in the world unless you are very careful, when you put me back, not to let a breath of wind arise from the place where I am buried." The boy heeds the words. He tries to put the uncle's remains back as delicately as possible, but it's of no use. A puff of air escapes from a crack in the soil as the boy returns the body of his uncle to the earth. This single puff of air, the Kumeyaay claim, is the cause of all the sickness in the world.

*

Every epidemic follows the same basic course. Exploiting some change, it perplexes and momentarily gains purchase on a population. From there, it either recedes or becomes another among the multitude of endemic conditions that make up the landscape of illness and health with which people must contend. While medicine identifies and strikes at the cause of the rot, epidemiology works through inference. Like John Snow investigating the cholera epidemic, we don't need to see the pathogen to be able to stop it; we just need to know that people drank water from a particular well and then died. It's a strange science that way. The ultimate foundations of the world can remain a mystery to epidemiologists even while we set about to control them. We don't need to capture that elusive puff of air. We only need to find the crack in the grave from which it escaped and bury the rotting corpse for good.

Had I found the crack in the grave in Tijuana? My investigation had come a long way, but I had also made incorrect assumptions about the specifics of the epidemiologic triangle here that needed correcting. First, without much experience of the Zona and El Bordo, I had assumed that the women at risk of being overtaken by this amorphous social pathogen were essentially a closed population: a group that was largely fixed, with few new entrants. The truth, though, was that Tijuana was constantly in flux, like a body regenerating cells yet retaining its cohesion, and the population of potential victims was constantly changing. The maquiladoras employed roughly two hundred thousand people across Tijuana, and more than half were women. Worker turnover—from injury, death, or burnout—was high, and the industry was expanding: in 1990, around five hundred maquiladora firms operated in Baja California, but by

2001, that number had nearly tripled. Migrant women were drawn here, many of them unable to find legal work. That meant that the population at risk was constantly being replenished, even as older women like Rosa found themselves inching closer and closer to the end of the line.

Second, I had assumed that the environment ended at the border. This was perhaps my most egregious error. In fact, it was the loosening of the border through NAFTA and its subsequent tightening against the flow of humanity after the drug war that had altered Tijuana's environment and contributed to a sudden decline in the number of Americans flooding the city, to the point that women were forced to take more chances with a rapidly dwindling pool of clients, to whom they gave more of themselves in desperate attempts to stay paid and alive.

Third, I began this investigation assuming that I would be dealing with hard-line cops and ferocious cartels caught in binary conflict. In reality, those relationships were protean and had contributed in more subtle ways to the environmental shifts that influenced the spread of the epidemic. Rosa had put it best: there was a shamelessness that seemed to come and go, and with its movement women found their safety increasing or decreasing. During periods of shamelessness, the collusion between police and cartels seemed to grow as the rule of law waned. Rosa and Susi had referred back to the period of the late 1990s and early 2000s as a particularly shameless time, and this lined up neatly with when Tom first began his research in Tijuana. That being said, it was also a time when the number of women killed in the city was relatively low despite the everyday violence they faced: in the year 2000, Tijuana's female murder rate was 2.5 per 100,000. In the early 2000s, the city was stable until twin tragedies—the attempted takeover of the police department by cartel operatives and the 2008 drug war—scrambled the established order. By 2010, women were being murdered at a rate of 25 per 100,000. Violence exploded at levels unlike any the city had seen before. Environmental shifts had allowed an epidemic of femicide to get out of control. While by 2012 the murder rate in Tijuana had slowed, it nevertheless remained elevated, high above the epidemic threshold. Rosa described this period, the brief respite after the spasms of the drug war, as a less shameless time. But then, for some reason, a new wave of shamelessness emerged, plunging the Zona and Tijuana into a tailspin, the overall murder rate improbably spiking once again, reaching close to 101 homicides per 100,000 in 2017, while the rate for killings of women reached 40 per 100,000.

Fourth, I underestimated the breadth of control cartels could exercise. Tijuana was rife with all manner of uncomfortable truths, from an HIV epidemic to the brutal slayings of women injecting drugs in picaderos. How did cartels maintain control over their fiefdoms in the city? And, more importantly for the femicide epidemic, how did they maintain control over the city's women?

Finally, I was still unsure of how to define the social pathogen. Think of the definition of "pathogen" in John Last's *Dictionary of Epidemiology*: "any organism, agent, factor, or process capable of causing a disease (literally, causing a pathological process)." Like so many entries in Last's tome, here was a tidy definition designed to establish a sturdy foundation for epidemiologic practice (there's nothing epidemiologists like more than watertight definitions). What I understood from the entry was that a pathogen produced binary outcomes: either it infected a person, spreading the epidemic, or it didn't. Under that logic, some women in Tijuana would succumb to the social pathogen and then see their lives and bodies destroyed while others would escape it somehow. There was no middle ground.

I've consulted Last's dictionary more times than I can count, and I read that concise definition of a pathogen over and over as I tried to make sense of the epidemic of femicide I was tracking. It wasn't until much later that I even considered the words in parentheses: "any organism, agent, factor, or process capable of causing a disease *(literally, causing a pathological process)*." What was a "pathological process"? After some digging, I found an article in the *British Medical Journal* (*BMJ*) titled "Diseases Are Really Just Examples of Pathological Processes." The author, a general practitioner from Hereford, England, had written to the journal to quibble with what he believed was an overly reductive way of defining disease states. As he put it, "There are very few diseases that one either definitely has or has not." Asthma, for instance, is a spectrum of breathing disorders that on the margins is exceedingly difficult to define, especially given that all of us might at some time start wheezing as a result of external stimuli. Humans can harbor the influenza virus but fail to ever present with symptoms of the flu; if the pathogen is circulating in your system but you don't feel anything, does that mean you are sick? This way of thinking about pathogens was revelatory. I had always assumed the kinds of infectious diseases I studied could be clearly defined based on whether a virus was present or not. But about 25 percent of people infected with

hepatitis C spontaneously clear the virus, meaning their bodies naturally find a way to stamp out viral copies in their bloodstream without
the aid of modern medicine. Does that mean they are diseased? HIV-
seropositive people who have suppressed the virus in their blood to the
point that it is undetectable (and therefore untransmittable) also
demonstrate how oblique the boundaries between the presence and
absence of disease can be.

In Tijuana, was it correct to say that some women had been infected
by a pathogen leading to death while some had not? If I followed the
thinking of the general practitioner from Hereford, then framing the
issue in those terms was overly simplistic. The point he was making—and
which John Last implied in his entry on pathogens—was that illness and
health exist on a continuum rather than being set against each other in
a binary system. From what I had seen, it made so much more sense to
track a pathological process—a number of factors driving the death of
women in the city—rather than to try to isolate one distinct pathogen.
Just like the police and the cartels, the boundaries between the two sides
were hardly fixed.

I had conceptualized the social pathogen in many different ways: It was
a kind of coming together of forces like poverty, despair, and violence that
had coalesced during a period of heightened ruthlessness in Tijuana to
become a potent killer of women. Or, it was a social system that degraded
women and worked to undermine them, but that had become deranged,
out of control, and had subsequently let a frenzy of death loose. I liked
Rosa's definition best, and it hinted at the understanding of a pathological process as a gradient: the social pathogen was a kind of shamelessness, coming in waves over time, that led people to indulge in multiple
destructive impulses.

What's more, this pathological process didn't spread through Tijuana
spontaneously. The city—the epidemic's environment—had for decades
stoked its reputation as a place where erotic fantasy and sexual need could
be first separated from moral constraints and then fulfilled, and it was
helped along in this task by depictions of Tijuana as a place where a wholly
different morality ruled. This reputation had benefited the complex structures of the sex trade. But as the trade withered, the environment of
the Zona shifted and the boundaries of what was morally permissible
became more fragile. Though this epidemic was unlike any I had studied
before, there were nevertheless useful parallels here to other epidemic

origin stories that I could draw upon, despite how different they might appear at face value.

The technological leap in Chinese farming that occurred in the mid-sixteenth century produced higher rice yields and expanded the prosperity of the empire. But it also placed ducks and pigs—the former a reservoir for multiple viruses, the latter an efficient mixing vessel for viral components—into close proximity on Chinese farms, which produced the common flu, among the world's most tenacious and successful pathogens. The Spanish flu was once just a collection of separate viruses residing in birds, horses, pigs, and humans, until these multiple pathogens somehow cohered, sometime in the nineteenth century, into a virulent and deadly new agent, killing tens of millions. In both cases, epidemics bloomed after multiple pathogenic components were synthesized. This basic phenomenon, the combining of disparate agents into a single pathogen, is often critical in amplifying virulence.

This syncretism—the combination of pathogens through new pressures and opportunities—was exactly what had occurred in Tijuana as well. It was the reason so many women of the Zona and El Bordo had lost their lives and were now missing. Here, though, the pathogen wasn't made up of fused viral components in pigs and ducks but consisted of the behaviors of different sets of men in power working in some kind of murderous harmony. Corrupt police. Violent cartels. Desperate johns. HIV on shared syringes. Each of these, better understood together as a pathological process, lay on a spectrum of virulence that might allow a host to survive her assault, or be killed, or end up being infected. It was only when the shamelessness overtook Tijuana in the late 2000s and beyond that this pathological process escalated in frequency and intensity until, from an epidemic perspective, these behaviors were effectively working in concert like a new hybrid virus, their virulence amplified as they more efficiently killed their hosts. Tijuana had witnessed not only an epidemic of femicide but the emergence of a new syncretic agent of death. That meant that even for those women who believed themselves immune, the downfall could be swift as the city shifted under their feet.

*

Ana moved warily through the El Cuete offices and sat down across the table, daintily removing her purse and placing it next to her on a chair. She looked across the table shyly. I was there with Teresita, a Mexican doctoral student who had joined our division at UC San Diego, whose presence at these interviews always tamped down their inherent awkwardness. We both smiled back at her but it was Teresita she responded to. Everywhere I went in Tijuana, despite becoming more and more comfortable in the city, I couldn't escape the fact that I was a clean-cut white guy who spoke only rudimentary Spanish and who, despite my best efforts, stuck out like a sore thumb. I always felt slightly humiliated when I hung out with my Mexican friends because we would be accosted by vendors hawking wares in rapid perfectly accented American English, something I'm sure didn't happen when I wasn't around. I was the mark dragging everyone else down.

Ana was large and delicate, with the face of a young girl and a natural acquiescence that drew me toward her reflexively, perhaps to balance the sense of retreat that she projected. The day we met, in January 2015, she was exquisitely made up, her skin glowing under the creamy texture of meticulously applied foundation. She was twenty-six years old but looked younger. Unlike Rosa and Susi and so many other women I had met here, Ana had been born in Tijuana, though like the others she had quickly found herself enmeshed in the margins of the sex trade.

Tentatively, in a whisper, Ana explained that she had been fourteen years old when it all started. That was when, she said, she was taken into the care of a "mister"—a pimp—along with seven other girls her age. "It was a house that we rented, and all the girls used to pay the rent, but he was the one that handled us."

"Handled you?"

"Well," said Ana, "let's say that he was the one who moved us. We had to give him the money—we were all minors, but we all used to work." In Tijuana, these houses mimicked the setups at the grand cartel-run brothels in the heart of the Zona but on a much smaller scale. The women and girls were recruited and ostensibly protected from danger while having their movements steeply restricted. In Ana's case, the surveillance from her mister was so intense that she was, along with the other teenage girls, a prisoner, living by a simple routine. It went like this: while in the house, they waited and watched TV. Then a call would come in and she and the other girls would be taken out, often to a hotel in the Zona, to service clients. As the mister sourced a larger network of contacts, Ana was shuttled to more remote destinations for isolated parties. This back and forth was never freedom, only work. When she was taken outside, it was always under the mister's watchful gaze.

Ana's best guess is that her move from hotel-based sex work to private parties occurred in the years right before and during the corrupt mayoralty of Jorge Hank Rhon (2004–2007). These were also the years that the Tijuana Cartel consolidated power in the city, including through the infiltration of the police department. The ascendancy of the cartels meant that Ana's clients were drawn from an increasingly exclusive pool. "Well, they would take us to houses or ranches around Tecate or Ensenada in a van," she explained, listing towns about a thirty-minute drive from Tijuana. "And the mister used to come with us and stay at these parties while we worked. The parties were all made up of narcos."

"Parties with narcos?" Teresita asked. "How could you tell?"

"Well, because we could see everything," Ana replied. "They had so many guns and drugs, and they would do drugs and we used to have to do drugs with them too." Even at twenty-six, Ana radiated innocence and fragility, as if she could be broken if handled too roughly. Looking at her across the room, it was near impossible to imagine the vulnerability she would have exuded a decade ago when, as a teenager, she stepped warily out of a van and onto the doorstep of a secluded desert ranch at dusk.

Ana shrugged. "I didn't feel safe, but I would go anyway," she said. "I mean, I was scared that something could happen to us; you could see how people had gotten killed around those houses and ranches pretty often, because of drugs and all that." Wherever she went, she was forced to yield to the desire of others, without much input into what was going to be done to her body. "Basically, they would pay and you had to do whatever they wanted."

"And if you didn't," Teresita asked, "what would have happened?"

Ana paused, then spoke quietly. "I don't know," she said, exhaling deeply. "We could get killed or . . ." Her words trailed off.

"Did something like that happen while you were there?"

"Well," she replied, "one time they hit a friend and left her there all beaten up, but they never killed someone in front of me." The threat of violence and the history of previous killings at the ranches were enough to keep her in line.

During this time, in the early to mid-2000s, cartel ranches were a prime target for rivals seeking to test the power of the prevailing overlords. Ana experienced these conflicts firsthand, describing the episodes as "pure violence," with her and the other girls sometimes caught in the battles. "Yes, pure violence," she repeated. "Just narcos with guns everywhere. We were in a ranch in Ensenada once, and they started to shoot each other and we were right there with them—we were in a truck and we got stuck in the middle of the crossfire. Nothing happened to us, but they killed some of the narcos. We left before the police got there." In this climate of fear, negotiations around sexual services were left to Ana's mister, who would, crucially, decide whether she could use a condom or not. In practice, she rarely did given that the price went up if she didn't use protection, a common situation among sex workers in Tijuana and elsewhere that ratchets up their risk of acquiring HIV. Avoiding disease was further complicated by drug use; Ana recalled having pills put in her drinks by her cartel clients, and nights becoming a blur. "You wake up and you don't even know what happened."

My heart ached as Ana described those places, isolated and wild. Hers were the memories of a child among adult predators, her only source of protection a man who acted in concert with her clients. Picturing her in those situations was horrifying. At the same time, as a scientist, I considered whether her story fit or upended the epidemic model I was constructing about women in the city. On my first day in Tijuana, when Susi and Patty had showed me the desolation of the canal and Susi had described her past as a hit doctor, I had—even without consciously realizing it—been developing a classification system to understand women's trajectories through the city's various sources of danger. So where did Ana fit in? Susi and Rosa expressed a relative fondness for the late 1990s and early 2000s, when Mexican police officers, military from both sides of the border, and a steady influx of American tourists flooded the Zona and kept them working; that time of shamelessness when the paraditas would fight each other in the street, clients were easy to rob, and the everyday violence of the place was palpable. The money they made sprung from the chaos and disorder of the neighborhood, which drew a steady stream of tourists to the place, but that era of shamelessness also produced risks: one false move, or simply being at the wrong place at the wrong time, could mean death. The margin between living and dying, which for most of us feels enormous, had been worn away to a transparent layer so thin that oblivion was always within view.

Ana had been insulated from the chaos of the street in the closed house where she was forced to live and the remote cartel ranches where she was sent to service men. But this highly organized existence was just another pathway leading her and those like her toward a pathological process—a synthesis of violence, HIV infection, and drug use—that was killing women. Was it more dangerous working clients on the Zona's streets or being stranded in the silent desert night at the mercy of narcos? The shamelessness of the street attracted clients looking for risky sex. The closed house/narco-ranch system, though, was where shamelessness was distilled down to its most potent form, placing women's bodies under the absolute control of Tijuana's cartel overlords.

There was another side to Ana's early days of servitude. In Tijuana, no grift can ever really last unless all players are given their tithe. Aside from the narcos, Ana's other regular clients were the police, who would check in every month with the mister at the small house in which she and the other girls were kept. "They knew what was going on there: that we were all underage," Ana said. It was a common arrangement, just another deal made among the daily multitude: "[The mister] would pay them with women." By forcing Ana and the other girls to service police officers, the mister was able to delicately thread the needle between satisfying cartels and keeping the police at bay. Of course, this was a time when the two forces were often indistinguishable, as Bañuelos had described to me in such great detail: the time of good cops and bad cops existing side by side, shady men walking into the police academy in the morning and leaving that same afternoon with a gun, a badge, and a uniform. Beyond allowing the mister to continue his business undisturbed, the kickbacks to the police also had the effect of placing an extra layer of control over Ana's life. With cops as silent partners in the enterprise, Ana's chances of escaping went from near impossible to nonexistent. She remembered a time when two of the girls tried to flee; the beating they received was savage. But even if they had been able to make it into the city, the police would have hunted them down and returned their captive bodies to the small house, where they would return to the room with the blinds drawn and the TV on.

Eventually, though, and against the odds, Ana was liberated. It is a testament to her mister's cruel effectiveness that her freedom was only secured after he extracted a carefully negotiated price. The man was a client—a narco—who had taken a shine to Ana and had fallen in love with her despite the fact that their intimacy was transactional. While Ana was sure money changed hands to secure her release, she was never privy to the details. Still underage, she was led out of the house by her new partner into a kind of freedom that she hadn't known in years.

Years into her sex trade career despite being only seventeen years old, Ana had managed to get out at an age before many women started selling their bodies. She was with a man who loved her and who had put up money so that she could be free to love him in return. They had a child together, a boy that Ana still cares for. After the routine of forced confinement, supervised journeys into the desert, narco parties under the cold moon, and monthly visits from the police, she had finally, in a way, broken free.

As Ana shared the details of her release, it struck me as a stroke of good luck in an otherwise unhappy life. As she continued to talk, though, I realized that luck had played no part in this new chapter. The forces that had aligned to weaken and enslave her as a child were the same that brought her that bit of good fortune. "I felt safe with him," Ana said of her new husband, whom she described as caring deeply for her. "But I was also scared because I would think, 'They are going to get me when they get him.'" The milieu in which her husband worked was not lost on her: he was a soldier of the cartel, their house littered with piles of drugs and cash. Ana's escape from the mister's closed world was in fact just a reordering of her place within the same system. And while she was happy and loved the man, she left her old life fearful for the future. She did not know who "they" were, exactly—other narcos or police aligned with forces that opposed him—but she knew that it was a matter of time. They were going to come for her husband, and when they did, they would get her, and her son too.

One day around noon, after two years of marriage, the police came to Ana's door. "They took him outside, and I thought they were going to take him to jail," she said. He was a criminal, after all, and the alliance between police and narcos had become more complicated by 2006, during the runup to the Mexican drug war, as the resident Tijuana Cartel had split into warring factions and the Sinaloa Cartel had moved in to take advantage of the chaos. The result was the final breakdown of the plaza system in Tijuana, with men like Ana's husband, caught in the middle of newly warring factions, paying the price. "They told me that they were going to take him to jail," she said. "'Go and find him there,' they said. But it wasn't true."

Instead, "maybe six blocks away," she said, "they *levantarlo*." That word is all too common in Tijuana. It means, roughly, "to disappear someone." Ana has no doubt that while the executioners may have worn police uniforms, her husband's disappearance and murder came at the order of rival narcos. "After they killed him, they broke into our house looking to see if he had left something, guns or drugs. They were policemen, but they came and stole everything that he had there. They knew everything about him."

"Do you think the police were involved somehow with the—"

"—with the narcos?" Ana asked, cutting the question short. "Yes," she said grimly. In that scenario, trying to extract justice for her husband's murder was impossible. "They denied it," she said of the police. "They said they didn't do it, but I know they were lying." With her husband killed and a son to raise, Ana had no choice but to return to the sex trade.

Ana's story wasn't one of luck, of reversals of fortune, of being in the wrong place at the wrong time, or of any other cliché that we tell about the unanticipated paths our lives take. Hers was a story of being taken into the sex trade and forcibly submerged under the weight of the powers that controlled it. Is it right to call what she tasted at the age of seventeen, her marriage to a cartel foot soldier, some kind of freedom? Can we call the *levantar*—the taking of her husband—unlucky, when she prophesied its coming from the very first day that she was transferred from the mister's house to his? We want to be the agents of our own narratives even if they end in failure, because at least we can find some meaning there. But after a decade in and out of the sex trade, at the age of twenty-six, Ana was too unsentimental to believe that she had ever exerted real power in her time with the mister or her husband. She had seen enough. She knew it was a lie.

At some point after he sold her, Ana's mister was sent to prison. His incarceration and her husband's murder meant that she was freer, in a way, than she had ever been before. During that time she had grown into adulthood in a world that was, while dangerous, at least familiar. "I used to make so much money," she said mournfully, reflecting on the changes since she returned to the trade. "Eight years ago, I would have around ten clients per day. Now I only have one or so." Rosa had said almost exactly the same words to me when I first met her; both their livelihoods had withered as the drug war kept johns away from the city. Nevertheless, Ana was adamant that she was in a better position than ever to avoid danger. "I don't work for anyone anymore, so I decide if I want to take a job or not," she said. "Anyway, most of my clients these days are familiar; I already know them. I feel fine in that sense."

Like Rosa, Ana had seen the changes in the Zona up close. While Rosa believed the shamelessness was still increasing even after the worst of the drug war violence had passed, Ana understood things differently. When she spoke to me, 2014 had just come to a close, a year when the proportion of female murders among the city's total homicides had dropped by about half from its peak five years earlier. "Well, before they used to kill people everywhere; you could see it around the city," she said. She paused for a moment before continuing, considering her words carefully. "I don't know if I feel safer, but before [the Zona] was full of narcos and you don't see that anymore," she said. "But maybe it's just the fact that I got out of that environment. I don't know."

There was one other piece of the puzzle for Ana. The data about women and HIV risk in Tijuana were unambiguous. If they injected drugs, like Susi used to do in her wild days in the Zona, fewer than 10 percent would probably become infected with HIV. Of women who injected drugs and also worked in the sex trade, at least 12 percent acquired the virus. Ana didn't do drugs: she had only taken them under duress in the days she served the narcos, which reduced her risk of becoming HIV-positive. While she still sold sex, she was her own boss, meaning that she was in a better position to negotiate whether her clients used condoms or not. And she had started getting tested for HIV during her pregnancy in order to protect her unborn child. After the boy was born and her husband was murdered, she continued to come regularly to health clinics for free condoms, regular testing, and safer-sex education. She had done what she could to minimize her risk of becoming infected and avoid at least that aspect of the pathological process.

It wasn't a happy ending, per se, but there was a gentle neutrality to Ana that suggested to me some inner peace, however small. I got the sense that she believed the worst was over, and from a probabilistic point of view, that seemed likely to be true. She was no longer a child, a captive, a tool of the narcos, or the monthly tithe paid to police. She was no longer the wife of a doomed man. She was a young woman with a son she loved, living in a city she knew intimately, and working in an industry with enough experience to do it on what amounted to her own terms. And perhaps most of all, she seemed to have no illusions about the dangers she had faced or those that were to come.

*

The tortuous path of Ana's adolescence and her inability to break away completely from the sex trade—her body instead being transferred from one mode of control to another and back again—was a reminder of how quickly the Zona could overtake a person's attempts to extricate themselves. Until Ana, I was so steeped in the statistics about the health of the Zona's women that I hadn't much thought about how they might find a way out that didn't involve death. And yet, Susi and Rosa were both more than twenty years Ana's senior and their lives appeared from my vantage point to be relatively less dangerous than they had once been. Susi, at least, had found a way out through the research infrastructure in the Zona that had been built up by Steffanie, Tom, and others. She was still in a way reliant on the sex and drug trades for her livelihood, but at a remove, and she was inoculated by her steady job and abstinence from drugs. Still, she remained tied to the decades-old network of drug users and sex workers that she had cultivated amid Tijuana's hidden places. I wondered if Susi was ever tempted to rejoin that scene in earnest, to unburden herself of her responsibilities and start hustling on the street again. Unlike Susi, Rosa had no distance from the action; she was still hanging onto her rung of the sex trade to ensure her survival. Rosa's and Ana's inability to escape the Zona made what Susi managed to pull off seem even more exceptional and more fragile.

That wasn't to say Susi hadn't experienced loss. The names of her dead friends, told to me when I first came to Tijuana, were seared into my memory like an incantation. La Paloma, La Paniqueada, La Osa, La Lobita, Angie. Knowing Susi meant knowing ghosts; not just ghosts of people but of long-forgotten bars and hotels, of street fights and wild parties, of scenes registered in no official history but that made Tijuana something of what it was. They were all half-finished stories, as if Susi couldn't muster the energy to remind herself of how they really ended. But as I worked to define the femicide epidemic, I needed to know whether conceptualizing it as the product of a multifaceted pathological process rather than a single pathogen made sense, and that meant pushing Susi to remember things she probably didn't want to. Susi's friends were a microcosm of the population at risk of succumbing to the epidemic of femicide. They were all women who had been living in and around the Zona and who were all variously involved in the vice economies here. Knowing what had killed them would help me test the soundness of my hypothesis. It was another of those unpleasant moments when women's bodies became the currency of scientific inquiry. That meant convincing Susi to tell me not only how her friends had lived but how they had died.

*

Susi and I ordered steaming bowls of seafood pozole in a restaurant a few feet from the Tijuana Arch, which stands at an intersection leading to the main tourist drag of Avenida Revolución in one direction and the women of La Coahuila in the other. It was an unseasonably cold spring day. Teresita joined us; she was savvy enough to navigate Susi's rough Tijuanensis slang. Better yet, while Susi was mostly indifferent to me, she adored Teresita. I asked Susi to finish the story of La Paniqueada; I knew she had been murdered, but I had never asked Susi about what had happened next.

"So a client killed her?" I asked. Susi nodded. "And did you ever hear who the client was?"

"No," Susi replied, "they never found him. The people running the hotel knew the client who had killed her, but they didn't do anything." She looked at Teresita and me. "People here don't really care about people like that. They know that sex workers steal money from clients, so . . ." She shrugged.

With Teresita's help, I asked Susi whether all her friends from back in the day stole from clients. "Not all of them," she said. "the *putos* in the *fuerzas especiales* [the Mexican Special Forces] were always hanging around the Zona Norte." Even with them off duty, she explained, their presence made robbing clients difficult. "But the *placas* [local police officers] would help the paraditas," she said with a smile. "The cops would detain the paraditas who stole and release them two or three streets away. Their boyfriends would pay off the police officers to keep the cycle going. It was a business."

"Why would the police officers help them?"

"Because they were pretty and they would have sex with the officers." Plus, it meant a little extra income for the police. From Susi's perspective it was as simple as that: the corrupt cops like pretty women they can control, so an individual officer makes a decision to look the other way when a woman commits a crime, knowing he'll get both money and a brief spell of sovereignty over her body. What the police did to the paraditas as the Special Forces lingered nearby didn't constitute the most important risk factor responsible for the femicide. But it was a way to normalize their violation. It was a constant state of play, habitual interaction between agents in a closed system. It was the same system Rosa had described, with police storming hotel rooms hooded and priapic, violating with impunity.

We finished our soup and ordered some tacos and beer. "What was La Paniqueada like?" I asked gamely.

Susi snorted as she held a taco in one hand, a napkin in the other. "She was *perrucha* [bitchy]," she said, "and she looked like a guy. Because she was really into drugs she would pull her eyebrows and her hair out; she was always paranoid, thinking that someone was following her."

"Because of the drugs?"

"Yes, because of the meth," Susi replied. "She would use cocaine, crystal, pills—but she never used heroin. She would think that she had animals inside her skull and her body, and that's why she would always scratch her head. She was nice, though. She was my friend."

"How long did you know her?"

"For like twenty years, we always used to party together. And then she was killed in that hotel a block from here, the Hotel San Jorge."

"When was that?"

Susi paused and stared down at the table, frustration evident on her face. "I don't remember right because I started to be clean in 2001."

"So it was before then?"

"Yes, like in the late nineties."

"Did you stop using drugs because of what happened to her?"

"Not really." Her words, which had been coming at a rapid clip, ceased again as she stroked the fibrous scars encircling her forearm. "I stopped mainly because the wounds were in really bad shape. They weren't healing properly, and I had had them for many years, just like this," she said, raising her arm up for Teresita and me to see.

"Did it really hurt?" Teresita asked.

"Yeah, it was really bad. Also I couldn't inject myself anywhere else, and some days I would inject like twelve or fourteen times. Sometimes you're with someone that convinces you to use that much, and other times you depend on other people to inject you because you cannot do it by yourself anymore."

"So who would help you?"

"*Batos*," Susi replied, using a Sinaloan term that translates roughly as "dudes," "or La Paniqueada, or La Gringa [the American]."

"Who is La Gringa?"

"Angie." I knew how much that name meant to Susi and how quickly tears could spill at her mere mention. But despite knowing how close the two of them were, Susi had never told me how it was that her friend had died. Sensing the question coming, she cut me off. "She was killed crossing the Vía Rápida"—the multilane highway running alongside both sides of the canal—"when she was on her way to a shooting gallery. A car hit her." We sat in respectful silence for a moment. "I think the issue was the placas. That's how people get killed: because they are being chased by them."

"Where was she?"

"In the canal, at the picadero called El Chaparral [The Thicket]," Susi replied. El Chaparral is the shooting gallery inside the canal's flood vents that I had spied that first day in Tijuana, outside of which I had seen the lone woman standing before she had disappeared from view. Even as we were navigating through the chaotic traffic on the Vía Rápida and picking our way down the sloping walls, Susi had betrayed nothing of the fact that we were following the path her best friend took on the day she was killed.

"That's where I went with you and Patty," I said.

Susi nodded. "Yes, yes, back then, before the canal was cleaned out, people were hanging out there and the conecta [drug-dealing spot] at the big door was still there."

"What was Angie like as a person?" Teresita asked

A flash of joy passed over Susi's face. "She was my carnala [sister]!" she cried, "even though we didn't look anything alike. She was tall, she had blue eyes, she was blond; but still, she would say that we were sisters. I would eat from the same plate and we would do jales [jobs] together where we would steal from people. We looked after each other. I cried a lot when she died. I don't know how to tell you exactly, but I would like to perform a ceremony or throw flowers from the bridge above the canal because so many people die on the Vía Rápida and they never get a proper ceremony or service." With that, Susi burst into tears and both Teresita and I leaned over to console her. I could feel Susi's body shuddering as she wept. It was hard not to feel guilty about bringing up these memories.

Susi wiped her eyes and ate a little more, and soon she was her old self again, seeming to relish the memories of her friends in life rather than in death. "La Paniqueada, La Osa, La Lobita . . . they were all really feisty," she said with a smile, "they all had different personalities and different styles, but they were all cut from the same cloth." I pictured Susi with her girlfriends, running scams amid the chaos of what she had once called the "old-school Zona." "I would hang out with the dudes and steal a lot," she explained, "and the others would have clients." They all protected each other, she explained, pooling resources and backing each other up in the fights they often had with other workingwomen.

"So La Lobita," Teresita asked, "why did you call her that?" The name meant the She-Wolf, and even though I had tried to parse it, I had come up short.

Susi seemed to slip into some kind of reverie. "She was always around here, close to a place called Amor Latino. She used to drink a lot with men and would get drunk with them, and she was also really aggressive, and crazy. She was really pretty; she had dark skin, with nice features."

"But why did people call her La Lobita?" Teresita repeated.

"Oh." Susi seemed dumbfounded by our ignorance. "Because she was really hairy, especially her legs." With that she let out a long belly laugh.

"And what happened to her?"

"I don't know," Susi sighed. "I think she was selling drugs and something went wrong. She used to sell meth, and I don't know what happened to her after."

"Do you think someone could have killed her?"

"Yes," Susi said, finally. "She had an issue with drugs with the guy who she was dating."

"And La Osa?"

"La Osa"—the She-Bear—"is dead."

"Was she the one that you were telling me about, the one who was HIV-positive?" Teresita asked.

"Yes, La Osita," Susi continued, using the diminutive, "she was a paradita and she used to work next to a place called Las Charras—now it has another name—she would stand outside that place to find clients. Sometimes we would steal from clients or from drunk men who would pass by."

"And she died from AIDS?"

"Yes." Susi replied, her tone slackening.

"You didn't know she was sick?"

"No, I didn't know."

"Why did you call her La Osa?"

"Because she was big and strong," Susi said, laughing again, "and she had long black hair with one white lock; people always recognized her because of that."

La Paniqueada, murdered servicing a client in a hotel. Angie, hit by a car while running from the cops toward a picadero. La Lobita, the

She-Wolf, killed by her boyfriend over a drug deal gone wrong. La Osa, the She-Bear, big and strong, who died of AIDS. Tough women of the Zona, a wrecking crew too crazy and wild to mess with, their deaths coming from all sides. And there was one last friend that Susi had mentioned once but had never spoken of again: La Paloma, the Dove. Perhaps, though, that wasn't by accident. As Ana said, some people were *levantarlo*: disappeared. That left Susi as the sole survivor out of her group of six.

As we finished the meal, Susi regaled us with stories of knife fights with women and the friendships that arose in their aftermath, and of first meeting La Lobita, who quickly became a soul mate, in a bathroom stall in one of the Zona's now defunct brothels as the two of them did drugs and went *loquear*, crazy. The memories were still so present for Susi, the joy and sadness both overwhelming. I was transfixed, nearly shaking, as the magnitude of what she had experienced sunk in. The deaths of her friends, all living and working in the Zona, had come from multiple causes. It wasn't HIV, or murder, or being run down in traffic on the highway at the border wall. It was a multifaceted pathological process closing in on them from all sides simultaneously, driving an epidemic that took many forms to take their lives.

Before we got up to leave, Susi wanted us to know one last thing. Perhaps she regretted the way she had talked about La Osa, the fact that she had made light of her strength and ferocity. "She was also pretty," Susi said, looking us in the eyes. "All of them were beautiful."

*

There's another part of the Story of the Shooting Star, an early subplot easily lost amid the complexities of the sprawling narrative. For the Kumeyaay, the hero of the story is the grandson of the girl who bathes in the pond—herself the product of the incestuous coupling of the Sun and the Moon. By the end of his quixotic journey, his grandmother is a minor character in the drama, practically forgotten. Her role in the legend is limited to the story of her youth, when she was still just at the edge of her sexual awakening, before her belly was seeded by the Sun, her father. But as with many myths, there is another version.

The girl loves to bathe in a pond. Every morning she goes there with her older sister, feeling the cool water swirl as she dives. It's a quiet space for the two girls, safe and private. Unbeknownst to them, though, two young men from their village have fallen in love and spend their days strategizing about how to marry them. Too shy, the men are unable to approach the girls directly. So they ask the gopher, that fat and pesky rodent, to do it for them. He agrees, happy to be in on the action.

One day, the girls arrive at the pond. The younger sister, readying herself to leap into the water, suddenly senses a change. She looks down: the water that day is different—cloudy and troubled—and she becomes afraid. Her older sister, though, sees nothing amiss and tells her to ignore her childish anxiety. To prove that everything is as it should be, she jumps in first and swims around, unmolested. Upon seeing her older sister splashing around happily, the younger one follows her lead and jumps in as well.

She was wrong to ignore that abstract fear. Before dawn that morning, the gopher had come down to the pool and slipped into its depths, his musky fur turning slick and black amid the reeds. He had waited all morning, knowing that the girls would come as they did every day. The gopher is a carnal but patient beast. When the older sister enters the water, he remains still and invisible right beside her in the depths. But even he has his limits. When the gopher sees the younger sister's lithe figure penetrate the surface, he can no longer help himself; he gives a little kick and lets himself be carried by the current across the pond toward her, her legs catching glimpses of the Sun, her father, the light dappled under the murky water.

He comes near to her, so near that she can feel his presence, but she has no name for the sensation. He is furtive and experienced, unseen but felt, playing on the girl's own naïveté to infiltrate some part of her that she does not yet know. As he passes close under the water, all she knows is that something is very wrong. She runs screaming from the pond, terrified and violated, as the gopher darts away to hide again among the reeds.

Soon after, the girl gives birth to the twin heroes, the forebears of the Kumeyaay. And while some say it was the Sun that impregnated her as she lay open and willing in the desert, others speak about the deal made between the gopher and the young men. It is a deal that feels somehow familiar, with an inconspicuous creature negotiating the violation of a woman on behalf of men incapable of intimacy without domination, a go-between who quietly takes his own cut of the action, the deal carried out under the cloudy black surface of the water, within which both the perpetrator and his victim are submerged.

The myth is unclear about whether the twins are the progeny of the Sun or the rodent that lives under the earth. Perhaps the source of the confusion is simple: under the murky waves, as he swims toward his victim, her legs illuminated by the Sun, even the gopher might believe that he is the light shining in the darkness rather than the inky blackness that envelops her.

CHAPTER 9

Causation

I did not know Tijuana like Ana did, but I had a dataset that captured the knowledge of hundreds of people like her who navigated the city daily and were familiar with its sources of pleasure and death. By the spring of 2015, roughly a year and a half after I had begun working with Stefanie and her team, my analysis of police extortion among El Cuete participants was almost complete. On the one hand, I was building a model to see if being forced to pay bribes to police made people who injected drugs less likely to access addiction treatment. I was also mapping all the places where the study's participants said they interacted with police. The goal was to spot some kind of pattern across the city's *colonias* that could help explain why the level of uptake of methadone treatment among people who most needed it—heroin-dependent injectors in the city—was so pitifully low. I had quadruple-checked my analysis to make sure that I didn't repeat the statistical errors that Tom had flagged in my Vancouver research during my first visit to San Diego. Nevertheless, I was having trouble interpreting the results until I met Ana.

It wasn't so much her description of how endemic police corruption had become across Tijuana. That had been a constant refrain from Susi, Rosa, and Patty, and it was repeated hundreds of times in the rows of El Cuete participant data that had become a flashing fixture on my laptop screen. Instead, it was that Ana understood the police and the narcos to be largely indistinguishable. That's not to say that there weren't good officers; just that despite the attempts to rout the grifters from the rank and file, there were still grinning duos of beat cops looking to fill their personal quota by any means necessary. And like the cartels, benefiting from the misery of people who turned to drugs that they supplied, the police in the Zona relied on the underclass of injectors to both justify their presence and keep the bribes flowing.

Like a good epidemiologist, I had been seeking causal pathways in my model of bribery and addiction treatment access. And like any scientist, I had brought my own biases with me as I approached its construction. It would be so elegant if I could show that the police willfully targeted Tijuana's methadone clinics for cash, and that was—more than anything else—what I was hoping my analyses would reveal. There were signs, though, that it probably wasn't that simple: Susi was adamant that while cops hunted down people in picaderos, she hadn't seen that happen outside the methadone clinics. And yet, I was committed to the idea that the police were engaged in a conspiracy of sorts and thought that if I squinted at the data hard enough I would find it.

*

A certain uneasiness can bubble up when scientists present as overly passionate advocates for their chosen cause. Epidemiologists who have been working in the trenches with marginalized populations for years or decades can appear to have had their scientific objectivity whittled away by the empathy they feel for the subjects of their research. Some might number me among that rank. I've caught myself losing my cool in interviews about police brutality and government neglect in ways that would make my scientific mentors blush. It's not that they don't agree, necessarily, but there's a scientific tenor that one is supposed to muster, a way of speaking about one's research that implies a certain skepticism about its results. Just as your analysis is in principle the product of an unbiased assessment of the available data, your opinion about what the analysis shows is supposed to hew closely to the results and never speak beyond what the results demonstrate. For that reason, it's a cardinal sin of the scientific craft to come to an issue with a fully formed opinion and then undertake research in a way specifically designed to confirm that opinion. That pathway leads to doom, because it ultimately turns scientists into conspiracy theorists, people so fixated on an idea's truth that they ignore facts that don't agree with them and find spurious associations where none exist.

It's a legitimate fear, both for scientists and for those who rely on their
expertise to understand how a certain corner of the world works. The
truth is, of course, that all scientists harbor opinions, a fact that shouldn't
surprise or bother anyone. In fact, I mistrust scientists in my field that
don't seem to stand for anything except robust methodology. Honestly,
what's the point of endlessly refining your analysis if you aren't motivated
to right a wrong? Why bother employing the rigorous techniques of the
scientific method if the end goal is simply to bask in their elegance? This
feels more problematic to me than a scientist guided by empathy who lets
it overwhelm her every once in a while. The main reason is that it's hard
to teach compassion to those who only care about methodology. That, and
the fact that there are two central tenets of the scientific method that
ensure that a scientist's closely held opinion won't affect analytic outcomes:
self-correction and validity testing.

While other systems of knowledge may be either dynamic, systematic,
or fact-based, science somehow pulls off the feat of being all three at once.
It's that combination that bakes in the endless self-correction that makes
science so useful. When error enters into the scientific continuum (most
commonly through a peer-reviewed study) it may hang around for a while,
but the system's dynamism—its capacity to integrate new sources of data
and new approaches, and reconsider previously rejected conclusions—
means that errors will almost invariably end up being buried under a
deluge of better-produced findings. Science evolves to answer the most
pertinent questions that we pose in the most rigorous way. Those that are
most important will be the subject of greater scrutiny and, consequently,
will be less prone to error, and the answers to questions that we don't care
about will simply be forgotten. That process may take months, years, or
even centuries, but it will undoubtedly happen if the basic question is of
sufficient value to the human race.

Science is an architecture made up of an infinite set of testable truths,
and that's where the concept of validity comes into play. Validity in science
is considered in two distinct ways: as internal validity, which measures
how your model coheres, and as external validity, which measures how
well your results map onto the wider world. While they are largely
independent (and tested separately as a consequence), it's not enough to
simply prove one or the other. If you want to produce truly robust science,
you need to demonstrate that your research achieves both kinds of
validity.

Thinking back to the model airplane as a stand-in for a statistical model, internal validity means demonstrating that all the airplane's pieces fit together nicely. If you came across a model airplane that was missing a wing, you'd be right to assume that the model was incomplete. If instead, one of the wings had been taken from a different model set, was larger than the other, and was haphazardly glued onto the airplane's chassis, you'd be right to conclude that the model lacked coherence. In the same way, statistical models that are missing key variables or confounders open themselves up to error; the plane won't fly with just one wing. If instead, statistical models have forced-in variables that have nothing to do with the outcome you're studying, they won't accurately represent its true nature; the plane won't fly if one wing is bigger than the other. Getting that balance right—making sure all the right model pieces are included, and making sure that no extraneous pieces have been added—is the essence of internal validity.

It's not enough, though, to make a model coherent and thereby achieve internal validity. If you carefully build your model airplane piece by piece, making sure everything fits together perfectly, but you end up with a tiny plastic race car, something is amiss: the whole point of a model is to represent something real. That is why scientists seek to prove the external validity of their results, which involves testing that a model accurately represents a truth out in the world. That's why model airplane enthusiasts are always on the hunt for more detailed sets: despite knowing that they're only building representations, they nevertheless want to build the best one possible. So it is (or should be) with epidemiologists: we want our statistical models to reflect something true about the populations we're studying. After all, that's the only way to make sure that the science can have an impact in the real world. What's the point of building the best model airplane possible if it doesn't actually look like an airplane?

It might seem simple to achieve both internal and external validity. The problem is that unlike people who build model airplanes, epidemiologists don't always know which pieces belong to which set, and even if they're able to build a set using all the right pieces, they're not always sure what the real airplane looks like. That makes it hard to know whether an epidemiologic model is externally valid or not. That conundrum is made more difficult when the population of interest—that group of people you want your model to represent—doesn't want to be found, as is the case with the epidemic I was studying in Tijuana. Despite these challenges, epidemiologists need to do all they can to achieve both kinds of validity while being transparent about where their models fall short.

The upshot is that while an epidemiologist might start an investigation with strong opinions, carrying it through to a meaningful conclusion will require her to employ scientific methodologies. These methods, if used properly, will make her personal beliefs largely irrelevant to the process. Opinions are only really important insofar as they orient the initial direction of the research. If the science is undertaken with rigor, they'll be scrubbed out in the process of achieving validity.

*

I had all of these thoughts in mind as the fall of 2015 approached, the sun cooling slightly and strange chaotic winds rising up in the wake of its retreat. I had spent the last season tinkering with the statistical model of police bribery and methadone maintenance therapy, which was populated with data from Tijuana's underclass of opioid injectors. I had a clear sense when I started about what it was that I would find: Methadone costs money. Tijuanenses who were injecting heroin would probably want access to addiction treatment. The practice of police extortion would rid people of the cash they needed to pay for the methadone and scare them away from even going near clinics if police were present. In my statistical model, this all had to be simplified down into a straightforward hypothesis: that people who paid a bribe to police would be less likely to access methadone. It was simple and it made sense.

I was wrong. Despite the opinions that had motivated me to do this work and my hope that the model could be used to support a tight narrative about the damage done by policing in Tijuana, the final results were exactly the opposite of what I expected. After a careful process of entering potential confounding variables into my model, the only variable that was significantly associated with accessing methadone was, it turned out, police extortion. That is, people who paid a bribe to police were more likely, not less, to access methadone. I checked my statistical code; I considered different confounders; I even triple-checked that I hadn't mistakenly flipped the definition of methadone access so that when participants reported "Yes" they actually meant "No." Nothing changed the model's results.

What did this mean? The most basic interpretation is that police bribery was somehow increasing access to methadone treatment and making the lives of the most marginalized people in Tijuana better as a result. For a certain class of beat cop in Tijuana, that validated what they presumably believed all along: brutal police tactics—even those that drifted into low-level corruption—were justified because they got people off the street and into addiction treatment. Of course, the other option was that my model was faulty because internal validity hadn't been achieved, making its statistical associations spurious. In short, maybe I had just built wrong.

After spending a few weeks reviewing my statistical approach, I had to conclude—despite the implications it had for the work our group was doing in Tijuana—that the model had been constructed correctly. The results were, as far as I could prove, internally valid. The El Cuete cohort was also thought to be roughly generalizable to the population of people who injected drugs on the street out in Tijuana, meaning that the results were probably externally valid too. Where did that leave me? I tried to think systematically about what I could do next. Because I had started as an epidemiologist with very little training in biostatistics, I got in the habit early on of assessing data using the simplest possible approach. That meant that I was generally more interested in looking at basic statistical information, like the difference in the proportion of an outcome between two groups, than at fancier statistical measures, like the odds ratios, relative risks, and confidence intervals that epidemiologic models generate.

So as I considered the notion that police extortion was a great way to make people access addiction treatment, I went back and looked at the rows of data from El Cuete participants. Roughly half of the study participants reported that they had paid a bribe to police in the past six months, amounting to a daily flip of the coin for those trying to survive in the Zona. I looked deeper. Caught up in the model's counterintuitive results, I had largely ignored a simple truth. More than 90 percent of the study participants used heroin, and about half reported that they needed treatment for their addiction. Nevertheless, only 8 percent of the sample— less than fifty people in total—had actually been enrolled in methadone treatment in the past six months. Almost nobody in the El Cuete study was actually accessing the medication.

One thing I had learned from my research in Vancouver was that the longer someone stayed on methadone, the more likely it was that they would eventually abstain from using heroin and other street drugs. For people who started on a course of methadone but couldn't stay on it for more than a month or two, the medication was basically ineffective. If there was anywhere to look for answers about what was really going on, then, that 8 percent was the best place to start. Knowing how long that small subset stayed on methadone could provide some clues about the exit ramps available to women and men addicted to opioids in Tijuana.

Focusing on the experiences of that subset caused my interpretation of the results to shift radically. Of that 8 percent of participants who made it to a methadone clinic (forty-eight people in all), 40 percent stopped treatment within six months, dropping the number enrolled and retained in treatment down to only twenty-nine people, about 5 percent of the total El Cuete sample. There were roughly five to ten thousand people who injected drugs in Tijuana; assuming that the external validity of my findings held, extrapolating my results to this group meant that only between about two hundred fifty and five hundred people were enrolled in treatment in the city. With numbers that low, the proportion of people who arrived in Tijuana and started injecting drugs was more than replenishing the proportion that stopped injecting through methadone. After all, Tijuana welcomes, on average, more than one hundred deportees from the United States per day, all of whom exit the gates at the border and immediately come face-to-face with the canal and its encampments. For many, the solace that heroin offers is too overwhelming to avoid, and the pain of dislocation from their home too great. That trauma and its succor was reflected among the 40 percent of El Cuete participants who were deportees and had started injecting once they had arrived in Tijuana. Making matters worse, 70 percent of the people who stopped their course of methadone prematurely did so because they ran out of money. For women who injected drugs—who, I found, were just as likely as men to be forced to pay a bribe—that meant one path out of the multifaceted femicide was blocked.

The results of the model showing that police bribery was correlated with methadone treatment access suddenly made a whole new kind of sense. If people who injected drugs were able to scrape together enough pesos to pay for the treatment (equivalent to about $6 a day), they might be targeted by police simply because they had money; after all, that's a pretty sizable sum in a country where the minimum wage amounts to about $3.50 per day. Additionally, once someone is enrolled in methadone treatment, they might be able to stabilize their addiction enough to gain a steady income. That improvement in their income might, in turn, make them a prime target for corrupt cops looking to line their pockets. Regardless of the specific pathway between police, methadone, and money, what the data made abundantly clear was that for most people, addiction treatment became too expensive to continue for more than a few months, and that if you were enrolled in treatment, chances were that you were more likely to come face-to-face with a cop demanding money. Given the abject poverty of the drug injectors enrolled in Proyecto El Cuete, it was difficult enough for them to find food and a place to sleep, let alone save enough money to self-medicate with heroin—and that's before being forced to pay bribes to police. Methadone treatment is more expensive than a daily heroin habit, so the money can quickly run out, meaning people return to the street and to heroin to get their fix. The stability and respite that methadone promises is illusory if you can't pay for it, and you can't pay for it for long if the police are taking your money. The cops who forced opioid-dependent people to pay bribes weren't helping to get people off the street and into treatment after all; their daily quotas were instead insidiously undermining the capacity of Tijuana's heroin injectors to manage their own addictions, which ultimately kept the chaos of the street roiling.

The paper I was writing was only one analysis in a sea of literature about Tijuana's drug-injecting underclass, itself just a niche area of study within the broader expanse of epidemiologic study of HIV and substance use. But like so much epidemiology, it was an act of bearing witness to a preventable horror: it described how vulnerable citizens are preyed upon by those in power and how cities fail to protect them from that predation. Like so many instances of bearing witness, it was mean-ingful only if those with the power to end the horror chose to do so. That last step was beyond my control. I was, though, relieved to have done something—anything—with the data. Early in my career, one of my graduate supervisors drilled into my head that among the many ways that scientists could act unethically, one of the most overlooked was also the most common: collecting data from marginalized people on the vague promise of improving their lives and then failing to do anything with the intimate information they provided. Epidemiologists, according to my supervisor, carried a moral imperative to publish their research because it was the best tool they had to bring about improvements to the populations they studied. Analyzing people's data and turning the find-ings into a peer-reviewed manuscript, in his view, was the most basic epidemiologic ethic. In that light, the study on bribery had fulfilled a basic responsibility to women like Rosa, Ana, and the hundreds of others who shared their secrets with strangers in small white rooms in the heart of the Zona Norte. It was a start.

I put the finishing touches on the paper and circulated it to Steffanie and the others on our research team for feedback. Then, I dove into maps of the city that had been painstakingly populated with hundreds of dots splashed across the city's many colonias. Each dot represented some kind of interaction between an El Cuete study participant and a police officer, with the dots divided into four shapes. A red triangle meant an arrest, a green circle meant a summary detainment, a blue diamond meant a physical assault, and a purple cross meant a sexual assault. The shapes and colors overlapped and swirled around each other, forming ligaments that extended along Tijuana's main thoroughfares, the occasional cluster of sexual assault and arrests popping up in remote areas of the city. I followed the dots and found, to my surprise, a cluster of physical assaults and detainments in the neighborhoods of Los Laureles Canyon, right near Oscar Romo's civic art project, the Korean-owned maquiladoras, and the slums that had come to life in the canyons below. Another long string of dots of all colors—red, green, blue, and purple—ran like an artery along the canal, pooling in greater numbers right where it met the U.S.-Mexico border, near the section of the Vía Rápida upon which Angie had died running from the police; what she was running from suddenly became clearer. And then, right up against the border fence just west of the canal, inside the boundaries of the Centro delegación, dots covered the small area of the Zona Norte like an overflowing cyst erupting with toxins, the mass marked by purple crosses denoting instances of sexual violence at the hands of police, numbering in the hundreds.

The sheer scale of the violations was shocking, as was seeing that the carnage pooled in the red-light district. It was as close to the femicide's pathological process made manifest as I had encountered to date: instances where violence, the prerequisite for killings, had been exacted upon the El Cuete study's women. Beyond the fear and trauma that each of those encounters represented, I wanted to know how this wave of assaults might restrict women's access to addiction treatment. The idea that cops staked out methadone clinics didn't ring true for Susi, even if I had discovered a circuitous pathway by which their casual extortion doomed people to continue injecting drugs in Tijuana's picaderos and public spaces. It was proof that something more insidious and systematic was happening, and I wanted to see how deeply embedded in the functioning of the city it had become. An idea had emerged as I had worked through the El Cuete data on extortion. Basically, police behaviors didn't necessarily have to be intentional to place people in danger or to block their means of escaping a scene that was slowly killing them. From my research in Vancouver, I knew that the presence of a single parked police car in front of a life-saving service like a supervised injection site could act as an insurmountable barrier to those who needed it. I wondered if the same was true of Tijuana: even if cops weren't intentionally targeting the clinics, simply being nearby would surely deter people from visiting, especially given their reputation for extortion and so much worse.

Through a colleague who worked at one of Tijuana's health agencies, I managed to get my hands on the addresses of the city's addiction treatment centers, including the location of its two methadone clinics. I input those addresses into a map of the city and superimposed the location of the police interactions that participants had reported. I then created a buffer of a few hundred feet around each of them, figuring that police action within that buffer was likely to discourage people from accessing treatment. I set the statistical code so that ten or more instances of police arrests, detainments, or assaults within the buffer zone around a treatment center would turn it into a bright red circle, with fewer instances of police action turning the buffers orange, and only one or two turning it gray. I set the code to run and waited for the new map to generate. When it did, I scanned the map once again, this time looking for red circles. There were clumps of orange and gray circles strewn across the city, but there was only one circle that glowed red, and it was around the lone methadone clinic in the Zona Norte.

I had expected overlap between the places where police action occurred and where the treatment centers were located, but I hadn't expected the geographic relationship to be this stark. That wasn't to say that the map showed that police were targeting the Zona's methadone clinic; on that, I had no reason to disbelieve Susi's expert opinion. What it did make clear, though, was that the combination of sexual assaults, arrests, detainments, and beatings by police was carried out close enough to the clinic that it kept people away. Those that accessed it, I had already found, were more likely to be forced to pay a bribe, which now seemed unavoidable given the intensity of the police presence revealed by the map. In the study on bribery, 70 percent of Proyecto El Cuete participants who stopped methadone reported that they had done so because they ran out of money; another 20 percent because they couldn't easily access the clinic. The map, showing the cluster of police assaults that held a close orbit around the Zona's lone methadone clinic, explained both findings.

What's more, the analyses made me realize that my orientation to the femicide had been too reductive. Epidemiologists are so interested in proving causation, perhaps because it's so difficult to do and so satisfying when you are able to point at a factor as the sole source of illness and death. Beyond the hard numbers they generated, my twin analyses were a reminder that things can end terribly without anyone intending them to. In the Zona, power was clearly exercised intentionally by those who possessed it. Women's bodies aren't dismembered and scattered by accident. Hooded policemen don't just find themselves raping sex workers in hotel rooms. They are motivated to use whatever power they possess to bolster their position and satisfy their desire. Even so, police didn't seem intent on stopping women from entering into addiction treatment. And yet, somehow, the cops themselves were the single greatest barrier to people staying in treatment. Once I pulled back the lens, though, and saw patterns of behavior replicated across the city on the map, a new sense of the place was unlocked. There was a whole other level of systematic power obscured by accounts of a single corrupt police officer shaking down an injector or a narco taking a cut of the action in the Zona. The point wasn't the uniqueness of these stories but their similarities.

The city was a living organism, an entity made up of systems that worked together and separately to create the conditions that dictated the lives of its populace. The mapping of police brutality spread across the city like blood vessels, leading away from and toward the heart of the action in the Zona Norte and the canal. Here was one system among many. Another was the network of addiction treatment centers that attracted police and those they preyed upon, where the police then repulsed those seeking help. The system of enforcement was in chaotic competition with the system of care. A third was the maquiladora industry that ringed the canyons of the city, an employer of primarily women workers whose numbers could always be replenished by the tens of thousands of migrants that landed in Tijuana each year searching for steady factory jobs; it proved elusive for many, which is one reason the Zona remained so well stocked with young paraditas standing out on its narrow streets. But Tijuana was also a drug-trafficking plaza, an increasingly important one as the cartels operating here—the Arellano Félix Organization, the Sinaloa Cartel, and the Cartel Jalisco Nueva Generación—sought to take advantage of the stumbles of their rivals and keep the state at bay through force and guile. And so, different picaderos were controlled by different cartel actors with different drug supplies and different rules; these picaderos were the venues where HIV was passed between women and where they died of overdoses. While the picaderos stand like sentinels across the city, they cluster in and around the Zona, just like the addiction treatment centers. Both attract cartels who vie for control of the sex and drug economies as well as police who both protect and disrupt their activities. All of this left the Zona's women with a diminishing population of johns. All these actors sought their own ends, but just like variables in a model, intentionality was irrelevant; the only outcome that mattered was their impact on the host population.

If a pathological process had really taken hold in Tijuana, then the Zona was the epicenter of infection, the place where multiple pathogens were spawned, which then drove a complex epidemic of femicide that radiated out across the city. Staring at the map of Tijuana, that made sense to me. The city was sick, and its citizens were finding themselves succumbing to illness and death for reasons that seemed to them haphazard. And yet, in aggregate, those singular causes of death—the decision to share a needle, take that client, run across that highway—were metastasizing into something else entirely. An epidemic.

Start the outbreak from its beginning. Women come to Tijuana to find factory work but are doomed to inhaling toxic fumes in the maqui-ladoras or in their homes in the canyon slums. The pollution slowly kills them. If they complain, they are simply removed from their jobs and left destitute. So the system is static, unchanging, the women slotted in or left behind. For those denied legal work, the red-light district beckons, where the cheap drugs are as ubiquitous as the pain. Both pull women deeper into the city along routes that thousands of others have taken, though everyone's path here always feels unique. Once ensconced, barriers compound their escape. The city's ecosystem functions like any other, with the movement of the vulnerable dictated by scarcity and predation. Women, many of whom are migrants, broke and desperate, quickly learn who the apex predators are: the police and the cartels. Like many predators, they are in competition, at turns collaborating and in conflict with each other, the nature of their interactions determining the safety of women's lives. For the cartels, the women are disposable, to be consumed or used as props in displays of mass terror. So women run into darker and darker hiding places in the city—the picaderos or old beat-up hotels where neither the cartels nor police can find them. These are the places where they can die of overdose, or rape, or of furtive needle sharing, often carried out among strangers. They may want to stop using, but addicted women can't access treatment centers, so they stay on the streets, unwilling to risk their lives to get clean, remaining trapped where they are.

Even if that situation were static, it would be sufficient to kill women. But Tijuana was as complicated and protean as a human body, with autonomous systems operating without the knowledge of the whole, the entire structure constantly changing. An infected body, Tijuana also had hidden reservoirs where, like the HIV virus in the gut, a pathogen lurked undetected. The stresses on the city intensified and abated, with grave consequences for those Tijuanensis women living through these periods of change. The gravest of these was the steady decline of the sex trade, which forced women into impossible choices. Whereas before the launch of the drug war and the pullout of the U.S. Navy, women could avoid the worst impulses of the city, after the wholesale client base retreated, they began to face double, triple, and quadruple binds: their lack of income from a dwindling clientele pool forced them to choose johns who were sick or crazy, their potential for violence flaring like a beacon. For some women it was too much and they eyed the drug trade, dangerous but profitable under the control of a set of squabbling cartels. With less money, those women who sought to overcome their drug dependence found methadone too expensive; for those who could afford it, a corrupt police force made sure they wouldn't be able to for long. Those overlapping systems spread like blood vessels carrying cells devoid of oxygen, choking the land and its inhabitants.

The Mexican author Sergio González Rodríguez, in his investigation of the death of women in Ciudad Juárez, another notorious border town, described the churn of these types of city-wide systems leading to the death of women as a "femicide machine." It was as apt a description as I have heard to explain the relentless efficiency with which a city can destroy its own.

*

By the end of 2015 I had known Susi for two years, even if we remained essentially mysteries to each other. I had been thinking so hard about the epidemic and its pervasiveness that I had come to assume that it was inescapable. It's rare, though, to find a pathological process that eradicates all of its hosts. The purpose of all forms of life—even viruses, which some consider living creatures—is replication. Highly virulent pathogens are often less successful at transmission because of their murderous effectiveness. If an infection kills you too quickly, like Ebola, the virus might not have enough time to jump to somebody else. If it can linger and replicate without doing too much damage, like the common cold, it will become ubiquitous. While I was convinced that the pathological process I was investigating was deadly, it would not have been able to maintain its foothold in Tijuana if it ended up killing absolutely everyone it encountered. Susi, it appeared, was the one that got away: of the six friends that rolled together through the Zona in its heyday, only she had survived. What had set her apart?

The story Susi told was that the wounds that perforated her arm had made it too painful to inject anymore. The bracelet of thick scars running from her wrist to her elbow attested to the intensity of the physical trauma she must have gone through. She began to seek care for her wounds, she said, and then, as HIV was running rampant through the sex worker population in Tijuana—the women with whom she shared dirty veterinary needles she began to fear that the infection would kill her. This was just a few short years after the U.S. Navy had started sending hundreds of thousands of condoms to sex workers in Tijuana, hoping to flood the city with prophylactics in a roundabout attempt to protect its own troops from infection. Already receiving wound care, she took the next step and was tested for the virus.

Susi's diagnosis came in 2001. "I got sick, you see . . . it was then that I was very sick, but in those [first] three years, I didn't want to take the medicine." Unbeknownst to Susi, La Osa was also HIV-positive, neither ever revealing their status to the other, which exemplifies just how stigmatizing the disease was at the time. Unlike Susi, La Osa died, which makes Susi's survival seem that much more miraculous. Somehow, she wrenched herself away from injecting drugs; in her telling, it was the stigmata that covered her arms that ended up saving her from dying. Her friends didn't have the same wounds, so many of them continued to use and share syringes among themselves.

Breaking away from addiction can feel like an impossible task: in those moments when all is lost and you have denied yourself the only sacred joyful feeling available, you must also remove yourself from many of those you love and depend upon for support because they are still using and could tempt you back. For many, recovery from drug addiction means exile, from a community and a home. Treatment centers are often

self-consciously alien, exotic, the expensive ones made to look like facsim-
iles of an antiquated time when life wasn't so complicated and the right
way forward so obscure. Mown grass. Mild footpaths. Attentive well-clad
staff. In Tijuana, the treatment centers—the cheap ones, the outliers, the
uncertified and unregulated—resemble prisons in form and function; the
only difference being that in these centers, the moral argument for incarceration has been amplified to its limit, because instead of punishment
they offer the illusion of total recovery.

In 2003, Susi spent a year in La Morita on the east side of Tijuana, an
addiction treatment center where they finally convinced her to start
taking her HIV medication. She was committed to starting a new life, to
staying out of trouble and the Zona Norte. These were the years that the
drift from her friends began to really take hold. The crew of cast-off
women—self-described paradita, *tecates* (injectors), *bajadores* (thieves),
and hit doctors—began first to disassemble and then to disappear. "But
even then," Susi said, "I still came to this place to sell things during the
night. I kept on coming here, and I would ask myself, 'Well, am I never
going to get out of here? I don't use but I keep on coming.'" The Zona
kept calling her back; from the bridge above the canal she would look
down at the encampments below, never sure if that was the night she
would finally descend into the polluted murk. More than a decade later,
the burning desire to return to those places remained.

*

The U.S. Navy's self-imposed exile from Tijuana came after rising violence
from the Mexican drug war overran the city in 2008. I had assumed that
the loss of the Zona's reliable wholesale client base—over one hundred
thousand American military personnel stationed across the border to the
north—had been the environmental shift that had let a pathological
process loose. It made sense in principle: without these tens of thousands
of potential customers, the margins on Tijuana's vice economies were
stretched even further, with women forced to take greater and greater
risks to maintain a living wage. That would have left everyone in on the
action with less money and, consequently, with greater desperation. It was
just like the 1930s all over again, when the repeal of the American prohi-
bitions on alcohol and gambling had ended Tijuana's monopoly on both,
leaving the city destitute and reeling.

The trouble was, the timing didn't quite line up with what I had been
hearing from the women who had been living in Tijuana over the past

few decades. The last period of shamelessness that Rosa had identified began in the early to mid-aughts; that was also when Susi's life reached that axial moment and her path diverged from those of her late friends, with her trip to La Morita instead of down the canal wall. While the sex trade had without a doubt declined steeply after the U.S. military's retreat in 2008–9, the portrait of the Zona that Susi and Rosa had painted of that earlier time—fewer American tourists, the disappearance of off-duty police and Mexican soldiers from the bars along the strip—already described a place in an advanced state of decay. While it was impossible to uncover the annual revenue brought in by the women working in Tijuana's semilegal industry (let alone their counterparts in the larger informal trade), there were other ways to catch glimpses of the waning fortunes of the sex trade. Cross-border traffic flow, for example, is a good proxy measure of visits to the Zona given the outsize role of U.S. citizens in keeping Tijuana's sex trade afloat. Comparing the volume of pedestrian traffic across the border year after year could therefore help pinpoint the moment when the Zona's downturn began.

In 1997, the earliest year for which I could find data, there were 83 million crossings recorded at the Tijuana–San Diego border. By 2000, that number had risen to 91 million; a year later, in 2001, total cross-border flows reached over 100 million. In 2003, the number was up again, reaching 110 million. But in the ensuing years, a strange thing happened. By 2005, one year before President Calderón's initial strikes against the cartels and three full years before the Mexican drug war was officially launched, traffic had regressed to 97 million; by 2007, before the bloodshed had reached Tijuana, traffic was down again to 84 million. In 2009, the year the navy stopped allowing its personnel into Tijuana, only 71 million crossings were recorded. At the end of 2012, after the worst of the first wave of violence had receded, and four years after the official launch of the Mérida Initiative, only 70 million crossings took place. The thickening of the border had run its course, insulating the Unites States from Mexico and, more importantly, preventing its people from exploring their dark fantasies within the boundaries of La Coahuila. But when did that thickening start?

In the waning years of the 1990s, local civic leaders on both sides of the San Diego–Tijuana divide began seriously considering a bold proposal to unlock the potential of the region. After a century of expansion from the free and easy movement of people and goods, the border between Tijuana and the United States had become something of an afterthought. The need for a barrier had receded in the minds of those who lived on either side; it was an anachronism from a more fearful time, but the combined Tijuana–San Diego region was on the brink of coming into its own as a truly binational economic and cultural power-house. There were so many issues that bound Tijuana to its American sister city, and so many of the region's problems—industrial pollution of the Tijuana River Estuary, the cross-border cycle of waste tires finding their way from Mexico to California's beaches, and useless trade restrictions that slowed the flow of capital and goods—could only be dealt with collectively, by undoing the border fence's cleaving of this one great cross-border metropolis. At its best, the pairing of Tijuana and San Diego was an economic dream: where else could one find cheap labor, high-tech engineering, manufacturing infrastructure, and exceptionally generous trade regulations, all perfectly located to supply a thirsty American consumer market? The only obstacle was the international boundary. That made the next step obvious: get rid of the wall.

By 2001, a binational group of civic leaders and captains of industry was publicly floating the idea of removing the border fence entirely. The group's efforts reflected new thinking since 1993, when President Bill Clinton authorized the building of a physical barrier to divide Tijuana from San Diego. The slatted fence Clinton erected was an anachronism that dragged Tijuana and San Diego back in time, all the way to 1924, when the U.S. Border Patrol was first created to protect Americans from their Mexican neighbors (who at that time had just emerged from a decade of revolutionary war). Regardless of the fence's lack of utility, it was for Clinton a necessary political act: the North American Free Trade Agreement (NAFTA) was to go into effect the following year and required the support of lawmakers suspicious of anything that looked like a weakening of American border security. Within a decade, though, regional civic leaders from both sides of the political divide recognized the impediment to progress the wall had become. Discussions about not only if but how to remove the fence gathered steam. There was simply no reason to keep an artificial divide in the middle of an urban center that increasingly understood itself as one singular place. It was time to let Tijuana and San Diego embrace.

When airplanes flew into the twin towers of the World Trade Center on September 11, 2001, there was more than enough information circulating that Al Qaeda had been plotting an attack on U.S. soil. While there are constant threats to America's security, it took just one successful attack to set the system awry. The mathematical functions that underpin many epidemiologic models assume that the relationship between variables will remain predictably linear. For example, every person infected with measles produces twelve to eighteen secondary cases; that ratio of primary to secondary cases is known as the disease's basic reproductive ratio, and it will hold steady if conditions remain stable. Under certain circumstances, though, variables will interact to produce outcomes that are nonlinear and therefore difficult to predict. September 11, 2001 is one such nonlinear event, like Angie's last step onto the highway, which turned a living person into a dead one. Most epidemiologic models assume smooth (continuous) changes, so unforeseen (discontinuous) shifts can cause those models to break down. The power of terrorism comes from the fact that it is a discontinuous outcome, a sudden jarring shift in a system that feels like a catastrophe. The use of asymmetrical tools of combat, unlike the grinding wars of attrition where armies creep slowly to conquer land, is designed to produce decidedly nonlinear outcomes. In the case of 9/11, those outcomes rippled out across the American empire, sharply transforming it in ways with which we are still grappling.

For the binational civic leaders peering across an antiquated border fence toward their sisters and brothers on the other side, the dream of tearing down the barrier and letting the region fulfill its true potential was last dreamt on the night of September 10, 2001. After that, there was to be no formal coming together of Tijuana and San Diego. The century of collaboration between the two cities would no longer culminate in their union. Instead, people on both sides watched as the rusted slatted fence became a double barrier reinforced with a concrete wall, with a demilitarized zone placed between the fence and the wall for good measure. While walls are meant to affirm the sovereignty of two neighboring parties, the scale-up of the militarized border apparatus in the wake of 9/11 revealed an entirely different truth about this place.

Tijuana retains the seductive charm of those way stations set up by empires to serve their own kind. It is a Casablanca or a Macao, and like those cities it brims with a palpable, double-edged romance, a colonial town holding a mirror to the true face of the empire while purveying those darker needs that can only be sated at the empire's hazy edge. And like those other cities, Tijuana is also a place of dreams on the verge of coming true or falling apart, a transient meeting place bridging the wealth of America and those that work to supply it. The difference is that Tijuana is the southern tip of a network of religious communities that stretched all the way up to Los Angeles before the Spanish-American War. The imposition of the U.S.-Mexico border in 1848, at the site where Francisco Palou placed a wooden cross near a rock in 1773, ignored the natural fraternity of this Dominican enclave and the Franciscan settlements to its north. Once severed, Tijuana took desert dust and an overbearing neighbor and sought to do what it could to survive. After 9/11, its neighbor ran from its arms, and dust is not sufficient to sustain a city.

The catastrophe of that day, that discontinuous outcome that tipped the United States into a state of panic, laid bare the intimate bonds that existed across the border fence. As the U.S. recoiled from the outside world and from those within its own walls that exhibited otherness, Tijuana saw its lifeblood—Americans and their fantasies—dry up; on November 25, 2002, President George W. Bush created the Department of Homeland Security, one of the largest reorganizations of the federal government ever carried out. The department fulfilled its mission at the border, if we can assume this mission to have been the isolation of America from the dangers of the outside world. It would take a year or so for the new security apparatus to get up and running, which explains the decline in cross-border traffic beginning in the mid-aughts instead of immediately after 9/11. In 2006, on the basis of the 9/11 Commission's recommendations, President Bush passed the Secure Fence Act, mandating the construction of 850 miles of multilayered barrier at the southern border. In 2007, the Western Hemisphere Travel Initiative required all American citizens to start carrying a passport when reentering the United States. Again, the border thickened, and again the human traffic crossing into Tijuana dissipated. The decades of easy come and go between the two sides, the idea of the border as an outdated fiction on the verge of being dismantled—it was all brutally ended with the construction of the second wall, concrete and very high, impenetrable and opaque.

While walls stifle the flow of goods and people between two places, they also increase the transfer of one particular phenomenon across the divide: fear. The wave of anxiety that emerged in the United States after 9/11 suffused American culture and politics. There was a term Oscar Romo used to describe the makeshift shelters constructed in the slums under the maquiladoras. Pointing to the waste tires, garage doors, and washing machine casements that made up these homes, he described it all as a kind of vernacular architecture, a style of building rooted firmly in the needs and materials of those who lived in Tijuana's canyon shantytowns. The border wall dividing Tijuana and San Diego is the greatest example of the vernacular architecture of America's post-9/11 era that has been constructed to date. It is a feat of engineering undertaken with the full force of the country's military-industrial complex and animated by extreme collective angst. The sheer folly of imposing ten feet of standardized concrete upon a rough and wild landscape stretching across miles of desert, mountain ranges, rivers, and swampland betrays the depth of the wound the United States sustained after the twin towers fell. While the fever dream of a continuous border wall was never made manifest (it was shuttered after cost overruns revealed the impossibility of the project), it runs from Tijuana east, covering 580 miles. The portion of it built in Tijuana nevertheless cleaved the city from its sustenance and broadcasted American fear into a Mexican town that was, for the first time in its history, isolated from the United States.

That was when murder, that component of the pathological process, moved the femicide from outbreak to epidemic. In 2000, less than 6 percent of the murder victims in Tijuana were women. In 2003, the year the Department of Homeland Security began operating, that figure had increased to 10 percent, despite the fact that the overall number of homicides in the city stayed relatively constant, at roughly 300 per year. In 2008, the year the Mérida Initiative was officially launched, more than 20 percent of Tijuana's murder victims were women; that proportion has remained either equal or higher every year since. That's counterintuitive, as the military offensive should have increased the proportion of men killed given that narcos are almost exclusively male. And yet Tijuana's women were increasingly the victims.

Killings were not the only facet of this larger epidemic that these women would have to navigate after the environmental shift. In 1995, Tijuana's HIV epidemic was still largely contained, with HIV prevalence at 0.5 percent among the city's female sex workers (including those that injected drugs), well below the threshold of 5 percent (the standard for HIV set by the World Health Organization). Within just one year—2005 to 2006—the prevalence of HIV doubled among a sample of women who inject drugs in Tijuana but stayed the same among drug-injecting men. Overall, 11 percent of women who worked in the sex trade and injected drugs were infected with the virus, while only 2.5 percent of men who injected drugs were infected. The epidemic threshold had been smashed, but only for the half of the population that was female. The virus's basic reproductive ratio is two to five cases per single case of HIV, meaning that it generally spreads quite slowly relative to highly virulent diseases. A doubling of prevalence in one year among only the female half of a small marginalized subpopulation is a striking epidemiologic phenomenon, and it calls to mind John Snow's search for the cause of the cholera poisoning only half of the households in London's Soho district. By 2006, across the entire city of Tijuana, scientists estimated that as many as 1,295 Tijuanensis women were infected, equivalent to 263 HIV cases per 100,000 women. Among the city's 10,000 sex workers, 436 were believed infected with the virus. The HIV virus had spread rapidly through the bodies of Tijuana's women in the years shortly after 9/11.

The retreat of the U.S. Navy from Tijuana wasn't the beginning of the environmental shift. It was the coda on a process that had started with 9/11. The spread of American fear into Tijuana was quickened by the barriers that rose up at the border. Then and only then did that era of shamelessness that Rosa and Susi described emerge, which allowed a pathological process consisting of many component parts to increase in virulence: police corruption and assault, cartel violence, fewer but more ruthless johns, the risks of savagery and disease at each encounter increasing as the prices for women's bodies dropped. But that wasn't all. Crystal methamphetamine began to show up alongside heroin and cocaine, increasingly destined for Tijuanenses rather than just American consumers. Women were chased like game into oncoming traffic. Bodies became more useful to deliver narcomantas than as vessels for life. All of it stemming from American fear.

Tijuana was an imperial way station that had seen its fortunes plummet because of the perverse actions of a man and his acolytes living in Afghanistan's mountainous Khost Province, many worlds away. Their fear of annihilation was sent as a projectile into America; that fear, transmogrified, found its way to another fringe of the empire, the city of Tijuana, in the form of a vernacular architecture of barriers. And so the city declined and the fear spread unchecked, eating first through the city's economic fabric and then into its moral center. Here was the origin of the environmental shift that preceded the increasing virulence of the pathological process that had been lurking in the Zona for some time. After that, the women who lived there found themselves, suddenly, facing an emergent femicide.

I had found that puff of air rising from the grave in the Kumeyaay's Story of the Shooting Star, and had come upon Saint George's plague-spreading dragon; I had found the axial point when an epidemic was unleashed. But after mapping Tijuana's ecosystem and tracing the catastrophe that let the pathological process spread virulently, I was left with a looming question: how do you begin the inoculation?

PART IV

Containment

CHAPTER 10

And Yet They Love Them

Europe in the late nineteenth century saw the flowering of post-Enlightenment scientific positivism, which amounted to a belief that rational thought had a practically limitless capacity to solve vexing social problems. In this paradigm, reason was an unstoppable panacea that would be the basis of a well-designed, wholly modern society. It was a time when humanity was on the cusp of taking charge of its destiny to become its own worshipped god. While hyperbolic, this hubris seemed plausible to the citizens of major cities, given the rapid innovations in urban planning and architecture—meticulously planned neighborhoods, vast public works, mass transit—that they were witness to in European centers like Prague, Berlin, Liverpool, and Budapest. But outside of the cities frothing with change was a countryside still resistant to the brutal reordering of society that positivist thinking demanded. Instead of highly ordered agricultural communities designed through scientific equations, rural Europe still greeted visitors with scenes of death and decay in full bloom. This is no lyric description: out there, in the fields upon which herds of cattle grazed, the rotting corpses of cows and sheep—felled by an enigmatic plague—lay like unshakable reminders of humanity's failure to conquer nature and its constant companion, death.

It wasn't for lack of trying. Sheep and cows had been dying from a mysterious disease for thousands of years, and farmers had become well equipped to spot the signs of its onset: a high fever and blood pooling around the mouth, nose, and anus. These symptoms presaged a coming death. Animals that died in this way were buried in the fields, deep down in the earth, on the assumption that submerging diseased corpses in soil would protect the healthy. But despite these burials, other animals continued to fall victim to the plague. Worse, if the farmers dragged the bodies of diseased animals away, they and their families could find themselves quickly succumbing as well. Even factory workers whose only contact with livestock was handling wool began to wheeze, vomit, cough up blood, and die if the wool came from diseased sheep. Dead animals were left to fester, spoiling otherwise bucolic landscapes. Farmers, fearing for their lives, went bankrupt as their herds died off. This plague—whatever its cause—was a rotting reminder of the limits of rational thought at a time when reason claimed to be all-powerful.

The French chemist Louis Pasteur exemplified the belief that science could wrestle nature and win. By the 1880s, he had already identified the cause of rabies (a virus), revealed that bacteria in beer and milk produced a sour taste (which could be removed by boiling), and saved Europe's silk industry by successfully eradicating muscardine, a fungal disease that afflicted silkworms. But these victories weren't enough. Pasteur also set his sights on solving the age-old dilemma of rural Europe's most tenacious plague. While scientists throughout history had tried to pin down the causes of the disease, until Pasteur they had all been stumped by a simple yet intractable piece of the puzzle: how was it possible that an infection could be transmitted to new hosts when the corpses of the victims were buried deep under the ground? It should have been impossible given that disease vectors need living animal reservoirs to pass from victim to victim. By all laws of nature, placing six feet of earth between an infected corpse and new hosts should have been enough to stop the spread.

Pasteur brought two innovations to his investigation. The first was to recognize that there had to be a biological mechanism that brought the pathogen to the surface of the earth, where it could continue to spread through populations of sheep, cattle, and humans. Of course, he needed to prove it. So Pasteur, who obviously didn't mind getting his hands dirty, went into fields where infected animals were buried and collected large soil samples. Inside, all he found were earthworms, wriggling dumbly through the earth; when he examined them in his lab he found that their excrement contained a pathogenic agent that they had ingested as they had slowly engorged themselves on animal carcasses. That pathogen we now know as anthrax.

Pasteur's second innovation was to then cultivate the anthrax bacteria from the blood of infected animals and inoculate them with heated—and thereby neutralized—bacterial antibodies. By doing so he created one of the world's first live vaccines. Pasteur's work wasn't just important science. It was hugely consequential in securing the economic future of European farming. There was an important symbolic dimension too: the identification and curing of the anthrax epidemic demonstrated that science could defeat the morbid disorders of nature, even the complicated riddle of a plague that escaped from the bodies of entombed animals to infect those still walking aboveground. He had sealed a noxious crack in the earth.

*

In the aftermath of 9/11, Tijuana saw its fortunes decline as the border became increasingly unpredictable. American tourists, unwilling to risk long waits at the border to return from this America-loving Mexican city, simply stayed away. In the Zona and across Tijuana's many tourist haunts, brothels, drug-dealing spots, and cantinas, business plummeted. Far from the scenes of carnage at Ground Zero in New York City, the attack perpetrated by Osama bin Laden and his collaborators had driven a wedge between the people of Tijuana and their most loyal customers.

There was one bright spot, though. Tijuana's pharmacies have a long established reputation as purveyors of cheap and easily accessible pharmaceutical drugs. Staffed by smiling sales associates in white lab coats, these legal drug dispensaries have filled a gap for Americans running up against the astronomical costs of the U.S. health care system. Valium, OxyContin, Viagra, and other prescription drugs are still sold in Tijuana at cut-rate prices, a practice that pulls in massive profits for the city: in the late 1990s, it was estimated that one in four U.S. residents traveling to Mexico brought back prescription drugs, with the cross-border trade in Tijuana worth millions upon millions of dollars each day. After 9/11, the trade suffered briefly in the immediate aftermath of the attacks, when uncertainty and fear dampened the bustling border traffic. That lull in sales would be short-lived.

On September 18, 2001, just one week after the attacks, when Americans were still catching their breath, a second catastrophe ratcheted up the mass anxiety that gripped the nation. Multiple American congressional offices and media outlets across the country reported receiving letters in the mail containing a fine white powder. One letter delivered to a tabloid newspaper in Boca Raton, Florida, was opened by the paper's photo editor; within days he was dead. The powder was anthrax, and the letters—which claimed to be from Al Qaeda—were classified as weapons of biological warfare. It was terrorism at its most effective: nobody doubted the virulence of the pathogen, but the scale of the attack was completely unknown. Theories abounded that the anthrax-laced letters were a second wave within a greater terrorist plot to destroy America. That made the work of Louis Pasteur, with his hands covered in soil and earthworms, more relevant than ever since his discovery of the pathogen over one hundred years earlier.

Within days of the anthrax attacks, Cipro—the brand-name treatment for the bacteria—became a highly sought-after commodity. Across the United States, a run on the medication ensued, followed by reports of widespread shortages. And so, while Tijuana was largely shuttered in those weeks after 9/11, one glaring exception stood out. As a *New York Times* article from October 20, 2001, reported, pharmacy windows along Avenida Revolución were full of signs advertising the latest craze: WE HAVE CIPRO, they read. HIGHLY EFFECTIVE AGAINST ANTHRAX. It wasn't uncommon in those heady weeks for tens of thousands of dollars to change hands as Americans made bulk purchases of Cipro before heading back into the zone of fear across the border. Even though Americans had abandoned Tijuana, the city resolutely continued to provide whatever balm its northern neighbors required.

*

Tom Patterson made his career inverting expectations. Recruited by the U.S. military to combat the AIDS epidemic in the early 1990s, he was among the first to argue—and among the first to do so successfully—that focusing prevention efforts on the population at risk of acquiring HIV was tantamount to trying to inoculate the entire world. Instead, people already infected with the virus, who constituted a population much smaller and easier to define, had to be the starting point for a strategy to eradicate the disease. It was an uphill battle at a time when HIV-positive people were generally seen as social pariahs responsible for their illness. And yet Tom, through reasoned analysis and unceasing pressure, worked with others to cut through the stigma of the day to help transform the U.S.

government's approach to dealing with the epidemic. What he and his colleagues also recognized was that the only way to convince public funders to reorient prevention toward those already infected was to strip the disease of any tinges of morality. After all, as with today's opioid overdose epidemic, the only effect that moralizing has on a public health crisis is to slow the response and thereby fail to prevent mass death.

Tijuana is no stranger to stigma. In fact, it has cultivated its stigma to great effect, leveraging an outsize reputation for libidinous behavior and permissive immorality into a steady source of income that has lasted more than a century. The city's welcoming of sinners has long acted as a pressure valve for Americans, a place to blow off steam. After, the visitor returns home stripped for a time of the lusts that had wormed their way through a well-adjusted life and threatened to eat through its very fabric. It is an inoculating city, an antibody of sorts, giving tourists a taste of darker pursuits that might, if taken in too high a dose, destroy them.

Tijuana's upside-down system of morality was a perfect match for Tom's approach to epidemic problem-solving. He had begun working in the city in the early 2000s without worrying about what was and was not considered appropriate. Instead, he focused his energy on establishing a research infrastructure that could rapidly identify and address the needs of sex workers who were infected with HIV, as well as those at risk of acquiring the virus from them. Sex workers are sometimes referred to as a "hidden" population, meaning that their information isn't easily captured by a census or government health survey. In that light, it was a testament to Tom and Steffanie's success in Tijuana that I was able to connect with so many women here who were participating in the research studies they had established. More importantly, the women I met had all been enrolled in clinical care simply through participating in research, which avoided the ethical pitfalls that can ensnare even well-meaning scientists. Despite these accomplishments, Tom recognized that there was a subpopulation even more hidden and stigmatized than the sex workers of the Zona Norte, a group of people who stood at the intersection of multiple epidemics in Tijuana: johns.

From the early days of his work on the HIV epidemic in the U.S., Tom had focused on those subpopulations that were easily identifiable and at greatest risk of spreading the disease. In Tijuana that meant, naturally, studying sex workers. But because women were primarily becoming infected by their clients, Tom also concluded that asking women to change their behavior set unrealistic expectations. In the tiered trade that exists throughout the Zona and stretches across the city at large, women often have too little leverage to demand that their clients use condoms. If they live and work at the big clubs or in closed houses, they have to balance institutional desire for profit with their own need to remain healthy. If they face disadvantages—poverty, drug addiction, and social isolation—that tends to lean the balance of power toward their clients. This is not to say that every transaction invariably ends with women having sex without protection. Ana and Rosa had so far avoided becoming infected and were at least partially able to dictate the terms of exchange with their clients. But at the population level, there were enough women engaging in risky sex work—a group that was increasing in size with the dwindling of the Zona's client base—to continue spreading HIV. With these restrictions on women's decision-making, Tom figured that the solution would have to involve convincing clients to voluntarily change their sexual behavior. It was a risky strategy, given that nobody knew much about what kind of men made up the client base in Tijuana. Who were they and where did they come from? Why did they visit the Zona? Were they all willing to pay a premium for condomless sex? And, crucially, did they care at all about the women with whom they coupled?

Tom's decision was counterintuitive, given that everybody—himself included—assumed that the men who were coming to Tijuana to party, do drugs, and pay for sex would have zero interest in participating in a public health study. But rigorous methodologist that he is, Tom was also intent on connecting the dots between the many populations among whom the HIV epidemic was spreading. "Obviously the clients are a big part of the equation when you're studying sex workers," he told me one day over the phone. "And I thought, 'Let's give it a shot.'" That casual gloss obscures the time-consuming work involved in establishing public health surveillance of a brand-new population. Beyond the many weeks of grant writing, there are months of waiting on decisions from government institutes, which typically fund fewer than one in five projects of this kind. In the unlikely chance of success, the research has to pass an ethics review board, which can take another few months, before any actual work is initiated. Only then, roughly eighteen months to two years after a project is conceptualized, can the work finally start. That's when the hard part of staffing up and somehow recruiting participants from a population that nobody knows anything about begins. It was that last stage that worried Tom the most as he approached the launch of data collection in October 2008.

As part of my own research into the Zona, I came across an online forum of clients—"mongers," they called themselves, short for whoremongers—dedicated to sharing tips and stories from Tijuana. Some of the posts covered the basic logistics of getting into the city ("Hope to see a few of the bros in TJ this Friday night . . . Let me know if we can car pool."), while others shared advice about the perils of regularly buying sex there. One post from September 2007 was typical of the advice on the site: "Lice eggs are tiny spiky things like specks of dust. They will attach to your body even if your pubic area is completely shaved. Lice are tough creatures. I doubt you can drown them. I used OTC ointment with fine lice comb but it did not work completely. The eggs kept hatching waves after waves and the lice kept coming back. Finally I used prescribed Lindane ointment over 2 weeks and got rid of all the eggs."

As the years passed and the drug war made its way to Tijuana, the forum's tone changed. One post from June 2008 signaled a shift among the mongers, who had moved from recommending specific sex workers in the Zona ("I found Michelle standing near the exit. She's a tall, lanky girl with dark hair and the sweetest face anywhere.") to commiserating about its dangers ("TJ does scare most people shitless with all those federales wearing face masks, black fatigues, toting machine guns, raiding the bars in La Zona Roja [another name for the red-light district]."). It wasn't hyperbole: in April 2008, just two months earlier, seventeen narcos were killed in a shootout between warring factions of the Arellano Félix Organization that took place steps from a row of squat maquiladoras near Tijuana's eastern city limits; in the wake of the street battle, the city was on edge and military and quasi-military law enforcement brigades had since then been patrolling constantly. According to Tijuana's downtown merchants' association, only about 150 tourists visited the area each day in 2008, a drop of almost 99 percent from three years earlier. At the time, a long and active thread emerged among the mongers complaining about stepped-up border security, with self-serving accounts of clients being forced to justify their day trips across the border to suspicious U.S. Customs and Border Protection agents ("I was harassed by an agent. He could smell the chicas' perfume in my clothes and became very jealous."). Another post, from July 2008, was titled "Federales Raid": "I took up Country John's [the handle of another forum poster] suggestions and tried out Las Pulgas club, a civilian disco club on Revolution. I was ogling and contemplating my moves on some of the sweetest-looking civilian chicas on the dance floors when the Federales swooped in wearing their black uniforms and face masks, aimed their machine guns, stopped the music and checked out ID's of hundreds of people in the club . . . So my take is that the Federales are just not screwing around for nothing. I just hope the Mexican government can manage to clean up the crime, violence and corruption so the people will have a better life. We just cannot give up our fight against evils." Another, from October 2009—the same year the U.S. Navy barred its personnel from visiting the city—was uncharacteristically brief: "La Zona Roja was sparse and quiet. Not too many people on the streets like years past."

Around this time, a squabble broke out between some of the clients on the forum, with one (Country John) accusing the forum's moderator (One Wing Low) of placing the community in danger through his rhapsodic accounts of Tijuana's sex trade: "He's really trying to bring some more mongers into La Zona Roja despite the whizzing bullets and the headless dead bodies that keep showing up . . . Wonder if he's getting his free quality-control fucks off the paraditas in the alley??"

If the monger forum was any indication, Tom's fears about recruitment were well-founded. The men who posted online appeared interested only in the prowess of the Zona's women during bouts of transactional sex; the worries they expressed about the security situation in Tijuana were centered entirely on their own safety. Around the same time, in the fall of 2009, though, a commenter called Libra 7474, perhaps reacting to the flood of accounts of violence in the Zona, sought to move the normally coarse conversation in a new and surprising direction: "Hi guys, I am reading a fascinating book called *Sex Work and the City: The Social Geography of Health and Safety in Tijuana, Mexico* by Yasmina Katsulis. I think it's a must-read for anyone interested in the subject—it is a well-conducted research." Corny jokes about the joys of qualitative research with sex workers ensued.

It was into this milieu, with clients fleeing the city in the wake of violence and hassles at the border, that Tom launched his study, which he dubbed Hombre Seguro (Safe Man). It had looked like an uphill battle when he was conceptualizing it in the years before the violence hit the city. By the time data collection was set to commence in 2008, with the death toll spiking, it looked like a near-impossible undertaking. But Tom soldiered on, hiring field staff to approach men in the bars and brothels of the Zona who looked like they were there to buy sex, while also syncing up with a network of *jaladores* (Mexican slang for "cooperative people"), local fixers who arranged sex workers for tourists, with the aim of recruiting a total of four hundred men. On paper, the enterprise sounds ludicrous. "When we started this project I expected that to be the case," he told me, referring to the difficulties of finding men sympathetic to his research, "but I always thought that I'd like to be able to look at all the segments of HIV risk populations in Tijuana." However outlandish it may have seemed at the outset, when Hombre Seguro finally launched, it became clear that Tom had tapped a hidden fount of knowledge at the epicenter of the city's HIV epidemic.

Tom sort of chuckled to himself in disbelief as he reminisced about the launch. "These guys—many of them were really anxious—they lined up out the door to participate. And much to our surprise, they felt that they had been ignored, and they were just hungry for information. There was a vacuum there, and we were at the right place at the right time." In that context, the ribald and misogynistic posts I had read on the monger forum obscured a deeper issue. Under the jocular veneer of their stories of sexual conquests, the posts betrayed the mongers' collective fear of catching disease, being arrested, or ending up bloodied and beaten by the Tijuana police. It was a fear of being engulfed by the chaos of the city.

Tom's study tapped directly into that anxiety by providing clients with HIV testing, while also communicating that the knowledge they brought to the project was critical to developing a safer system of prostitution in Tijuana. A later phase of the study even trained the clients themselves in safe sex techniques and provided them with education and basic treatment for HIV and other STIs. While the men might have been "hidden," they had a unique perspective on the epidemic, Tom figured, and their opinions were critical in figuring out the maximum points of impact to control the spread of HIV in the Zona. Tom subsequently found that 4 percent of the clients he interviewed tested positive for HIV, with those who used crystal meth more likely to acquire the virus. The clients, as Tom had hypothesized, were a significant reservoir of HIV in Tijuana. More troubling, they were, through their families, a potential avenue to a generalized HIV epidemic that reached beyond the Zona and across both sides of the border. Like the earthworms delivering anthrax from beneath the soil's surface, the clients were unwitting vectors hidden amid the darkness of the Zona.

The publications that Tom and his team produced from these studies, which include testimonials from clients, paint a complex portrait of how sex, drugs, and fear—the latter resulting from the fact that many of the men had been deported from the United States to Tijuana—intersected to spread the virus. The anxiety and isolation of these deportees, many of whom had been born in Mexico but had lived their entire lives in the U.S., is palpable, especially juxtaposed against the neat clinical language of Tom's scientific prose. "Loneliness . . . immense loneliness. That this city cannot fulfill," said one recently deported client when asked to describe why he paid for sex. "The way we live our lives here in TJ, in this little area," said another, referring to the Zona, "you live a fast life anyways. We are hustling to survive, so every day that you live is a risk. Having sex without a condom is part of that. If you don't want to have risks in your life, you need to go somewhere else." That expression of fatalism had another common manifestation: "Normally I try to keep safe; but if I'm drunk or high, I don't care in the moment. Then later I think, 'What if the girl has an infection?' Especially in this part of Tijuana . . ."

Salvador, a vendor in the Zona Norte, was one of those clients enrolled in Hombre Seguro. An amiable man in his late forties, Salvador described his habitual purchase of sex as a natural consequence of spending time in the neighborhood. "I sell things here you know, *chácharas* [junk], secondhand clothes, so that's how I get to know [the sex workers]," he said, speaking over a small table in one of the interview rooms at the El Cuete offices in the Zona Norte. "They buy my things, they ask for money, I give them money, and that's how we start having relations. Sometimes they don't have money, and I can offer them a place to stay for two or three days." Salvador first moved to the Zona in 1991 and had witnessed the contraction of the neighborhood's fortunes since then, as well as the ways in which the desperation of the Zona's sex workers constrained their capacity to avoid acquiring HIV. "If women charge five hundred pesos [roughly twenty-five U.S. dollars] and they're offered one thousand pesos to not use a condom, well, I think they take it. I think they shouldn't do it. And the clients—I mean sometimes they have families, you know? And even if you are a client with a woman that just went to the clinic, you never know because they can get [HIV] at any moment." As a crystal meth user, Salvador was worried about the kinds of risks he faced even just sharing a pipe with his paid companions. "You don't know if the person you're smoking with is sick or if it's you, and passing the pipe around can get the others in trouble. Imagine that this happened? It would be my fault." That lack of information about the hidden dangers he faced was the reason Salvador decided to join Hombre Seguro. "I was really interested in [HIV risk], and also to be able to explain all this to my kids, and to be able to tell my friends, to have an opinion. Now I can explain to someone what this is all about, and it's not only about putting a condom on or taking something to cure yourself: The point is to be careful. To avoid all these diseases, right? And then to know what to do if you get infected."

Salvador wasn't typical of the sort of client I had pictured when I began work in Tijuana. His life was as tied to the Zona as the women he paid for sex, unlike the mongers who cruised down for a night at the big clubs like Hong Kong or Adelita's before returning home to the United States. He was poor and local, and he spent his days hustling just like everybody else around here. More than anything, Salvador exuded a sense of concern for the women of the Zona. This place was his home, after all, and they were his neighbors. Unlike the boasting mongers online, Salvador was plain about why he paid for sex: he was lonely and yearned for human connection. He also considered himself as inextricably linked into the same informal economy here as the women he paid to be with, and the transactions that brought them closer—be they of money, drugs, or a temporary place to stay—did nothing to reduce the meaningfulness of their time together. Perhaps they even enhanced it, given that both parties were facing the same long odds.

Despite using crystal meth and paying for sex, Salvador wanted to make it clear that his own behavior and intentions were different from those of other clients. "People get transformed when they use drugs," he explained. "They might seem like regular people, but once they are intimate with sex workers, they change—they act totally different. There have been so many cases here of women being assaulted and killed by clients. And that's just one of the risks that women face."

As he talked, Salvador kept returning to the lives of the women he paid, largely glossing over his own experiences of poverty and risk in the Zona. "I get concerned because some women get sick. For example, a little while ago a woman—a sex worker—died." He looked somber. "She never looked sick, but there was a period of about fifteen to twenty days that I didn't see her, and I heard after that she'd died. And what happened to her? Well apparently she had tuberculosis and I believe that was because of her partner: if you smoke [crack] together, you can get infected, you know?" This was exactly the kind of information that participants in the Hombre Seguro project learned. At that moment, the full weight of the situation seemed to hit him. "I think it's just too fast."

While I didn't doubt his sincerity in supporting women's health, Salvador's decision to join Hombre Seguro was evidently related to fears about his own health—exactly the motivation Tom had hoped to tap into. "Well, I met these guys [the project staff] and they invited me in," Salvador said, "and I started to get more interested, to learn about things that I only knew about superficially. For example, we talked about the HIV; I only knew it by name, but I didn't know what it was and how you could get it. I needed more in-depth information, right? It's good for me to know all that because I'm exposed to it."

Salvador claimed that Hombre Seguro had been instrumental in improving his relationships with the women he paid. "Sometimes I tell them, or even just make a comment like, 'Have you ever been tested for this and that?' It's something that I do now. I do it to protect myself and help them, right? To just let them know, so they can recall that they need to take care of their health, be careful, and get tested periodically." He had also made an effort to educate those women who he thought were at greatest risk of infection, violence, or worse. "For example, I've seen really young girls around and I tell them, 'Be careful, don't go with just anyone; go with someone that you know or let someone know where you are going to be.'" He sighed. The Zona was a dangerous place, and he was just one person. Or perhaps he was acknowledging his own participation in the machinery of sex work that pulled women in and slowly devoured them. "That's all that I can really do."

The knot of intimate behaviors between vulnerable people taking place amid the desperation of the red-light district was exactly what Tom sought to transform. The first task was to untangle how clients and sex workers interacted. The next step was to find a way to rewrite the neighborhood's power dynamics sufficiently to allow sex workers to counter, even in the smallest of ways, the risks that the base economics of the district imposed upon them. That research had started, for better or for worse, in a post-9/11 Zona, when the thickening of the border had tightened the stranglehold the Zona held on women. That situation had produced an epidemic of HIV among sex workers, among whom less than 1 percent were infected before 2002 and as many as 12 percent were infected after 2006.

By the time that I started my research in Tijuana in 2013, when the epidemic of femicide was expanding at an accelerating rate, Tom and Stefanie (along with a slew of other researchers) had turned their lens on the root causes of violence against sex workers. What they found was exactly in line with what Salvador and Rosa had been telling me all along, as well as with the casual misogyny I had seen on the monger message boards. Among the five hundred sex workers the team interviewed, those that had been assaulted all shared a few select factors: they served foreign clients, used drugs with their clients, and worked on the street. These were women like Rosa.

Tom had no illusions that Hombre Seguro, a stand-alone study with a modest number of participants, would somehow reverse these systemic causes of the femicide on its own. The program was just one part of a larger edifice being built to protect those at risk of succumbing to the epidemic; the four hundred clients enrolled in Hombre Seguro were a small fraction of the tens of thousands of men who bought sex in Tijuana. And yet, it was clear that Salvador—just one well-intentioned local client—had been empowered by basic scientific knowledge that many of us take for granted but that nevertheless had a profound impact on how he related to women. When asked whether he now used condoms, he became animated. "Yes, yes, of course! Before you couldn't find them, but now there's more access. Before if you wanted to use a condom you would have to buy it, and if you didn't have money—well, you simply wouldn't use one. I used to have sex without condoms," he admitted, "but now I can tell you that I definitely use them, because of what I've learned here: it has made me more conscious that I need to use them."

Salvador's change in behavior was just a small part of building an architecture grand enough to shelter women in Tijuana. While scientific advances like vaccines rightly get the lion's share of the media attention on disease prevention, these biomedical silver bullets are rare. In the meantime, epidemiologists content themselves with building a patch-work of interventions to control the shifting patterns of epidemic expansion. It can at times feel like a deeply unsatisfying way to solve problems, especially when the answers are simple and appear to be within your grasp (free condoms and safe sex education). But when those at risk of dying have been forgotten before they're even dead, simple answers are illusory. The price to save lives is always too high when we'd rather remain ignorant that these people exist at all.

Salvador continued talking about this neighborhood, his home for the last thirty-five years, and it was clear that he was also attuned to the changes Rosa and Susi had told me about, though at one step removed. "Sometimes there are periods with less drugs, but they always come back, eh? I actually think there are more now, because there's always a new type of drug." He had watched one drug in particular take over the neighbor-hood. "Crystal," he said firmly. "Before, you couldn't find it, but [the Zona] has changed a lot." Despite using crystal meth himself, Salvador was adamant that its emergence as a drug of choice among clients had put women in danger. Meth, he pointed out, made clients aggressive and hyperactive, leading to violence against women that could quickly escalate into deadly force.

From his perch on the sidewalks of the Zona, where he peddled his cháacharas, Salvador had also had a front-row seat to the retreat of American tourists in the red-light district. "Well, maybe fifteen or twenty years ago, you would see so many people—tourists, people from the other side—and all the bars were full, day and night. Now you don't really see people here, no tourists; and why?" He looked across the table with a keen expression. "Because of the police." Salvador was convinced that the overwhelming police presence in the Zona—a phenomenon that Susi had noted began in the early aughts—was the neighborhood's death knell. "They are the ones that drive people away," said Salvador. "They steal from them if they see an American, and if they see him drunk they detain him and take his money. The police know everything—they know who steals, but they don't do anything. I've seen it myself: they don't do anything at all." I thought back to the mongers on the message boards and their fears of getting busted coming down to party in TJ after the drug war began. "So: what happens? Well," Salvador continued, "if there's people coming from other places, the police know that they have money. They take their money, they detain them, and take them to jail, and they charge them more money once they get there." The constant grift had, according to Salvador, worn away the reputation of the neighborhood as a place to have a little harmless fun. "If I lived on the other side," he said, "I wouldn't come, because I'd get robbed and abused. Not anymore," he said, shaking his head. "They might even kill me. No, no."

As the conversation came to a close, Salvador became wistful. "It was different," he said of the Zona. "I'm telling you. Like, twenty years ago and before that—there was money for everyone, more people here to use drugs. Now you can see even the girls say, 'It's empty.' During the weekends it's busier, but the rest of the time this place is like a ghost town."

We said our goodbyes and Salvador politely excused himself. He lumbered down the steps and back out into the street, off to retrieve his cháacharas or to find some love somewhere amid the small bundles of drugs and money changing hands across the neighborhood. As he left, it struck me that I had gotten so used to thinking of the final movements of dead women in the Zona; Susi's friends or the women of the El Cuete cohort that had died, their data scrutinized posthumously after that one last hit delivered via a needle, a car hurtling along the highway, or a man towering above them. Salvador was right. The Zona was a ghost town. With the tourists gone, it was easier than ever to glimpse the outlines of the spirits that still haunted it.

*

Hombre Seguro was typical of Tom's approach to the puzzles that he set himself. Over a decade after his first battles with the NIH to focus on vectors of HIV spread rather than potential victims, Tom found himself in a remarkably similar position: facing down an HIV epidemic—this time, localized around the U.S.-Mexico border—and readying himself to work with a risk population largely reviled by pretty much everyone. Talking to Tom, you get the sense that his openness to work with populations like johns isn't a consequence of compassion. Sure, he's a compassionate guy, but so are many other people. The difference is that Tom has a remarkable ability to remove extraneous noise from his scientific decision-making. Compassion, morality, anger, sadness, stigma: Tom is able to lock them all away and find the most effective solution. That detachedness is perfectly suited to his work in Tijuana, as it is to deciphering minute differences in the songs of the sparrows inhabiting Bay Area forests. A part of me thinks that Tom would have been happier keeping those headphones on and drawing out the strange and beautiful notation of birdsong, with its long horizontal lines and short diagonal inflections, in a quiet office somewhere far from the border, before HIV intervened.

As interdependent as Tom and Steffanie were, there was no doubt that their orientations to the problem of HIV were profoundly unalike. Where Tom is happily mild-mannered, you can always feel the emotional energy radiating off of Steffanie, and she has never in the time I've known her been interested in shying away from raising a ruckus to get things moving. Instead of setting aside her emotions in the pursuit of her goals, she employs her lingering anger creatively, letting it drive her work. While in a lesser mind that approach might taint the purity of the science, Steffanie knows better than anyone the vitriol and opposition that scientists face when working on issues of drugs and sex, so she bolsters her research against it like a soldier disassembling and reassembling a gun every day to make sure it still fires perfectly. She has faced down angry American congressmen, developed the early scientific foundation to support Vancouver's supervised injection site, and successfully navigated Tijuana's byzantine regulations to establish the El Cuete study, which has against all odds been operating in various iterations in the Zona Norte for almost ten years. While Steffanie revels in reliving these fights, the frustrations that Tom undoubtedly experienced across his long career have, in his retelling, been smoothed over like placid ripples barely disrupting a pool. Steffanie's past battles are fuel for future victories. It's a good thing, too: her unflagging energy makes the bleakness of the predicaments of women like Rosa, punished for their addiction and their poverty, feel surmountable.

Steffanie's desire to tackle the spread of HIV in Tijuana eventually collided with the recognition that people who inject drugs in the city could not change their behavior while being systematically brutalized by law enforcement. That's because so many of their daily rituals—sharing syringes, rushing injections, shooting up in hidden picaderos—were inevitable consequences of their fear of police brutality. So Steffanie adapted her attack. When I worked on my piece of the epidemic puzzle—quantifying that police bribery stopped people from staying on methadone—I didn't know exactly what, beyond bearing witness, my work was supposed to accomplish. I would soon find out.

*

Robertito sat in a small office behind a cheap laminated desk topped with piles of paper and a large chocolate clown. It was a narrow space contained on two sides by thin windows, one of which looked out into the central training area of the Tijuana police academy, the exact spot where cadets were transformed into officers of the law. The day I visited him, the indoor grounds were empty except for a black punching bag and a plastic mannequin employed to show cadets how to disarm uncooperative parties. Robertito smiled wanly as Teresita and I approached; he was pleased that we had come to him with questions about what it was like to be a cop in Tijuana. He gestured for us to take our seats and waved away another officer who had stopped by with a question. A large circular balloon printed with the words I LOVE YOU in English hung listlessly about halfway up the wall in the far corner of his office. It looked as if it had been slipping down from the ceiling for quite some time. It was a present, he said, from his wife. They had recently celebrated an anniversary.

Robertito, now in his late forties or early fifties, worked at the police academy as an instructor. At this point in his life, he was happy to have been given a desk job far from the action. He had earned it: for over a decade starting in the early 1990s and through the mid-aughts, Robertito worked as an undercover cop in the Zona Norte, ensuring that the neighborhood's simmering tensions never bubbled over into chaos. It was easier in those days, when drug trafficking and prostitution hadn't yet been so formalized to the point that all the players knew one another. "I used to patrol in the nineties, and police officers had control," Robertito said, "but after the corruption started to increase the police lost a lot of that." From behind his desk, he hardly recognized his old stomping grounds, now turned into a war zone. "When I was working in the Zona, I never had to deal with cadavers left in the streets. That's more recent. You can find a bag with a body inside," he said. "They leave messages now."

Robertito talked about his time patrolling the Zona, stories of wearing civilian clothes and fake beards and keeping a walkie-talkie hidden under his shirt. He made it sound fun. Back then, he was mostly tasked with making sure that women selling sex stayed inside the confines of the Zona so that the trade didn't spill out into the rest of the city. It was low-level policing work, with the understanding that it was preferable for everyone that the quasi-legal system self-regulate rather than have its business subject to strict enforcement. "Those operativos were mainly to prevent petty crime downtown, not to pursue more serious crimes like drug trafficking," he said. Looking at Robertito, with his epaulets and short moustache, I had trouble picturing him blending in unobserved, especially given that women like Susi and her gang of friends would have been attuned, as a matter of survival, to every face hanging around the Zona. Robertito conceded as much. While working undercover allowed him to bust small-time operators committing robberies or stealing from tourists, the women of the Zona quickly clocked him. "In the case of sex workers, yes," Robertito said, "you detain them so many times that they recognize you completely." Instead of trying to police their behavior, Robertito started chatting with the women he met, even when he was supposed to be detaining them for transgressing the invisible geographic boundaries of the sex trade. Robertito wanted to share the story of one of those encounters with us.

"The case of this woman is that I saw her and she was really depressed," he said, as he leaned forward, his elbows on his desk. "So she told me her story: she was from Tlaxcala [a small state east of Mexico City] and she started to work in a maquiladora. And one day when she was walking downtown, she met a guy and they start dating, and—well, they were both young, and after a few weeks he proposes to her that she move in with him. And she tells me that she wants me to give her advice because her partner left her and took all the money that she made.

"Well, they had started to live as a couple and then this guy, he began to get angry with her, telling her that he feels frustrated because he cannot provide for her, and so he starts pushing her to . . ."—Robertito trailed off, as if even saying the words transgressed some moral boundary— ". . . because she tells him that she wants to help him. And well—he proposes to her to do it too," he paused again and gestured vaguely, "this and this. And she got mad at first, but then he tells her that a few of his friends have done it. Well, she accepts his offer and then, that's the moment when I understood why she didn't have any money with her. The boyfriend would pass by and pick up the money that she made during the day. He was controlling her. He took the money so she didn't have any economic freedom.

"After a few years of this arrangement, she gets pregnant. They move to his hometown so she can have her baby, and when they come back he brings one of her nieces so she can take care of their baby and the mother can go back to work. While she worked, her husband stayed home with the baby and the woman's niece, and soon he starts putting ideas into the niece's mind. That's when the process of replacing her starts. I know this because the woman showed me a letter that her niece had written to her, saying that she knew all about what the job was. When the woman tried to leave, her husband threatened to tell everyone in her family and, as you know, that is unforgivable; you can forgive anything to a woman except if she does sex work. That's just the way it is. With that psychological pressure the woman kept working, and at the end, the husband left with their daughter and all the money that she had made." The niece was nowhere to be found. The tragic arc Robertito described was familiar: a migrant woman drawn to Tijuana by the lure of steady work in a maquiladora, only to find herself diverted into the machinery of the Zona.

Like Arnulfo Bañuelos and Victor Alaniz, Robertito was also on the force and working the beat when Tijuana's municipal police department was infiltrated by narcos. "That was really the saddest period for me," Robertito said, his voice softening. "We were given benefits so we wouldn't say anything. Suddenly we received a one hundred percent increase in salary."

"Everyone?"

Robertito nodded. "I always tell this to my students: when I started as an officer you had to buy your gun, you had to fix your car, and we made very little money. That was the culture of the time. Now everything is different, and even with all the benefits that we receive people are still not happy." It was no understatement: Tijuana's municipal police are the highest paid in Mexico, but in 2017, 70 percent of Tijuanenses reported that they did not trust the force. That's no coincidence: to hear Robertito tell it, the hike in police salaries was made explicitly to keep cops compliant in the face of institutional corruption. "Something I learned is that a leader needs to keep his armed forces happy. If you keep the armed forces happy, you can ask them to stop doing something or ask them to do something else." He paused; it was apparent that Robertito was talking about Jorge Hank Rhon. "This part is really complicated and compromising because it's really sensitive." Robertito chose his words carefully before continuing. "In 2003"—the year before Hank Rhon was elected mayor of Tijuana—"a person decided to establish a type of monopoly. Back then, people would ask me, 'Who can I talk with to make cops stop bothering me?' They wanted to make a deal with a police officer, and when that deal was made, all officers respected that pact."

While Bañuelos and Analiz were hunting cops internally, Robertito was on the street, seeing the work he had been doing to keep the Zona safe undermined by the department's infiltration by criminals. "I was really surprised," he said, "because when I would detain someone I would get a call from the department and they would tell me, 'Let them go,' and I was like, 'But they are carrying all this stuff!' And they would tell me, 'I didn't ask you what they're carrying. I told you to let them go.'"

"Those orders came from above?" Teresita asked.

"Yes, from above," replied Robertito. "In 2003 to 2007, I mean—the narcos would do whatever they wanted. They would drive around like they were a part of the federal government. It was incredible, you couldn't even ticket them for parking illegally." As the collusion became normalized, Robertito's day job effectively came to an end. "What happened is that whoever was paying off the police would tell people, 'If they bother you, tell them you work for me.'" That left Robertito unable to make arrests or close cases. "It was like a monster that kept growing."

Dismayed by the changes, Robertito opted to enter the police academy to train cadets. After the counterintelligence operation of 2008, when hundreds of corrupt cops were rooted out, the department instituted a professionalized system of training to make sure the same calamity couldn't happen again. Gone were the days when just walking into the academy on referral meant you were given a badge and gun. Instead, after 2008, cadets were weeded out early with a battery of tests before formal training even began. While that was necessary to ensure that the local police department kept the cartel at bay, it had a knock-on effect on recruitment. When I spoke to Robertito it had been almost a decade since the counterintelligence operation, but the effects were still lingering. "With Hank, we had cohorts of three hundred new police officers every year because it was so easy to enroll," he explained, which was more than enough to fill the two thousand positions in the police department. "But now," he said, "we have cohorts of fifteen. And it's all because we have a lot of restrictions and many more requirements before people are allowed to enroll."

As we were talking, about thirty cadets had assembled haphazardly outside Robertito's window in the indoor training ground. Some wore sweatpants and T-shirts emblazoned with corporate logos I didn't recognize. The trainees were put through their paces by an officer who directed them to move as one through the vast space in a mob-like formation. Robertito explained that they were being trained in crowd-control techniques. The exercise was all very casual; the cadets were a mixed bunch, some concentrating deeply, squinting to follow orders, and others chasing the crowd, smirking and out of place as they tried to copy their neighbors. The formation collapsed, moved, and reconstituted itself across the corners of the training ground, some cadets never quite capable of mastering the pace. I tried to picture them out in the city, responding to a gun battle in the Zona or trying to outflank narcos taking over a picadero by force. I just couldn't do it. There was a naïveté to the group that left me feeling morose.

Here was the next generation of officers, to whom the beat cops currently patrolling the Zona would soon pass the baton. That meant that, barring some kind of cultural disruption within their ranks, the brutal policing practices I had reported on and analyzed would be handed down like gospel to these young cadets. Arresting, detaining, and sexually assaulting women near the Zona's methadone clinic would remain a standard part of the job. Shaking down drug users would continue to be part and parcel of being a cop in Tijuana. Money and drugs would be forced into the hands of officers, while the syringes that people used to inject themselves would continue to be destroyed under black leather boots.

It was that last action, the destruction of the needle, that Steffanie had identified as a key driver of the epidemic. Tijuana's police department's approach to preserving public order included destroying people's injecting equipment. It was misguided, at best. The fact is, if someone could be convinced to stop injecting drugs because of how dangerous it was, people in Tijuana would have stopped a long time ago. It just doesn't work that way. Rosa had talked about la malilla, the little pain, withdrawal symptoms from opioids that become so unbearable that all other dangers—a beating from police, the risk of getting HIV from a used syringe, a massive abscess forming after polluted canal water is used to mix drugs—fade into the background. In that context, the efforts of Tijuana's cops to literally stamp out needles had only led to more widespread sharing of equipment, and that meant that the risks of HIV infection had multiplied.

In 2013, Steffanie sought to identify the factors that made sex workers who used drugs in Tijuana more likely to have their syringes confiscated or destroyed. These were the women who shared needles in Tijuana's picaderos and then shared them again with their clients. They were, like the johns Tom was tracking, a bridge population, which is exactly what it sounds like: a group straddling two communities, which puts them in position to expand the reach of an epidemic in multiple directions. When Steffanie analyzed the data, she and her team found that half of the six hundred women they were following had had syringes destroyed by police in the past six months. They were also about two and a half times more likely to be HIV-positive. These results were shocking but predictable, because syringe sharing is an efficient transmission route for HIV. What nobody expected to find, though, was that these women were also thirteen times more likely to report being sexually abused by police officers. Here again was the femicide epidemic, trapping women with composite pathogens, edging them closer to death.

Robertito was certainly proud of the culture of police professionalism that he had helped craft after 2008. The reality was that the subset of police that patrolled the Zona maintained the belief, whether consciously or not, that women's bodies were expendable. Where most would have looked at this situation and seen structural forces too resistant to allow for change, Steffanie saw an opening.

The key was in reimagining who the victims of Tijuana's brutal policing tactics really were. As long as police saw women who sold their bodies and used drugs as subhuman, motivating individual officers to change their behavior would be a dead end. What Steffanie and her colleague Leo Beletsky—a public health lawyer (and a friend of mine) who has long studied the intersection of policing and HIV—came to understand was that there was another potential bridge population that believed that it had been ignored. From the perspective of this marginalized group, sex workers and drug injectors were the vectors, not the victims, of the epidemic. This was a population that—despite wielding guns, badges, and enormous power—saw itself as vulnerable.

Forcing people to hand over syringes for confiscation is a critical moment, like sharing a used syringe or paying for sex without a condom, that places someone at risk of HIV infection. Strange new trajectories through which a life can move present themselves in those moments, trajectories that have the power to irrevocably alter one's sense of self and with whom one belongs, all based on whether a copy of the virus successfully jumps from one bloodstream to another. If it does, in the science of epidemiology, you cease being just a policeman. You become, instead, a vector.

If the widespread stigma against HIV-infected people at the border couldn't be dismantled, Steffanie and Leo set out to at least use it to their advantage. Instead of preaching to police about the merits of harm reduction and public-health-oriented approaches to drug use, they instead exploited the police's favored tool—fear—which had so pervaded the Zona in recent years. Though sex workers and drug injectors were regularly terrorized by police, it turned out that individual officers themselves were scared of the risks they faced in the midst of these shakedowns as well. When Steffanie and Leo investigated what the police actually knew about HIV, they found a situation similar to that of the clients in Hombre Seguro: their knowledge of how infection occurred was practically nonexistent. What the police were scared of, though, was handling syringes. This was Steffanie and Leo's entry point into changing police behavior and it set the stage for Proyecto Escudo—Project Shield—a police education program that used officers' fear of infection from needlestick injuries to instill a culture shift within the Tijuana Municipal Police Department.

Proyecto Escudo was, at its root, an offer. Steffanie and Leo's team would provide the police department with occupational hazard training, which would lower the risk that officers would acquire HIV on the job. This would lead to a healthier, happier, and more effective police force.

The best part was that the training, to be provided by experts on HIV prevention, would cost the department nothing. How could they say no?

The HIV prevention strategies with which Proyecto Escudo equipped officers just happened to line up perfectly with the tenets of harm reduction that Steffanie and Leo have spent their careers seeking to advance. After all, as a police officer, the most effective way to prevent yourself from accidentally getting jabbed with an HIV-infected needle is to avoid handling the needle at all. In turn, the easiest way for an officer to avoid handling needles is to stop confiscating them. With that in mind, the Escudo training instructed officers to instead link people who injected drugs with addiction treatment clinics in Tijuana. It was an approach to the problem that, on paper at least, would make the lives of officers easier, put a dent in the city's HIV epidemic, and reduce the public disorder caused by drug injecting. If the police were looking for a less dangerous way of doing their job, Escudo offered them a solution. After railing against police brutality for years to no avail, Steffanie and Leo had managed the impossible: they'd infiltrated a police department using a kind of public health subterfuge to orchestrate a massive culture shift.

I was largely unaware of Proyecto Escudo during the first years of my time working at the border. As my direct supervisor, Steffanie wanted me to focus on the task that I had been assigned, which was establishing the scientific evidence on the link between police brutality in the Zona and access to addiction treatment. I was single-minded in that pursuit, but Steffanie saw the whole game. Unbeknownst to me, one of the pieces of leverage she brought to her early meetings with the police was my work on the systematic extortion of drug users by the police in the Zona Norte. I wasn't in the room, so I only know that she presented it to the senior officers of the department—people including Bañuelos and Alaniz—but not what was said. I imagine, though, that the evidence I gathered fed neatly into the larger argument that she and Leo had honed; namely, that the best way for the Tijuana Municipal Police Department to stop public drug use was for officers to stop antagonizing people who needed help entering into addiction treatment. Knowing Steffanie, she would have strategized that coming armed with evidence that the police were engaged in extortion could be a useful way of leveraging power in the negotiation.

Whatever means she ultimately employed, they were successful. Not only did the departmental brass allow the Proyecto Escudo training to be delivered, they made it mandatory. That meant that not only the cadets who ran half-heartedly through their paces outside of Robertito's office window but the entire force, more than two thousand officers, would be taught that taking needles from people who inject drugs was the wrong way to clean up the streets. That amounted to a huge victory against the spread of HIV in Tijuana. Crucially, Steffanie and Leo also made sure that police officers themselves would be the ones delivering the message to their peers, improving its chances of sticking. Bañuelos, who had witnessed firsthand the department's slide into corruption and reemergence from the grip of the cartels, was especially critical in making sure that police throughout the ranks bought into the program.

Robertito, like all officers, received the training. "I'm interested in what we are doing with Escudo, because the idea is to learn from things that do not work," he told Teresita and me. While the assumption in our division at UC San Diego was that the project would prevent HIV infection among people who injected drugs, Robertito believed the training had had an impact far beyond its original mandate. "For example," he said, "our security policy, the fact that we try to prevent crimes by detaining everyone who has a specific look—homeless or addicted—well, clearly it hasn't worked, and if we keep doing that nothing is going to change." Robertito went on and, using a vernacular I didn't expect, described how he now understood the Zona as a "laboratory," within which he had made systematic observations about human behavior since being enrolled in Proyecto Escudo. While I had grown comfortable with that kind of detached objectivity in scientists working in my field, it was jarring to hear a police officer use the same kind of dispassionate speech when discussing human lives. I just hoped it didn't foreshadow an even more brutal police force. As Robertito continued talking, I was relieved to hear that this way of thinking had moved him in the opposite direction. "Usually, addicts are not violent: they'll commit a crime but not a violent one. The fact is, the addict is going to find a way of getting his money to buy drugs, and obviously if someone gives him the chance to do it without committing a crime, he'll take it." For Robertito, at least, Escudo had revealed a path to navigate the obstacles of the Zona without crushing those caught underfoot.

The cadets outside Robertito's office abruptly laughed and clapped their hands as their training came to a close, their footsteps and chatter echoing sharply through the hall as they broke ranks. The sound would have ricocheted differently had the department been able to attract three hundred new bodies rather than just fifteen each year, but such was the state of Tijuana that even working for the highest-paid police force in the country wasn't incentive enough to counter the threat of cartel violence. "We are afraid," Robertito admitted, "but we need to come to terms with that reality, right? I mean, we're police officers. If you want a comfortable job you should look somewhere else. This one requires a lot of responsibility and a lot of sacrifices."

Robertito would soon be standing in front of a classroom teaching the cadets about the city—his laboratory—outside the academy's walls and how each of them might protect themselves from its dangers once they were thrown into its fray. I hoped, as we all did, that his teaching would be enough to overwhelm their temptation to participate in the cycle of graft, to surrender to their baser instincts, and to roam the city after hours, their faces concealed by hoods. Tijuana needed a way to inoculate itself from powerful men spreading fear. It needed a way to bury those components of the pathological process—police brutality, cartel violence, and tweaked-out johns—instead of letting them rise to the surface to spread. At the very least, Escudo was turning officers, who represented just one component of the femicide epidemic, into antibodies. It remained to be seen whether the vaccine was effective.

CHAPTER 11

The Bottom Line

Epidemiology is like augury. Both create blueprints of the world using complex systems of knowledge grounded in arcane wisdoms. Both are attuned to connections between seemingly distal moments in space and time, a capacity that imbues the epidemiologist and the augur alike with the power of prediction. Like augury, epidemiology requires a ritual binding together of different elements for reasons that others cannot foresee. The presence of these phenomena must first be intuited and only then, through the strange alchemy of model building, can their power to portend events be realized. Variables, the raw materials of the science, are simply omens by another name.

I started working in Tijuana five years after the U.S. Navy forbade tens of thousands of its personnel stationed in San Diego from consorting with the women of the Zona Norte. This was almost a decade after Tom and Steffanie had first set up shop in the city. I came to Tijuana after post-9/11 fear had caused an environmental shift, unleashing a pathological process on the women of the Zona. In its wake, police corruption and assault, cartel murder, and the violence of ruthless johns—all pathogens that had long lingered in the Zona—had become more shameless and virulent, overrunning the neighborhood to such an extent that femicide had become a normalized phenomenon. I arrived as this epidemic was cresting and I bore witness as it risked transmuting into the epidemiologist's ultimate defeat: an endemic condition.

This is how it might end. The slow but creeping expansion of HIV among the Zona's sex workers, those who injected drugs in particular, would continue to result in their deaths. The casual extortion and sexual violence perpetrated by the police and the narcos would grind women down and make it impossible for them to change their circumstances. The dearth of clients visiting the Zona would cause women to continually take greater risks on bad dates. These were the primary aspects of the pathological process, agents of destruction that, at a population level, forced women down the same narrow paths toward death, but there were secondary elements too. Women hit by cars while running for their lives. Unexplained disappearances. Blood infections. Overdoses. And despite all of this pain, the supply of women—migrant women—was continually being replenished by the promise of steady employment in Tijuana's maquiladoras despite the industry's bait and switch, in which women are hired as workers on a subcontract until they are no longer healthy, at which point they are discarded. This is how an epidemic expands; not just because of one mechanism but through a confluence of factors that synchronize to propagate illness and death. It's the reason epidemiologic models account for multiple omens: there are always, no matter how hard one tries, hidden elements shaping the epidemic's course; and they are always changing.

One factor that I had heard little about in Tijuana until four years into my research was fentanyl, that hyperpotent opioid that has been saturating street drug markets in the United States and Canada since about 2005. On August 25, 2017, the Mexican military reported a bust of a major shipment of fentanyl—thirty thousand pills worth tens of millions of dollars—destined first for Tijuana, then the United States. Around the same time, Tijuanenses who relied on the street drug market were starting to complain about strange purple opioids being sold by new suppliers at the city's conectas. From what I had seen elsewhere across North America, it was only a matter of time before Tijuana would see fentanyl arrive in earnest, a spike in the already high rate of overdose death inevitably following, a new pathogenic component to be added to the mixing vessel.

I had witnessed the flowering of Tom and Steffanie's efforts to prevent HIV in Tijuana, with its advances, retreats, and lateral moves. I had seen Steffanie's canny decision to move from criticizing the police in published research to cajoling the chief of the Tijuana Municipal Police Department face-to-face to end the cycle of brutality. I had learned from johns enrolled in Tom's study about the mournful kind of love that can exist between two people brought together by desperation, money, drugs, and desire. And I had learned from Susi, Rosa, and Ana about the limits of change in a city controlled by criminal actors and beset by violence.

For all the looking back I had done to determine when the epidemic of femicide began, there was one aspect that I had yet to investigate. Tom and Steffanie had shared the story of their failed first hire, the dojo-owning medical doctor, who embodied the multiple identities typical of residents of a city that exists in a kind of schizophrenic state of bination-ality, stretched and torn between two countries. But beyond that, I knew little about how they had managed to negotiate this city as outsiders at a time when its corruption and violence imbued every interaction with a double meaning. I had learned so much about how pathogens emerged to propel the epidemic. And yet, I knew nothing about how the protec-tive factors keeping women alive had been nurtured. Before Proyecto El Cuete, before Hombre Seguro, before Proyecto Escudo, how had Tom and Steffanie avoided being outwitted by the hidden powers operating in this chaotic city?

*

With his expertise in behavioral psychology, Tom's endgame had always been to design an intervention that could directly empower women who sold sex—especially those who also injected drugs—to safely navigate the daily perils of the Zona. Condomless sex, needle sharing, and sexual violence loomed steadily over the neighborhood; these were the traps that women had to avoid if they were to remain HIV-negative and alive. Tom's plan was to develop a behavioral training program that made sense to the women facing these threats. So, in 2004, Tom's nascent research team started doing field outreach in the Zona, soliciting the neighborhood's working women—the paraditas and ficheras—to join what he was calling Mujer Segura (Strong Women). Unlike with the concerns Tom would later have when recruiting johns for Hombre Seguro, he was confident from the start that the women of the Zona would want to participate in this study. Mujer Segura was launched in the same year that the PrEP trials in Cameroon and Cambodia were halted as a result of ethical lapses, and if Tom's approach had mirrored that of the trialists in those cases, perhaps things would have ended differently. But Tom made sure that Mujer Segura participants were provided with HIV testing and person-alized clinical care, in addition to an honorarium. Unlike the PrEP trials, the women in Mujer Segura were also asked to actively participate in crafting an intervention that could prevent their risk of HIV. Tom's openness to learning from the women themselves went a long way in fostering their willingness to engage.

The Zona advertises its permissiveness garishly, the paraditas' bloodred miniskirts stark against the neon purple and white of the sign outside Adelita's. The faux gold highlights of the entrance to the Hong Kong Gentleman's Club share the spotlight with the sun piercing the muted green of the palm trees that line Calle Coahuila. Off the main drag, side streets like Calle Primera are a clash of dusty pinks, maroons, and yellows, with low-hung brothels jammed tightly against discount pharmacies and abandoned shopping centers. People mill around slowly in the heat or take temporary refuge in the shade. Women stand listlessly outside of curtained bars, from behind which the muffled sound of *cumbia norteña*, with its sparc accordion and heaving beat, can sometimes be heard bouncing against empty walls. You get the sense that everyone is waiting—for the sun to set, for their shift to start, for a favorite girl to step into her regular spot.

The neighborhood is a collage of architecture and people, both of which look as if they've been roughly thrown together. So you can forgive Tom for assuming that there was no central gatekeeper standing guard over the daily transactions of sex, drugs, and money as his team fanned out across the streets and alleyways to recruit women. Of course, there were sentries everywhere, thousands of eyes reporting to those with power about what was happening on the street below. And when the Tijuana Association of Bars and Cantinas, which regulates business in the Zona Norte, discovered that Tom was making unauthorized incursions into their territory to ask about HIV among the neighborhood's working-women, they became displeased.

It is difficult to know where to place the bar owners' association among the factors influencing the femicide epidemic. On the one hand, despite its recent swoon, the red-light district is still one of the major economic engines of the city, though it is dwarfed by Tijuana's continuing agglomeration of maquiladoras. On the other, the cozy relationship between the sex clubs, narcos, and police in the Zona Norte obscures the line between legitimate business and illegal activity. The brothels and strip clubs, while formally sanctioned, are still predicated on a simple business model: the exploitation of women's bodies. The official "zone of tolerance" that encompasses the Zona, though, has led to at least a few modest improvements in the lives of the neighborhood's sex workers. The most obvious was a bespoke public health system for sex workers—instituted in 2005 during the mayoralty of Jorge Hank Rhon—that provided registration cards to women who undertook monthly physicals and quarterly HIV tests. Those that didn't abide by the rules or who received a positive HIV test were, under the system, barred from carrying a registration card and forced to pay a fine. This being Tijuana, there was a catch. While the system was designed to improve the reputation of the city's women, the women themselves were made to pay the fee for the medical visits. While about eight thousand women initially signed up to receive registration cards when the law was passed, few returned for follow-up physicals. At around three hundred U.S. dollars per year, it was just too expensive for most.

For all of its faults, the registration system did make plain one important truth. While most Tijuanenses studiously avoided admitting it, Tijuana's sex trade brought value to the city in the form of millions of tourist dollars per year. The health cards were an initial feint at regulating the trade, along with the use of commercial police to provide protection to the Zona's clubs. According to Victor Alaniz, those officers hired by the brothels were only there to provide security, not to act as the hired muscle for criminal organizations. But in a quasi-legal zone of tolerance, what exactly constitutes criminal behavior? Cartels operated openly across the Zona to the point that old-school police work like the kind Robertito engaged in was largely useless. The narcos were both investors in the sex trade and suppliers of the drug market that arose alongside it. The two often went hand in hand, at least according to Rosa, Ana, and even Salvador, all of whom described drug use among clients as a part of the job for women. Though the exact nature of the relationship between the cartels and the sex clubs remains unclear—owners? Partners? Clients? De facto licensors?—it's evident that the clubs, the cartels, and the police all benefit economically from the arrangement. Susi and Ana, who both spent decades in the Zona, had told me repeatedly that the brothels and the cartels were effectively one and the same.

As soon as the bar owners' association found out about his research, Tom's field recruitment ground to a halt. Shortly after that, Tom received an invitation to meet with the members of the association in person. While the scope of the drug war violence that would soon be unleashed on the city was unfathomable when the invitation came in 2005, Tom nevertheless had no illusions about the stakes of crossing dangerous men in Mexico. So it was only after some hesitation that he agreed to take the association up on its offer and meet in a place of their choosing.

As he crossed the border by car and pulled up to the meeting venue, he was greeted by an unexpected scene. The informal gloss of the Zona, its casual disorder, had completely evaporated in the area outside of the appointed venue. "We went to the place where the meeting was," he explained. "It was a pretty large restaurant. On the outside of the restaurant there were Mexican police patrolling. The restaurant itself had been completely cleared out—there was nobody there, and they made a little square of tables in the middle." The cops would have been commercial police, straddling the line in Tijuana's zone of tolerance.

"Inside the restaurant," Tom continued, "there were the bar owners sitting around the table with me and the two people accompanying me." They weren't alone, though. While he had been made to walk through a security perimeter of police officers outside, it turned out that the cops were only the first line of defense. "Around us were a whole group of gentlemen in trench coats and whatnot that had Uzis and other guns under their jackets . . . and not so under their jackets." Tom, stepping through tighter and tighter concentric circles of enforcement, finally found his way into the heart of power in the Zona, a scientist surrounded by men with submachine guns.

Tom was there to talk about a virus, and this would not have been the first time that the bar owners would have had it brought to their attention. After all, the U.S. Navy had conducted its own research into the spread of HIV in Tijuana and had even launched a mini-Marshall Plan that included shipping eight hundred thousand condoms per month into the Zona back in 1988. But that was over a decade earlier, and the navy's own research, which was carried out by Mexican collaborators, had found zero cases of HIV among the Zona's sex workers. Having struggled for that long to maintain Tijuana's reputation as a safe place to buy sex, the members of the bar owners' association would have been keenly aware of the damage any blemishes to that record could exact. Tom's incursion was surely unwelcome, given the potential his work had to disrupt the well-oiled machine that the Association had so studiously maintained. Even the suggestion that an HIV prevention program was being implemented—though it might reduce the risk that women in the Zona were infected—was bad for business, because it implied that there might be something for clients to worry about in the first place.

Tom knew all this, but he still gamely tried to make his case, a towering foreigner standing under the gaze of hardened entrepreneurs, trying to use science to salvage a chance at protecting the lives of the women who sold their bodies on the streets outside. "Well, I gave my usual sort of geeky academic presentation of what the study was about," Tom said, unsure of how to relay his prediction that an HIV epidemic was about to explode across the Zona. "And they all sat there and nodded their heads very nicely." Then, he remembered, there was a pause; they sat in silence for a moment. "And then the head of the bar owners' association turned to me and said, 'But Dr. Tom, why would we want to be involved in this study? What is in it for us?'"

From his early days chasing white-crowned sparrows through the forests of the Bay Area and observing primate interactions behind glass, Tom has had to justify his study of behavior to a wide cross section of interested parties. His entire career—indeed, the heart of his work—has revolved around gaining a better understanding of people's motivations so that he can help them reduce the risks they face. Perhaps it was this capacity—call it strategic empathy—that helped him do away with his own interests in that moment so that he could fully understand the rules of the game he was playing. "I guess I was quick enough to realize these are businessmen," he said. "And I thought, 'This is a business, and their commodity is women. Women they are selling. Sex workers.' So I said, 'The reason why you'd want to involve me is because I'm going to teach your women how to stay healthy, and because of that you're going to make more money.'" The owners sitting across the table, a few men and one woman, considered his response for a moment. Then, Tom recalled, he heard the magic words. "'Fantastic. You can work here in Tijuana.'"

With the blessing of the Tijuana Association of Bars and Cantinas, Tom was able to quickly harness the unique perspective of sex workers to stop the spread of HIV in the Zona. Perhaps the owners had already recognized that it was only a matter of time before the rising prevalence of the disease among the women of the neighborhood would become too high to conceal. Or perhaps it was Tom's initial intrusion that had forced the association to reckon with a problem they would have preferred to avoid. In any case, a few months after Tom's meeting, the sex worker registration system was put in place. Regardless of the system's flaws, which limited its capacity to actually curb women's risk of acquiring HIV, the powers in the Zona had evidently decided that it was more strategic to acknowledge the epidemic than to ignore it.

That initial meeting in the cleared-out restaurant, which Tom described as burned into his memory, set the stage for HIV prevention work that would continue in the Zona over the next decade and beyond. Mujer Segura, the study that Tom was asked to defend, spawned Hombre Seguro. With rich data from these two populations at the epicenter of the epidemic, Tom then launched Mujer Mas Segura (in English, Safer Women), an intervention centered on helping women hone strategies to better negotiate condom use and avoid sharing needles with clients. As part of the intervention, sex workers put together a video called *Contamination*, in which they presented risky scenarios they commonly encountered while working and then shared tactics to avoid HIV infection during those perilous moments. The program also gave women the opportunity to come together to discuss their jobs, engage in role-playing, and educate their peers on how to access clean needles and condoms.

Tom undertook a randomized controlled trial of Mujer Mas Segura, carried out concurrently among sex workers in the Zona Norte and in Ciudad Juárez, between 2008 and 2010. The study randomized women in both cities to receive either a standard sexual and injection-related risk reduction training or an interactive training that had been designed with participant input (to ensure its ethical responsibility to its participants, Tom did not include a control group wherein participants were denied access to any risk reduction intervention). Amazingly, after two years, about 50 percent fewer women in the Tijuana group who received the interactive intervention became infected with HIV and other STIs compared with women in the control arm who received the standard risk reduction training. Tom and his team also saw the proportion of needle sharing among women drop from absolutely everyone—100 percent of participants at baseline—to about 5 percent at the close of the study. These kinds of results are practically unheard of with behavioral interventions, especially those carried out in the midst of a drug war.

Since the publication of the project's findings, Mujer Mas Segura has been expanded to twelve cities across Mexico, mostly in the northern border region, where HIV among women is still rampant. Whatever fears were on his mind as he walked through the cordon of commercial police and the ring of armed mercenaries that day, Tom's instinct to dismiss moralizing and focus like a laser on what had to be done paid off in the ultimate scientific currency: human lives saved.

*

Tom and Steffanie's research galvanized the citizens of the Zona to wrestle back some control over their bodies from the powerful forces that put them at risk. Salvador credited his own change in behavior to the combination of greater access to condoms and the knowledge about disease risks he gained from enrolling in Hombre Seguro. Ana also pointed to easier access to condoms and HIV testing—both made available through the El Cuete study and from local health authorities—as critical to women like herself who relied on selling their bodies for survival. "I feel that it has helped because I know I'm healthy," she told me. Prior to joining the study, the only other time she had been tested was when her son was born, almost ten years earlier, despite having worked in the sex trade since the age of fourteen.

The first time I met Rosa in that small interview room in the El Cuete field offices, she had rattled off the many ways that staff members had gone out of their way to help her. "Once, they diagnosed me with human papillomavirus and every day they called me," she said. "I got surgery, and they paid the two thousand dollars that I needed." Aside from being eligible for Steffanie's flagship study on account of her drug injecting, Rosa had, by dint of selling sex, also been invited into Tom's research. "The project, Mujer Segura," Rosa said emphatically, "supported me in everything." At the time she had described in clipped terms the changes in her behavior that had resulted from the project. "They always have free condoms, every time we need them, do you get me? I used to share needles; I even used to sell the needles, the used ones, to drug users that had *la malilla*. In the crappy hotel where I live, people have TB, hepatitis. I mean, you can tell when a person is sick, so imagine using the same needles? Oh, no, not anymore. I have learned so many things. I go to all these talks and I don't do all the shit that I used to do."

*

Alejandro Lares Valladares sat on a steel chair with his elbows on his knees, listening intently as a man named Darwin described in exquisite detail the ways in which injecting drugs improperly can end up killing you. Wearing a white button-down shirt and semitransparent braces on his teeth, Alejandro—who in perfectly accented American English insisted on being called Alex—had the air of a man not quite grown up but happy to enjoy the ride until he got there. Seated next to him was Dr. Nora Volkow, a Mexican-born American psychiatrist and the director of the U.S. National Institute on Drug Abuse. That job title gave her immense power in setting the direction of future scientific research on drug addiction in the United States, if not the world. It was 2015, and both had come to Vancouver for a biannual meeting of the International AIDS Society, a gathering that attracted tens of thousands of delegates from across the globe.

HIV infection from sharing used syringes, overdose from superpotent opioids, abscesses and blood poisoning from mixing heroin with dirty puddle water—all of these, Darwin explained, could be avoided if instead of injecting drugs on the street, people visited a medically supervised injection facility. Darwin pointed to his left and the small crowd looked over at a long steel counter set against a mirrored wall divided into twelve cubicles. Thin cardboard bowls filled with sealed alcohol swabs, blister packs of clean water, sterile syringes, and thin rubber arm ties were placed at the center of each brightly lit cubicle. These innocuous-looking supplies represented the central pillar of Vancouver's HIV prevention strategy. This was Insite, a medical facility that had been subject to a scientific evaluation that had generated over forty peer-reviewed scientific studies, one Canadian Supreme Court victory, and a decade of advocacy on the part of the thousands of people who inject drugs in Vancouver's Downtown Eastside neighborhood, also known as North America's largest open-air street drug market. The purpose of supervised injection sites is simple: get people who inject drugs on the street to do so indoors, under medical supervision, so that they don't acquire HIV and don't die of an overdose. In that, they have proven to be spectacularly successful. While overdose deaths have reached epidemic proportions across North America, not a single person has died after overdosing in any of the approximately 120 sites that exist in Canada and around the world.

It was Steffanie's research as a doctoral student in Vancouver that had first brought the HIV epidemic in the Downtown Eastside into the public's consciousness. Her paper, "Needle Exchange is Not Enough," was the first to report that almost 25 percent of people who injected drugs in the neighborhood were HIV-positive, and that among this population, the virus was spreading fast. At the time, she and her team recorded an HIV incidence rate of 19 per 100 person-years, meaning that for every one hundred drug injectors followed over the period of a year, nineteen were becoming HIV-positive, which was comparable to the expansion of HIV in sub-Saharan Africa.

Two decades after she first published those findings, her first major work in HIV research, Steffanie had returned to the Downtown Eastside, this time with Alex and Dr. Volkow in tow. The initial meetings with the police for Proyecto Escudo had gone well, leading to a memorandum of understanding between UC San Diego and the Tijuana Municipal Police Department, as well as the recruitment of officers like Robertito as trainers. After Alex was hired in December 2013 as the new chief of police, Steffanie had spied in him a potential ally and had worked assiduously to cultivate their relationship. Though their meetings were ostensibly about Escudo, it wasn't long before she was able to steer the conversation toward the potential benefits that harm reduction programs like supervised injection facilities could bring to Tijuana. Alex's trip to Vancouver—for which he was accompanied by Arnulfo Bañuelos and other senior officers from the department—was a final exclamation point on this argument. Steffanie had been planning for it a long time.

Alex had never been to Vancouver and would likely never have come had it not been for Steffanie. If Insite was the beating heart of Vancouver's response to its local HIV epidemic, Alex was the central node in Steffanie's plan to eradicate HIV among Tijuanensis injectors. As Tijuana's chief of police (officially, secretary of public security), Alex had the power to decide how much rope Steffanie would be given to alter the city's security apparatus. That made his support critical in determining how deeply Proyecto Escudo would actually penetrate the force. While you got the sense that Tom preferred to do any necessary dealmaking behind closed doors, Steffanie had a flair for the dramatic. I believe that it was the experience of choosing a career in HIV prevention after seeing both her best friend and her supervisor die of AIDS that opened her eyes to the power that bearing witness could have on influencing decision-making. Steffanie's strategizing had brought a harm reduction initiative to the doors of the Tijuana police department, with Proyecto Escudo prepared to infiltrate the Tijuana police force like a fifth column posing as an occupational safety training module. Bringing Alex to see firsthand how a commitment to harm reduction had curbed HIV transmission in Vancouver was a surefire way of sealing the deal.

I watched Alex as he looked around the facility. He was visibly impressed by the bright and clinical feel that the space exuded, particularly before it opened its doors in the morning and was still empty of clients. He asked pointed but not unfriendly questions about the site's capacity to reduce public disorder and listened politely as Darwin told him about the steady reduction in new HIV cases year after year among Vancouver's drug-injecting population. Standing in Insite, in the midst of the Downtown Eastside, meant being at the epicenter of a success story that Steffanie, Leo Beletsky, and the rest of the Escudo team hoped to replicate in Tijuana. While the hurdles were massive, it was worth a shot.

After the Insite tour ended, our little group wandered west through the Downtown Eastside toward the city's convention center, where the International AIDS Society conference was being held. It was a typically mild and sunny morning, the kind that always made me nostalgic for my childhood in Vancouver, the mountains across the bay a dark and verdant green against the light blue sky. I chatted with Alex and caught up with Bañuelos, who I hadn't seen in many months. While Bañuelos presented as the prototypical Tijuana police officer, a bit stiff and wary, Alex was looser, more like a glad-handing politician than a stern officer of the law. He looked remarkably relaxed despite being the person in charge of keeping the peace in Tijuana, and under whose watch, which began in December 2013, the official number of women murdered annually had almost doubled, from forty-four to seventy-four. As we walked, we struck up an easy conversation about the issues Tijuana was facing. I did my best to sell him on the potential role of supervised injection facilities as uniquely capable of addressing a number of Tijuana's issues simultaneously. Public injecting in the canal, the HIV epidemic straddling the border wall, the worrying increases in violence at picaderos: all of these, I argued, could be kept in check if Tijuana committed to a public health approach to drugs. Alex nodded along as he took in the bewildering scene around us, and I realized how right Steffanie had been to bring him and his officers here, to what had become North America's de facto harm reduction capital. We passed crowds of men and women begging for money and selling second- or third-hand products from dirty blankets on the sidewalk, and I was worried that the apparent disorder of the neighborhood would make him recoil. Alex surprised me, though, his demeanor never wavering, the words flowing easily between us.

At one point, when again I was waxing lyrically about the benefits of supervised injection, Alex interrupted softly. "You know," he said, "for me, this is a way to satisfy both the needs of Tijuana's business—" and here he made air quotes with his fingers, "and 'business' communities." I abruptly shut my mouth and nodded dumbly. The fight to get a supervised injection facility up and running in Vancouver had been pretty straightforward. On the one side was the Canadian federal government, which was opposed, and on the other were the advocates, among whom I counted myself. Sure, there were secondary players like the business improvement association in and around the Downtown Eastside that didn't like the idea of having people injecting at a medical clinic situated nearby their storefronts, but the battle lines were clearly drawn between a "yes" camp and a "no" camp. Alex's riff about business and "business" revealed a set of concerns unique to Tijuana that I hadn't even considered. Even after all the time I had spent there, tracking epidemics and learning about how power functioned at the border, I was still thinking like an outsider. In Tijuana, which desperately needed the sustained fight against HIV that Vancouver had waged and largely won, a supervised injection facility would be a much more contentious undertaking. Unlike Vancouver, the powers that would eventually sanction or forbid such a facility's opening would be hidden from public view. That process would surely require some version of Tom's submergence through concentric circles of security and power to beg for safe passage.

Alex was more than Tijuana's police chief. He was a fulcrum connecting the various layers of influence in the city. So much of the violence that arose at the border since 2008 was the product of cartels fighting it out for control of drug-selling spots across the Zona and in colonias across Tijuana. These were the same actors who killed police with impunity to amplify a message of fear. It was understandable that Alex and his comrades at the police department would feel some trepidation at the prospect of challenging the sources of drug-selling profits in the city. On the other hand, Alex had been tasked by Tijuana's mayor to get rid of the thousands of deportees who had congregated in rough encampments in the canal, many of whom eventually began injecting drugs there. He had followed those orders vigorously, a fact that he was keen to share with me as we strolled down Cambie Street and past Victory Square, a small urban park with a thirty-foot cenotaph that acts as the informal edge of the Downtown Eastside.

"You see," Alex said as we walked by, "our operations in the canal have cleared it of addicts, and public order is improving; maybe a site could help with that too." He was becoming exuberant; I was horrified. "They're all gone," he continued, "off the streets, and put in treatment." I had spent many years of my life trying to find ways to talk to police about harm reduction and to explain why classic policing tactics like rounding up drug users and smashing needles did nothing to stop people from injecting but only elevated the risks of doing so. The idea that someone could support both views simultaneously made me feel slightly crazy, and yet here was Alex doing exactly that. I tried to explain to him why one of those approaches—harm reduction—would lead to the kinds of outcomes he wanted, while the other—mass arrests and the targeting of drug users—would not, but he didn't appear convinced (though he was, in classic Tijuanensis fashion, too polite to disagree outright). Instead, he seemed genuinely puzzled as to why a combination of the sweeping raids that the police force had been undertaking coupled with a safe and supervised place for people to inject couldn't work. I tried to explain that harm reduction was based on trust between drug users and the authorities, and that operativos like those undertaken in the canal destroyed that trust, thereby making it very unlikely that people who injected drugs would ever willingly engage with services provided by the government. I described research I had done showing that drug law enforcement usually ended up increasing drug market violence rather than decreasing it. I told him about evidence showing that compulsory addiction treatment was basically ineffective and that in Tijuana, many supposed "clinics" were no better than labor camps, where staff forced their clients out into the streets to beg for change and then took their money when they returned. As he had throughout the day, Alex listened intently and asked considered questions that surprised me in their thoughtfulness. Perhaps it was wishful thinking, but by the end of our hour-long stroll, I got the sense that I had changed his mind. It was exciting, to say the least, that Steffanie had given me the chance to walk through the streets of my home city with a man who had the power to make things right in Tijuana.

By the end of the day, emails were circulating with photos of a smiling Alex, Tijuana's top cop, in a black T-shirt with the words INSITE SAVES LIVES emblazoned across its front. Steffanie's gambit was a success: Alex was all-in on supervised injection facilities. Regardless of how he thought they fit into the fabric of the city, the fact that he was convinced of their utility was enough. Their deployment within the police's larger drug control strategy was a problem for another day. I thought back to my first visit to the canal with Susi and Patty, when I had spied the lone woman, surrounded by a group of rough-looking men, moving furtively in and out of the vents of the canal's walls. I thought of Angie, Susi's friend, killed while being pursued by police. La Osa, who died of AIDS. La Lobita, killed by her narco boyfriend in a drug deal gone wrong. I thought of Rosa, keenly aware of the violence that crystal-meth-using clients were capable of, and the heroin addiction that caused her to seek them out. Women standing perilously at the edge of a femicide and being nudged over the line by a pathological process run amok. These were the kinds of women that a supervised consumption facility could protect. With Alex's support, there was reason to be hopeful that the deadly cycle might end.

I spent the rest of the day downtown, wandering in and out of conference presentations and catching up with old friends and colleagues. It was good to return home, if at least to be reminded that cities can change. The Downtown Eastside didn't become Vancouver's largest open-air injecting scene overnight. It was the product of decades of neglect, stretching back to the 1950s. Back then, the neighborhood had been the political, commercial, and cultural heart of the city. Forty years later, in the mid-1990s, that version of the Downtown Eastside had been largely gutted and its residents were succumbing by the hundreds to HIV. And yet, when the alarm was first sounded, and then when it was rung louder and louder by a growing chorus of people who used drugs, front-line agencies, and scientists, until at last the city took notice of the thousands getting sick and dying from HIV in its midst, an environmental shift took place that eventually put the epidemic in retreat. In 1996, the year before Steffanie first published her study of HIV spread in the Downtown Eastside, there were almost four hundred new HIV cases attributable to drug injecting across the province of British Columbia. By 2016, there were only sixteen. Intractable problems of poverty and inequity still exist in the neighborhood (most notably a growing epidemic of opioid overdose deaths that began in 2010 and has claimed hundreds of lives since). But people—thousands of them—were saved from HIV/AIDS by a combination of harm reduction, addiction treatment, HIV medication, and social assistance. That is a victory worth celebrating. If it can happen here, in Canada's poorest postal code, then it could happen in Tijuana as well, the forgotten city staring mournfully over the border wall.

The pieces were all there. A long-standing research infrastructure that quantified the scope of the epidemic as well as the extent of the pain that people were in. A local law enforcement agency that welcomed collaboration and appeared willing to support controversial approaches. A set of hidden power players who had no interest in wiping out the sex or drug trades (which they controlled, after all) but had shown themselves amenable to imposing some kind of order on the vice economies, as long as it allowed them to maintain profit. And perhaps the most important piece of all, which was also the one most ubiquitously felt across the city: despair. Tijuana had hit rock-bottom, violence flaring to the level of civil war in the streets of the Zona, the influx of American tourists trickling through the border wall dwindling a little more every day, and women yielding to riskier demands with the fatalism of those caught in a dying marketplace. In this bleak environment, where the status quo had so spectacularly failed, the risk of trying something new was basically zero. Perhaps that plague-spewing dragon could finally be collared and the epidemic forced to retreat.

Alex was no Saint George, but epidemics aren't really dragons either. In the legends we tell about them, dragons are always slain; epidemics will rage on endlessly if left unchecked. With Alex's help, though, it seemed finally possible that, like in Vancouver's Downtown Eastside, the environment in Tijuana could at last be shifted in a favorable direction, the pathological process made less virulent, and the hosts given the ability to shake off their fear of death. For a moment, finally, the omens appeared to point toward a brighter future.

*

Shortly after Alex's visit to Vancouver, a military convoy swept through the canal, pursuing men and women who ran blindly over its walls and into the traffic of the Vía Rápida, repeating Angie's fatal flight. "It's no-man's-land," he can be heard saying in an interview with San Diego's KPBS Radio when asked to justify the renewed brutality. "We are going to take possession of the entire river." In the photos that accompanied the coverage of the new operativo, Alex was back to his smart-looking police uniform, peaked cap and all, his braces nowhere to be seen.

CHAPTER 12
Endless Variation

The Pantéon Puerta Blanca is located a few hundred feet northwest of Calle Coahuila in a quieter section of the Zona Norte, the constant thrumming of the red-light district fading as one approaches its gates. It's a small and modest cemetery about the size of a city block, surrounded on all sides by a short unpainted concrete wall topped with a wire-mesh fence. A white cross adorns a brick archway at the main entrance, next to which an old woman sells votive candles and plastic flowers. Inside, the graves are set neatly along wide stone paths lined by large crosses that stand in the shadows of cedars, the tall trees providing some relief from the heat. Wind your way through the cemetery's paths for long enough and you will find yourself at a curious structure, a small redbrick mausoleum with crude and oversize toy soldiers stuck onto its flat roof. The cramped space below is adorned with candles, flowers, photos of young men and women, and copies of successful green card applications, all of it piled so high that there is hardly any room to move. This is the final resting place of Juan Soldado—Juan the Soldier—Tijuana's unofficial patron saint.

Juan Soldado, whose real name is Juan Castillo Morales, was a Mexican army private born in 1918 in the state of Oaxaca, in the mountainous southwest of the country. In 1938, he was stationed in Tijuana, where he would die. It went like this: on the evening of February 13, 1938, Olga Camacho Martínez, eight years old, disappeared. Her body was found a day later, bloodied and half-buried in an abandoned building, with signs of rape. That same night, Morales returned home to his wife, his hands apparently covered in blood. His wife alerted the police, and the future Juan Soldado was immediately arrested for murder. On February 17, 1938, he was executed in the Pantéon Puerta Blanca in the spot where his shrine now stands.

This linear narrative, though, conceals a murkier story. Morales was innocent, many claim, the proof being that even after the execution, young girls continued to be brutalized across the city. It was only when Morales's commanding officer was stationed elsewhere that the outbreak of femicide stopped. Rumor has it that this officer had framed Morales, and that Juan Soldado was as much a victim of his superior's menace as the young dead girls. Whatever the case may be, the hand of justice acted swiftly against him. In the days between the discovery of young Olga Camacho Martínez's body and Morales's execution, a mob formed outside the police station where the future Juan Soldado was being held, demanding that he be released for a public lynching. Calls for calm fell on deaf ears, and the mob, seized by an unquenchable bloodlust, began to riot. For seventy-two hours, Tijuana, then a town of only twenty thousand citizens, was engulfed in looting, violence, and flames. Both the city's police station and the city hall were burned, and the rioters sabotaged the local fire brigade's hoses, leaving the authorities helpless to stop the growing inferno. Despite the rising threat of Nazism at the time, the rape and murder of Martínez and the ensuing chaos in this modest desert town made front-page news across North America.

In a desperate effort to quell the violence, Tijuana's police force fired into the crowds, killing several people, an act that only inflamed tensions. At a loss to end the chaos, President Lázaro Cárdenas eventually gave in to the crowd's demands and ordered Morales to be executed immediately. This is the same Cárdenas, incidentally, who had made gambling illegal in Mexico in 1935, plunging Tijuana into an economic depression unrivaled in its history until the post-9/11 era. After setting the economic conditions for mass violence in Tijuana by denying the city its economic lifeblood, Cárdenas then ordered the one thing he thought would end it: more violence.

And so, Juan Castillo Morales was led, his hands bound, from the police station to the Pantéon Puerta Blanca to meet his final punishment. It was decreed that he would be executed by *ley de fuga*, the law of escape, in which guilty men turn their backs on a firing squad and run for their lives as the bullets chase them down. Morales's hands and feet were untied and he was told to face north, as the firing squad prepared itself. From his perspective, the border must have appeared tantalizingly close, only about a thousand feet away. The order was given, and Morales ran as fast as he could, hurtling his body toward the boundary; perhaps he thought that he might yet elude this morbid injustice and the bloodlust of the town that had risen up to destroy him. Under the heat of the desert sun, Morales glimpsed a sanctuary—America—and pushed his body to cross the threshold, beyond which he would be safe. Of course, it was an illusion. Ley de fuga is a pantomime designed to raise false hopes in order to make the punishment that much more severe. Morales fell to the ground, shot in the back, mere steps from the United States. And with that, Tijuana returned to some kind of calm.

It was this final sprint, forced upon him by the Mexican state, that transformed Morales, the alleged child rapist and murderer, into Juan Soldado, saintly protector of migrants. At his mausoleum at the Panteón Puerta Blanca, prayers are inscribed on stone plaques and ex-voto cards from grateful migrants and their families. "GRACIAS JUAN SOLDADO POR FAVORES RECIVIDOS LALO Y VICKI CASTILLO Y FAMILIA (Thank you Juan Soldado for receiving Lalo and Vicky Castillo and their family), reads one; GRACIAS JUAN SOLDADO POR LOS MILAGROS CONCEDIDOS BETO Y ANA (Thank you Juan Soldado for the miracles granted to Beto and Ana), reads another. A third reads JUAN SOLDADO GRACIAS POR DEVOLVERME LA VISTA Y LA SALUD (Juan Soldado thank you for giving me back my sight and health). The notes cover the entirety of the walls inside the mausoleum and those outside too, prayers from people desperate to cross safely into the United States, for whom Juan Soldado is known as the "lawyer of the impossible," a spirit whose own failure to cross the border, which ended his life, has made him the ideal protector of those who would follow in his footsteps.

*

When I began my research in Tijuana in 2013, the city was a cacophony to me. Between analyzing data from the El Cuete study, interviewing the women of the Zona, and looking back through Tijuana's history to reconstruct a baseline for the epidemic of femicide, there was little room to absorb how the city might be shifting under my feet. And yet, during my time at the border, new omens revealed themselves, presaging new turns in the epidemic.

In May 2016, I came across a study reporting on an outbreak of HIV infection in Chicago. The authors had analyzed differences in HIV virus composition among people who had seroconverted in the city over a six-year period. They then used phylogenetics—a science that studies genetic changes to understand how different forms of life emerge—to observe new strains of HIV arising as the virus mutated within the bodies of new hosts. By studying similarities and differences in the makeup of viruses among different people who were infected, the researchers were then able to determine how closely related the HIV strains were. That information was subsequently used to identify social and geographic links between actual people who had seroconverted and identify clusters of new cases among specific subpopulations: the more closely matched the virus was in two people, the more likely it was that HIV had been transmitted directly between them. It was a remarkable approach, the scientists pursuing changes in the composition of the virus like a thread through a labyrinth to uncover human interactions at increasing degrees of intimacy.

I sent the paper to Steffanie, thinking that we could use a similar approach in Tijuana to glean some useful data about where across the city new cases of HIV were emerging and among which groups. She replied to my email, as she did without fail, immediately: someone on the El Cuete team was already way ahead of me. "Sanjay is sequencing the last 7 el cuete seroconverters since they are believed to be clustered—patty says that most are going to the same conecta that was [relocated] from the canal and is reaching new clients," she wrote. "All were diagnosed by us in the last month, which suggests that there might be a major uptick in incidence coming. I have already alerted the health officials in tj and the DF [Mexico City]. It would be good to share this paper with Sanjay if you are amenable." I sent it off, a little disappointed to have been beaten to the punch.

The year rolled on. That spring, buckets of rain and torrential winds buffeted the region, and I came to my office at the UC San Diego campus one day (I had been upgraded from my windowless digs in Hillcrest) to find that a massive old eucalyptus tree had fallen onto a nearby faculty building, smashing its glittering steel letters and bending apart the beams that had held the structure in place. Eucalyptus, I learned, wasn't native to California and had been imported from Australia in the early 1900s for timber, the plantations abandoned after the wood was found to be too soft. The trees didn't belong here, their roots too shallow to hold fast to the desert soil when the hard rain upended the earth.

There were other signs of change in Tijuana. An operativo to clean out the canal, undertaken in the first half of 2016, was a short-term success for the police. The encampments of deportees injecting there were cleared away, this time ostensibly for good. Many of them were El Cuete participants, and Patty became increasingly distraught as they became (in the social science euphemism) "lost to follow-up." Their data were gone and their whereabouts unknown, as if they simply melted away. The prospects of a supervised injection facility had similarly been forgotten as Alex had gone all-in on a militarized approach to the city's drug problem.

Then, in May 2016, tens of thousands of Haitians arrived in Tijuana at a time when the city was still trying to accommodate the hundreds of American deportees who were being exiled here from the United States each day. Creole- and French-speaking, the Haitians had fled their homes after the 2010 earthquake there for Brazil, where they had found construction work in the lead-up to the 2016 Rio Olympics. Once the jobs dried up, they followed a land route—sometimes on foot—all the way from Brazil to Tijuana in the hopes of crossing into the United States, which had provided Haitians with a humanitarian visa waiver after the earthquake had destroyed much of their country. But on September 22, 2016, after thousands of Haitians had successfully crossed into the United States through Tijuana, the waiver was abruptly rescinded, America deciding that its charity only extended so far. That left thousands of Haitians in Tijuana with nowhere left to go. I began to see them along the pedestrian bridge that crossed the canal, men, women, and children with grim expressions, clutching plastic bags full of clothes and cellphone power cables. Patty drove me along a short street near her home in the Zona where a temporary shelter for Haitian migrants had been set up. Dusk was settling into night when we arrived, and I watched as a man pulled a garage door down over the front of the makeshift shelter building. Before he could secure it, I glimpsed hundreds of bodies lying on the ground set closely together in sleeping bags, an orderly congregation covering the entire floor. Dozens more sat on the curbs outside, checking their phones or just staring into space.

The year 2016 also saw Alex fired as Tijuana's chief of police (formally, he offered to resign). Starting in December 2013, he had been given three years to build on the security gains made after the worst of the drug war's violence had befallen the city. During his tenure, though, the homicide rate had steadily crept up. A news article about his firing quoted, curiously, the president of Coparmex, a Mexican business conglomerate, who stated that Alex had "built a strong relationship with society, and that is important. But what we need is someone with a stronger hand internally." Alex released a statement upon his resignation in which he claimed that he had brought about a "marked decrease in crime rates in all areas, except—I have to recognize—in homicides, due to armed attacks among small-scale drug vendors and dealers." It was a sign of just how violent the city was about to become.

In 2018, over 2,300 people were killed in Tijuana, almost twice as many as the year before, the highest level in the city's history. The murder rate approached 135 per 100,000, making it one of the most violent cities in the world, let alone North America. That included a 50 percent increase in the number of women killed since 2016. Meanwhile, just across the border in San Diego, the murder rate had dropped yet again to 2.3 per 100,000 in 2017, its lowest level in almost fifty years.

While the sheer magnitude of killings cast a pall over Tijuana, the city didn't feel as tense as it had during the first major wave of violence in 2010. That year, 1,257 murders had been committed, then an unprecedented level of murder. While 2018 smashed that record, I was told that the texture of the violence was different this time around. The daytime shootouts in the Zona, the grotesque theatrics of corpses hanging from bridges, the narcomantas left on charred bodies in burned-out cars: these were the hallmarks of 2010, when the Arellano Félix Organization, the Sinaloa Cartel, and other challengers were seeking to dominate the market by stoking fear.

The newest surge felt qualitatively different. With the entry of new players into the city like the Cartel Jalisco Nueva Generación, the city was being carved up into smaller and smaller fiefdoms, with specific conectas and picaderos becoming the primary targets. Establishing control in those drug-selling spots allowed the narcos a foothold into the increasingly lucrative local market for drugs, which was becoming just as desirable to the cartels as controlling the flow of drugs trafficked through Tijuana and into the United States. Rather than a repeat of the 2010 campaign of mass terror, the city was experiencing targeted urban warfare, with violence flaring in individual buildings and drug-selling corners in a slow and bloody war of attrition that was playing out in the margins, away from Tijuana's most frequented areas.

On one of my trips through the city around that time, a colleague and I followed a young man named Junior on a visit to a picadero near El Bordo, the border wall in view. We followed him through an alleyway, picking our way across a dirt road that had turned into deep mud after the recent rains. Across the street, a band of workmen were quietly building a fence in the morning's rising heat. Junior ushered us over to a short concrete wall and told us to peer into the lot on the other side. I did, but all I saw was the half-crumbled concrete footprint of a building now gone to seed. Junior was agitated that day and wanted to leave quickly. I figured it was because of his malilla. Later, my colleague, who knew Junior better than I did, explained what was really going on: earlier that week, Junior had been injecting opioids when two strangers had entered the picadero asking after the resident drug dealers. Someone pointed to three men, one of whom was sitting next to Junior. The strangers pulled out handguns and shot the men at point-blank range. The body of the dealer closest to Junior fell into his lap, and in that moment he believed that he was going to be killed next. Instead, the men pocketed their guns and left. There was a brief pause in drug selling at the picadero, but it lasted only a few days. Then new dealers set up shop.

Soon after, in early 2018, I saw Rosa for the last time. Unlike during our first meeting, her teeth-gritting impatience was absent; she was no longer trying to outpace her malilla. Instead, she was in a noticeably good mood, calmer and well rested. While her speech hadn't lost its hard cadence or roller-coaster expressiveness, she was in no hurry to cut our conversation short. Mired as I was in statistics and stories of women's deaths, I was singularly focused by this time on how the pathological process driving the femicide epidemic (police brutality, narco violence, and crazed johns) had cohered and increased in virulence, and the environmental shift that had preceded its emergence. I realized with a start during the interview that I had lost sight of the fact that women were actually eluding the epidemic. I had begun to assume that for women like Rosa, who only knew one way to make money, the end would come when their bodies could no longer raise capital and they took one too many risks with clients or drugs. But as we spoke that day in one of the cramped El Cuete interview rooms, she made me understand that there were indeed ways to escape, narrow paths though they may be.

Rosa untied an apron from her neck, folded it on her lap, and looked across the table at Teresita and me. As we said our hellos, Cyndi Lauper's "Girls Just Want to Have Fun" blared from a radio down the hall in the main waiting room. "I'm currently cleaning the hotel where I live," Rosa said, in explanation of the apron. "I work there with clients, but this is the first time that I'm actually working—cleaning."

"But you've always worked!" Teresita said.

"Well yes, as a sex worker," Rosa replied, "but I do real work now, I clean really hard, and it's good for me because I don't have a health card." She explained that police were stepping up their detainments of sex workers without registration cards and sending them to La Veinte (the municipal jail) for thirty-six-hour detainments. Rosa had found a way to avoid all that. "Instead," she said, "I receive a salary for cleaning and I find clients to bring to the hotel." The arrangement, while different from what she was used to, was working for her. She had also managed to cut down on her opioid use, from every day to just a couple of times a week.

Rosa always exhibited a deadpan gallows humor about her situation, but this time she earnestly appeared to be in a good place. There was a simple reason for that, she explained. She no longer feared for her safety despite the surge in violence that wracked the city. "The owners of the hotel are not *culeros*,"—assholes—"and they don't let anyone sell drugs inside," she said. "If there are no drugs, there's no danger from shootings or that type of violence. I mean, clients can get violent, but it's not the same, you know? Because the violence comes from narcos fighting over the Zona and the drug-selling spaces." Now in her midfifties and having exclusively performed sex work for the past thirty-odd years, Rosa—somewhat incredibly—had found a salaried job, was still attracting clients, and had achieved a measure of stability that shielded her from the worst of the dangers of the street. It couldn't have come at a better time, she explained, because the city's chaos had reached a fever pitch. "Nowadays," she said, "if you have five hundred pesos [about twenty-five U.S. dollars], you've got enough to pay to get someone killed just because they owe you money from drugs. That's what's happening right now. They even do it in the middle of the day." Rosa believed that the reason more women than ever were being killed was that the plummeting fortunes of the red-light district had pushed sex workers to try drug dealing as a way to make ends meet.

Here was a new layer in the uncompromising epidemic. Not only was there disease ("I think it's the AIDS," Rosa replied to a question about the greatest threat women faced in the Zona), overdose, police brutality, and murder at the hands of clients—the latest adaptation that women were taking to survive the Zona's post-9/11 environmental shift was opening them up to the ferocity of the drug trade, a sector that had been killing Tijuana's men for decades. Drug-related murder, never a major cause of women's deaths here, was now emerging as another component of the pathological process driving the femicide epidemic.

Rosa had seen its results firsthand. "This woman was found next to the Vía Rapída a little while ago in pieces," she said. "She was a friend. She used to work here as a sex worker and she was also a *tecata* [injector]. But she also used to sell drugs at a bar. And then, she was found killed and cut into pieces." Rosa's theory about her death was simple: "She had malilla and stole from the *narcomenudistas* [drug dealers] or owed then money."

When women entered the drug market, the narcos treated them just as they treated men: ruthlessly. The fact was, the stakes in the drug trade were so high, with three or more cartels battling it out for control of the Tijuana plaza, that the gender of victims was irrelevant in the face of the potential profits to be gained by controlling the market. "You cannot sell drugs where you want," Rosa explained, "because the cartels have really specific zones and conectas, and they don't care if you are a man or a woman."

"They don't care if you are a woman, they just don't care," she repeated, like a mantra. "Every conecta has women and kids selling drugs. They have boys and girls; it's really easy for the narcos to recruit them. Before, you would only see older people selling, like fifty-year-olds, or at least people in their twenties or thirties, and it used to be really hidden. And now, if you walk during the day or at night, even close to schools, they offer you everything—meth, heroin, everything—and most of them are kids."

The new drug-trafficking landscape had altered the environment for sex workers in other ways too. With the new cartels came new drugs: while crystal meth had long been available in the Zona, the takeover of picaderos and conectas by new groups with access to a different set of drug producers had flooded the city with the drug. "Before it was hidden," Rosa said. "But now you can see lines in the streets to buy crystal . . . they're worse than the lines for buying tortillas." She laughed heartily, but the truth was that the upsurge in crystal meth availability made her job harder for one major reason: while the drug made clients excited, it also made it harder for them to reach orgasm. This explained why Salvador believed that clients who used meth were the most dangerous kind. Rosa recalled one regular client who had switched to crystal meth and the terror that she experienced in the aftermath. "He was a good client, but that day he was really high—I think he was using Viagra combined with crystal, so he was so horny but he couldn't finish, which made him very mad. He was hitting me and hurting me, it was horrible." Susi, in one of her impish moods, had also once explained that sex workers that supplemented their income by stealing were having a much harder time doing so with meth-using clients because they were paranoid and would stay awake for hours. It was a far cry from the times when clients used heroin and reliably drifted into sleep, making them easy marks.

Rosa admitted that despite the violence, she had been tempted into drug dealing. "Last year, a guy came here and asked if I wanted to sell drugs—balloons [of crystal meth]—and I didn't want to, because I just didn't want to owe him money. But he left twenty-five balloons anyway, and I did sell some but I smoked others." Initially, Rosa hadn't understood what she was getting involved in, "but then I realized that he was a narco because I saw his gun; he was armed and I felt scared, so I paid him back for the balloons and told him that I didn't want to sell anymore." Given what had happened to her friend, it was, in retrospect, a close call.

We had been chatting relaxedly for almost an hour when Rosa asked what time it was, then hopped up abruptly and tied the apron back around her waist. She apologized: she was due back at the hotel to finish up her work for the day. After twenty-five years hustling the Zona, Rosa had found some kind of peace. Her home in the hotel was quiet—or as quiet as the red light district can get—but more importantly, she had found a place to weather the storm of violence that had once again gathered across the borderland.

*

On January 30, 2018, about a year and a half after Steffanie first mentioned the new HIV outbreak among El Cuete participants, an email with the subject line "Growing TJ Cluster" arrived in my in-box. It was from that same Sanjay that Steffanie had mentioned to me. Dr. Sanjay Mehta, MD, I discovered, was an impressive clinician and microbiologist with expertise in the evolution of viruses during their spread through a population. "That cluster we reported on last year is continuing to grow," he wrote, "and is up to 14 people." That meant it had doubled in size within a year and a half, a strikingly high rate of expansion.

The email had an attachment; I clicked it open and an image in triplicate appeared on my computer screen. Boxes and circles representing men and women enrolled in the El Cuete study were linked together by gray filaments, the whole apparatus cohering like a constellation in an astronomical map. The gray strands between the shapes were phylogenetic connections, instances where the strains of HIV were so similar that Sanjay could conclude that they came from a common source, meaning the two people had directly transmitted the virus to each other either by sharing needles or having sex. Subtle distinctions in the copies of the virus flowing through different people's bloodstreams also allowed him to infer where relationships were less immediate. In these cases, the virus had passed through someone else in the cluster first before moving on to a new host, the network expanding as HIV spread through a growing number of victims. Like my map of police brutality, Sanjay's map also overlaid a color scheme onto the shapes, ranging from beige to dark red. In my study, the deeper colors meant an area with a higher frequency of police assaults; here, bloodred shapes depicted someone who had had more than ten sexual or injecting partners in the past six months. There was one final piece of information. Stamped on some of the circles representing women, like a scarlet letter, was the acronym FSW—female sex worker.

Of the fourteen people enrolled in Proyecto El Cuete who had seroconverted over the past year, five were women; all but one of the circles representing a woman was stamped with FSW. The cluster of cases was roughly made up of three constellations connected by gray ligaments that stretched across the blank white backdrop of the pdf. At the center of it all, like a dying star erupting in a final burst, a gleaming bloodred circle stamped with FSW sent gray lines out to a jumble of other shapes, both men and women. Here was the center of the HIV cluster: a sex worker with more than ten sexual partners and drug-injecting companions connected to a growing community of seroconverters bound together by a virus steadily replicating in their bloodstreams. The virus itself was just a simple machine with only one function—to copy itself without end, the errors and mutations it generated along the way only adding to its power to cripple its hosts.

Until this cluster was discovered, the incidence of new HIV cases among El Cuete participants had been brought to a lull in part by the outreach that Patty and Susi had undertaken into the canal along with the efforts of other front-line harm reduction organizations in Tijuana that worked to distribute clean needles, condoms, and first aid to street-based drug injectors. Female participants enrolled in Mujer Mas Segura were even less likely than their peers to become infected given the intervention's remarkable effectiveness. Proyecto Escudo had also been showing promise in reducing the number of times that police destroyed needles. That change in police behavior had the potential to reduce the chances that people were forced to use the same needle to inject or to scavenge needles the way that Susi had done before she stopped using. Sanjay's mapping made clear, though, that all of these gains had not been enough. His map charted a surge that, if left unchecked, would rapidly expand into a renewed epidemic. I was shocked that HIV appeared to be accelerating rather than retreating, even after all these interventions. How could that be?

I stared past the colorful image of the cluster and into the blank background of the document. The constellation of seroconverters, bound together now for the rest of their lives, seemed like they were floating in a featureless landscape. But of course, the epidemiologic triangle requires more than just a pathogen and a host. Epidemics do not emerge out of a void. They are always driven by the dynamics of an environment, those curious facets of a place and people that make up real life as we know it. This new outbreak would be following those rules. And so, after doing a little digging, I soon learned where the environment fostering this emergent epidemic cluster was located. It was a new picadero on the outskirts of the canal that locals called Las Llantas. The Tires.

*

Patty had learned of Las Llantas through the Wound Clinic, a regular outreach service that she had initiated after encountering people at the El Cuete offices with increasingly ghastly abscesses and blackened open sores from injecting impure street drugs. Instead of restricting her care to those enrolled in the study, Patty decided to go to the canal and other locations where she knew she would find people who might need care. It was exhausting work, and it showed. Every time we met up, she was more beaten down by the endless needs of the people the rest of Tijuana was trying to forget. As the months passed, more and more people presented at the Wound Clinic when they saw Patty arrive with latex gloves and a folding table in tow, rolling up their sleeves and pant legs to show her their pain. But even as she began to build up the trust of her patients out in the street, the sores she was dealing with were becoming larger and more corrosive-looking, some wounds stretching from elbows to wrists, the product of some new kind of injecting behavior. Distraught at what she was seeing, Patty wanted to know more. After asking around, it turned out that some picaderos had been taken over by dealers from cartels selling new synthetic opioids, which turned out to be eating away at people's bodies from the inside after they were injected.

Black tar heroin, long the most widely available kind in Tijuana, is a sticky and unyielding substance that requires heating to about 165 degrees Fahrenheit before it liquefies enough to inject. Because of this process, using black tar heroin can actually limit people's exposure to impurities because they end up being burned away, while the drug's claylike texture also makes it difficult to cut with other adulterants like fentanyl. Even better, the intense heat needed to break down the drug is sufficient to kill the HIV virus. That means that people who inject with black tar heroin are also less likely to become infected with HIV even if they share syringes. But all of a sudden, El Cuete participants were telling Patty that black tar heroin was harder to find. That meant that as the drug war transitioned into a cartel street battle in Tijuana, the injecting scene was shifting along with it.

A dirty brown powder heroin, dubbed China White, had always been available on the margins of the city's street drug market. In 2017, though, it became the only type of heroin sold at major picaderos like Las Llantas. A variegated powder, the China White that was showing up in Tijuana was lumpy and crystalline and sometimes cast a purplish hue. It was a mixture of toxic substances that could burn through blood vessels like oven cleaner, and it was the reason for the grotesque and life-threatening wounds that Patty was seeing out in the street. Worse, China White doesn't require the same amount of heating as black tar heroin, meaning that the HIV virus, if present on syringes, isn't burned away during preparation. Here was the environmental shift causing the cluster that Steffanie and Sanjay had uncovered.

*

Colonia Postal, one of the oldest neighborhoods in the city, lies northeast of the Tijuana River Canal. Officially, it squats atop a high mesa about a mile and a half from the border wall, but it doesn't end there. As in many of Tijuana's neighborhoods, enterprising citizens have sought to expand its footprint along unyielding canyons so steep and perilous that it seems impossible that any structures built there could find purchase. And yet the neighborhood flows organically down from the top of the canyons to the canal, the chasms filled with cube-shaped bungalows, the sheer landscape miraculously transformed into dwellings. Postal was founded in the early twentieth century and is, basically, the final form that the shantytowns I saw in Los Laureles Canyon will take once they fully graduate from garage doors and washing machines to painted concrete walls and corrugated plastic roofs.

While Postal is largely indistinguishable from its surrounding colonias, one strategic advantage sets it apart for people who inject drugs: the neighborhood is equidistant to the canal, the Hospital Angeles Tijuana, and La Veinte, the municipal jail. Postal is also where La Casa del Migrante, one of Tijuana's main migrant shelters, is located. The canal, the jail, the hospital, and the migrant shelter; these four spaces are the gauntlet run by Tijuana's tecates (injectors) as they move through the city eluding capture and assault. That makes it the perfect place for a picadero. And while the "successful" 2016 police operativo to clean the canal had ended up dispersing people across the city, by 2018 Patty's team had been able to make contact with at least some of their lost participants. They had moved en masse, it turned out, to the area in and around Postal. At the same time, the influx of deportees from the United States remained steady, with over a hundred being exiled to Tijuana each day. Casa del Migrante was full to bursting with people with nowhere to go, many of whom had sunk into despair, rubbing elbows with drug injectors who had been displaced from the canal. Las Llantas had risen up to welcome them all.

While I knew Las Llantas was in Colonia Postal, actually finding it, which I tried to do in April 2018, proved challenging. Susi was the expert in Tijuana's hidden injecting spots and would have been my obvious guide, but I had been having trouble reaching her for months. That was a problem because Patty had warned me not to go to the picadero alone. Las Llantas had become a hot spot for murder, because what made it strategic for people who inject drugs also made it highly prized by the narcos who supplied them with their fix. After my day with shell-shocked Junior, witness to a massacre in a picadero on the other side of the canal, I heeded Patty's warning. Nevertheless, I spent hours driving up and down the narrow winding streets of Colonia Postal, eyeing every crevice along the side of the road for passageways. I wasn't planning to enter Las Llantas per se but I at least wanted a glimpse.

The only hint I had came from its name, so I scanned the neighborhood for telltale signs of tires, assuming these would be a surefire giveaway. As I drove up and down its steep and narrow roads, I realized it wasn't going to be that simple. Colonia Postal was utterly awash in waste tires. Discarded tires bulged out of the ground at odd angles, slowly being consumed by the desert dust. Every roadside path I came across was made of tires, some so old that they had completely fused with the ground like the exposed roots of an oak tree, betraying a vast and tangled network that lay beneath the surface. They were used as retaining walls and foundations for homes set along the steep ravines running almost vertically up from the canal below. At the colonia's peak, the streets were saturated with used tire stores. Stacks of tires, gleaming like new, were set in orderly fashion at the side of the road and advertised with colorful banners in a series of lots that stretched all the way to the border fence. My search was impossible: from what I could tell, the entirety of the neighborhood was Las Llantas. I left empty-handed, more puzzled than ever.

*

I redoubled my efforts to get in touch with Susi, hoping that she could guide me into Las Llantas, but she remained impossible to find. She didn't write emails, and though Teresita tried various phone numbers, nobody picked up. Worse, Susi had recently stopped working at the El Cuete offices and had moved out of her apartment. While it had been many years since she'd used drugs, those who knew her were worried about her potential for relapse once she became untethered from her job and her home. The last time I saw her, she was living in the Hotel Paloma in the Zona, which bore the same name as that one friend—La Paloma, the last of her gang—whose disappearance or death Susi chose not to tell me about.

For all the changes she was going through on the day of our last meeting, Susi seemed content, waving to friends along the street as we roamed the red-light district after a quick meal of shrimp tacos, excitedly talking about her plans for the future and her gripes about the past. Over lunch, Susi had finally told me about the first time she had met Angie, that friend whose death resonated most deeply. I assumed that they had found each other in the Zona Norte, but Susi corrected me. "I met her in San Diego," Susi said, describing an area on the outskirts of San Diego's North Park neighborhood, close to my apartment. "Angie used to live in that area, and back then she was crossing back and forth all the time." Susi explained that in the late 1980s, the drug-buying situation along the border was basically reversed. "You couldn't find heroin here," Susi said, "and with twenty American dollars you could buy enough heroin to last four to five days. Almost everyone who used heroin in the eighties in TJ would get it over there in the United States." That meant that women like Susi and Angie who worked in the Zona Norte traveled into the United States multiple times a week just to buy drugs, which they would then smuggle into Mexico to use. Only after heroin became more readily available in Tijuana in the early 1990s—around the same time that the homicide rates in San Diego and Tijuana were accelerating in different directions—did Susi and Angie stop crossing over.

*

With Susi gone, Patty eventually agreed to take me to Las Llantas. It was May 2018, and she was still trying to find participants that had disappeared after Alex's operativo. While going to the picadero was risky, Patty figured it would accelerate the process of tracking down those that had been lost to follow-up. Though Patty had never been to the site herself, one of her research assistants, a young man named Ephraim, clad that day in a golf shirt and Yankees cap, knew the way. The trick to finding it, he explained as we left the El Cuete offices, was to start at the top of the mesa and enter from above. I had made the mistake of trying to find it from the roads at the bottom of the hill near the canal.

Teresita and I tailed the beat-up El Cuete van carrying Patty, Ephraim, and the other members of her team as they wound their way from the hustle and bustle of the Zona, along the Vía Rapída, and through a series of switchbacks, roundabouts, and off-ramps to the foot of Colonia Postal, the border wall visible in the distance. From there, Teresita's pint-size car chugged up the hill in pursuit of the van and we laughed at the sound of the engine struggling with the steep ascent. Finally, we crested the mesa and pulled up to park a block away from a bright blue two-story bungalow that overlooked a quiet intersection just down the street from the Casa del Migrante.

"My grandparents lived at a shelter close to here when they first moved to Tijuana," Patty said as we assembled outside of the parked vehicles. "The very first shelter for migrants was just one colonia over in Libertad, which is the oldest part of Tijuana." From our vantage point we could see down to the canal below, empty and running headlong into the border, the wall's abrupt imposition visible, dividing the dusty and completely bare green-and-brown canyons on the northern side from the high ridge upon which we stood, which was filled beyond capacity with homes and people. If there was one thing that hadn't changed since I'd arrived in

Tijuana, it was the physical imposition of the wall. For all the talk of border security under the Trump administration, the architecture of division that separates Tijuana and San Diego—a double wall, a trench, and an overwhelming military presence deployed to stop intruders—was already so extreme that there was little more that could be done to physically convey America's deep desire to keep Tijuana apart.

As we walked down the street toward the blue bungalow, Ephraim warned me not to take pictures. "Those guys," he said nonchalantly, as we passed two men in white tank tops and cargo pants, one of whom held a chain attached to a large pit bull, "are the sentries." I learned later that they were known as *checadors*, or "checkers." A checador stands guard at a picadero, acting as both the site's muscle and its maître d'hôtel: they're the ones in control of who gets let in and who is told to move on. I thought of the old man who let Patty, Susi, and me in during that first visit to Las Palmitas; he would have been that picadero's checador. Once admitted past the checador, visitors seek out the *tirador* or "shooter," a combination dealer and site coordinator who sells drugs and injecting implements and collects rent. The visitor would then be sold the brown-and-purple China White that Las Llantas was known for. At Las Palmitas, the tirador had been the ancient woman with a collection of needles at her feet.

We passed the blue bungalow and Patty and I followed Ephraim as he peeled off toward the edge of the canyon to what looked like a dead end. As we turned to follow him, Teresita and the rest of Patty's team slowed their pace behind us and kept walking straight along the main road. I assumed that the blue house was Las Llantas and said as much, but Ephraim shook his head. "Las Llantas moves around," he explained, "sometimes it's below and sometimes it's in houses. Right now, the blue house has become the new Las Llantas, but it's only a part of it." I was confused but left it at that.

As we approached the dead end, I saw footpaths extending along both sides of the narrow street beyond the formal edge of the concrete. The paths plunged down the canyon face at a severe angle, leading away from each other. "Which path goes to Las Llantas?" I asked.

"Both," responded Ephraim with a shrug, "you can enter from either side." He waved mildly at Patty and me to follow and we headed down a set of uneven concrete steps to the left, all three of us picking our way carefully along the steep descent. I looked down to gauge how far the path continued, but I could not see its end. The morning sun had risen, but the path was partially covered by a canopy of succulents, cacti, and palms that filtered the light and moderated the heat. The steepness of the steps reminded me of Aztec pyramids I had seen in Teotihuacán, outside of Mexico City. We passed a couple of semivacant lots and cube-shaped homes, the terrain becoming more perilous as we continued down, the concrete gently receding with every step to expose a foundation made up, I realized, entirely of tires. We were close, I thought, and looked around to spy the specific building or abandoned lot in which Las Llantas was located. Piles of waste tires appeared in some of the lots we passed. I ducked under a tree branch, only to see a man in mud-stained clothing standing on the roof of a one-story dwelling, alone and trying to appear nonchalant as he stared at his shoes. "Hola," Patty called out to him in Spanish as we passed, "how are you doing today?" He responded with quiet pleasantries. "We're from Proyecto El Cuete; it's a public health study, do you know it?" she asked. The man shook his head. "Really?" Patty was genuinely surprised and laughed to herself. "Well, if you want to join the study we can help set that up; there are people at the top of the hill who can enroll you." The man mumbled his thanks then turned away to stare off into space. Later, I was told that he was another sentry, one of the informal layers of security that the cartels had introduced into this landscape.

We continued along our way, stepping aside to let a young man wearing a football jersey and bandanna pass us from below. He was hauling a heavy-looking orange bicycle, and Ephraim joked with him good-naturedly about the heavy load he was carrying up such steep terrain. The man half-grunted, half-laughed a response as the sweat poured down his cheeks and neck. He quickly disappeared up the steps.

We said very little to each other as we picked our way down, mostly pointing out hazards along the path, cognizant that we were effectively trespassing in a place that didn't officially exist, and that we had been allowed to do so only because we didn't appear to be a threat to business. My head swiveled from side to side at the shacks and lots, hoping to figure out which one was Las Llantas. None stood out, and Ephraim continued to amble down the structure, which was increasingly devoid of concrete and made up solely of stacked tire rings filled with dirt, the rubber squeaking and sliding under our feet. Up ahead, I saw the canal come into view just beyond the cars and trucks speeding along the Vía Rapída. I was disappointed; we were almost at the end of the path and we hadn't yet found Las Llantas. I looked back up the hill to see if we had missed something, then heard Patty call out from below.

"Hey, watch out," she said, "you shouldn't step there." Patty was standing further down in some weeds at the edge of a small roofless outbuilding, gesturing to the path just below my feet. I looked down. Amid the mélange of grayed and dusty vulcanized rubber, a large pool of blood had formed in a shallow well in the middle of a concrete-filled tire and was overflowing down the path. Half-coagulated, the blood at the edges of the pool had darkened to a ferrous maroon. Brighter streaks coated half a dozen of the uneven steps below as the blood dripped down. It was fresh—likely no more than half a day had passed since it had been spilt—and there was enough of it to suggest a wound serious enough to kill.

It was then that it hit me. Las Llantas wasn't the bungalow up above, or any one of the half-built homes that we'd passed, or the spaces in between: it was all of them. This whole area, from the top of the mesa to the canal below, was the picadero. It wasn't Las Palmitas, a decaying building in the middle of a scrap heap, or the half-destroyed vacant lot I had visited with Junior. After Alex's canal operativo had sent drug injectors fleeing across the city, this place had become a massive labyrinth entirely in thrall to Tijuana's drug market. All of the lots and the small shacks next to the concrete and waste-tire path, and the lots and the shacks beyond them, were a part of this strange new ecosystem.

Here was the heart of Sanjay's outbreak. It was a place where sex workers and drug-injecting women were being infected with HIV at an accelerated rate, the swapping out of black tar heroin with China White allowing live viruses to remain on syringes instead of being burned away. It was here that women were entering the drug trade at a time when the old rules of the plaza system had broken down to such an extent that Tijuana had become the most violent big city in North America and the fifth most violent city in the world. And it was here in Las Llantas that the drugs sold by the tiradors had a purplish hue because they contained fentanyl, that hyperpotent opioid that had caused such widespread overdose death in the United States that by 2015 the average life expectancy of Americans had declined for the first time in half a century. I was standing in the blank background of Sanjay's phylogenetic reconstruction of the outbreak, a place that had, like the outbreak itself, expanded beyond anyone's control.

We got to the bottom of the path and looked out at the canal and the city beyond. Patty pointed out the Agua Caliente racetrack, still owned by Jorge Hank Rhon, which was visible on the far side of the canal's sloping walls. "When it was still the Caliente casino, there used to be an airport there," she said, "where celebrities would come and go in private jets." We stood silently for a moment and I tried to picture what that era must have looked like, a time when Tijuana was a capital of glitz and glamour. After catching our breath, we turned and walked up a road to try to find the other path leading back up to the blue house on the other side of Las Llantas.

"Police come to this road, but they'll never go up the paths," Ephraim said. I asked if it was because they were afraid. Both Patty and Ephraim shook their heads. "No," he replied, "they just don't want to disrupt business."

The other pathway was even steeper, and the tires felt less securely fastened underfoot. I helped Patty as we labored to make our way back up to the mesa. Along the way, we passed a modest-looking home and I noticed a boy, no older than three years old, peering at me from a front deck. I waved at him and smiled; he stared blankly back at me and walked up to the edge of the deck to follow my movements closely up the path. Later, two women in their midforties emerged from a small home and greeted us politely as we passed. "Everyone," Patty said, as we finally made it back up to the dead end street near the blue house on the corner, "is involved. Those women we passed, they might not look like they control things, but if they didn't want you there, you wouldn't be able to stay." Rosa had told me almost exactly the same thing. We trundled past the blue house, and I peered through the open door to see teenagers, four boys and a girl, seated in a circle, the radio blaring in the background. "I used to have joy in this work," Patty said suddenly, "but the last Wound Clinic was depressing. Even participants who we used to joke around with are not smiling anymore. They are just killing so many people these days, killing and beating them. It used to not affect me inside but now it's tough," she said. "You get to know people and then they disappear; know them and then they disappear; know them and then they disappear . . ."

We got back to the cars and stood waiting for the rest of the El Cuete staff, who were having an animated conversation with the checadors. Eventually they said their goodbyes to the men and tailed us back to the vehicles.

"They told us there was a murder yesterday," one of the staff members said as she approached.

"We know," Patty responded.

*

Shortly after that day outside the Hotel Paloma, Susi disappeared altogether. There were rumors of a relapse, a return to drug dealing, and a
daytime fistfight in the Zona. As hard as I tried, I couldn't find out whether
any of it was true. The last I heard was a whisper that she had crossed
back into the United States and was living in an inpatient rehab center
somewhere in San Diego County, the border wall separating her from
home. Susi, with her stories of the old-school Zona and friendships born
out of knife fights with the paraditas of La Coahuila, of dumpster diving
for bloodied veterinary needles, a woman whose pride came from
knowing the hidden places accessible only to those who had experienced
true suffering, had finally left.

And yet, on that last day together, Susi had confided in me that there
was more to those early visits to San Diego than she had previously let
on. "I knew how to cross through the border without being seen," she had
said with relish. I asked her to elaborate. "I used to move *pollos*," she
explained. "I would hide under tractor trailers; it was so easy to cross!"
Susi, it turned out, had been a *pollero*.

"I used to *brincar*," Susi continued, using a word that means "jump"
but in Tijuanensis slang refers specifically to jumping over the border
wall, "to a *clavadero*." *Clavadero* translates as "nailer," and refers to a
house in which polleros gather migrants after successful border crossings,
from where they are dispersed across the United States. "There was a
clavadero at the corner of Thirty-Third and El Cajon," she said. This, it
turned out, was the spot where she first met Angie and where they struck
up the binational friendship that they would nurture in the Zona for a
decade. "Sometimes in one day I would cross one or two pollos," Susi said,
netting her about fifty dollars, enough to pay for her drug supply. It was
a far cry from the thousands of dollars now paid to smuggle people across
what has become a massive military checkpoint.

To Susi's many roles—drug user, hit doctor, thief, and outreach
worker—I could now add one more: pollero. Was it mere coincidence that
she had brought this up so soon before she disappeared from view? As
far as I knew, Susi had never been deported, so she was at liberty to cross
into the United States anytime she liked. Of course, there were always
gaps in the stories she shared, so the possibility existed that she had been
deported but chose to redact that part of her narrative. As the last of her
friends to survive, perhaps she understood that the femicide was never
at bay and that even in this era of border security, which operates like a

grotesque amplification of the ley de fuga, the safest option was to flee before the guns were at your back.

I tried to picture her in the United States, amid the manicured lawns and quiet, orderly streets of San Diego County, but my imagination let me down. I knew she had learned to inject in the U.S. and then parlayed that knowledge into a career as a hit doctor in the Zona. I knew she had met her soul mate, Angie, on the northern side of the border at a time when drugs were more plentiful there than in Tijuana. I knew that she had crossed back and forth for years, smuggling people and drugs as she clung to the underside of tractor trailers. But I still could not see her anywhere but here, amid the endless variation of the Zona.

Epilogue

On November 14, 2018, the first wave of a migrant caravan numbering roughly six thousand people arrived in Tijuana en route to the United States. The group had first come together in Honduras but had picked up numbers as it headed north, and it was made up of families and young men fleeing systemic drug-related violence. In the Central American countries of Honduras, El Salvador, and Guatemala, drug trafficking organizations had taken over large swaths of urban areas in a more vicious version of the PRI's plaza system; where the latter had relied on quiet collusion, the Central American gangs used a system of control built on the threat of ruthless violence for those who either opposed them or refused to join. As the caravan moved north, the migrants faced growing American hostility to their arrival at the Mexico-U.S. border, with President Donald Trump likening them to an invading army. In response, the leaders of the caravan settled on a path that led them to faraway Tijuana rather than to a closer border crossing. Doing so would land them in a city with a rich history of welcoming outsiders, located at a busy port of entry equipped to process thousands of asylum claims, however slowly. If, as was expected, the White House sought to block those asylum claims, so the logic went, at least Tijuana would be able to accommodate their needs in the short term. Tijuana was, after all, a city of migrants.

There were early signs that the caravan would be met with something less than open arms. The city's mayor, Juan Manuel Gastelúm, adopted the ubiquitous symbol of President Trump's ethno-nationalist movement when he donned a red hat emblazoned with the words MAKE TIJUANA GREAT AGAIN to announce his opposition to their arrival. "I apologize in advance to human rights organizations," said Gastelúm in his own defense, "but human rights are only for upstanding humans." On Sunday, November 18, 2018, Tijuanenses in the city's upscale colonia del Rio neighborhood protested the caravan's arrival; with shouts of "Mexico First," a crowd decried the flow of irregular migration, seeking, it seemed, to rewrite Tijuana's reputation as a place that would welcome all comers. The headlines generated by the mayor's performance and the protest established a narrative that Tijuana was as victimized by migration as its northern neighbor, and had responded in a way consistent with the xenophobia gripping present-day America. But the crowd in Rio was made up of only a few hundred people, hardly suggestive that the majority of Tijuanenses were uncomfortable with the new migrants, while Gastelúm's approval rating was mired at 4 percent, largely as a result of Tijuana's endemic violence. In that light, the mayor's antics seemed like a desperate plea for attention. Unmoved by these outbursts, the migrant caravan remained in the city, and authorities quietly began preparing to make their stay as humane as possible despite Tijuana's limitations. The open-air Benito Juarez sports complex, a gated baseball field in the Zona Norte on the edge of the Vía Internacional just steps from the border fence and three blocks north of Calle Coahuila, was seconded to shelter them.

The following Sunday, hundreds of migrants from the caravan began massing in the canal mere feet from the border. Some began to scale the fence, seeking forcible entry into the U.S.; they were met by an outsized show of force. In the weeks prior, President Trump had ordered 5,000 military personnel to deploy to the southern border to meet them at their arrival and, if necessary, beat them back. The day the migrants began congregating in the canal, readying for a run at the border fence, black military helicopters hovered lazily a few dozen feet above the San Ysidro border crossing; it had been temporarily closed to all traffic, the steady stream of cars replaced by a phalanx of border agents in riot gear facing south. The juxtaposition of a large and highly ordered military force on one side of the wall, and the destitute band of asylum seekers on the other, exemplified how charged the border had become since the post-NAFTA, pre-9/11 era when humans and capital were welcomed on both sides.

The border wall that separates Tijuana and San Diego is eighteen feet high in some places. The wide-open terrain on its northern side, flooded with searchlights at night, could not be emptier, making it easy to illuminate the brave and desperate who somehow find a way to cross over. The complex organization of guards, dogs, technological surveillance, and secondary detention at the San Ysidro border crossing is sufficiently byzantine to elicit both humiliation and terror among those seeking to enter America. The Tijuana–San Diego border has, more than anywhere else in the continental United States, achieved the goal of pure physical separation. It is a goal that previous administrations have worked toward, sometimes only rhetorically, but it has in recent years become a key plank of American state security.

Walls are a last resort when peaceful exchange with neighbors—the backbone of any successful community—becomes impossible. Frontiers are places of innovation, liminal zones where cultures can clash in natural experiments that generate confounding possibilities and unpredictable synergies. They are for that reason critical in enabling empires to evolve to meet new challenges. In the United States, the schizophrenic desire for impassable borders and free trade has sapped frontier zones of their creative potential. And perhaps the most powerful function of a wall is to deny the humanity of those who happen to be on the other side of it.

As the asylum-seeking crowd ran the fence in an effort to cross illegally, agents of the U.S. Customs and Border Protection shot tear gas into the canal, the canisters rolling down the sloping walls and into the trickle of polluted water that ran along its base. Scenes from that episode—mothers trying to revive children gasping for air amid the gas, others running through the pollution and smoke with small children in tow—suggested that the idea of a binational border region here had truly died. The titillating fear of the exotic that had lured so many Americans to Tijuana now made them turn their backs.

On the surface, the source of American fear is the city's drug-related violence, which most blame on the Mexican drug war. No matter that this drug war is funded by the U.S. government, via the Mérida Initiative, which has to date provided more than $1.6 billion since its launch by President George W. Bush. It is no coincidence that this is the same president who witnessed the security of America breached on 9/11 and, in the aftermath, reoriented the U.S. government toward total punishment of all those that exude otherness, both within and without America's borders. That included militarizing the U.S.-Mexico border, an act implying equivalence between America's neighbors, allies, rivals, and enemies alike. All were threats to its existence.

This is how migrant mothers and their children standing in the canal seeking to enter the United States can be shot at with tear gas by Customs and Border Protection agents. The irony is that the United States has long had the highest number of foreign-born immigrants in the entire world, with 19 percent of the world's foreign-born population living within its boundaries. America does not require protection from migration, or from cities like Tijuana, which is made up mostly of migrants; the country already resembles those seeking to enter. They will remain deeply embedded in the American experience regardless of how high the walls are built.

Despite the military response, the caravan remained in Tijuana, and the migrants returned to shelter in the Benito Juarez complex. Attacked by the country within which they were seeking refuge, the caravan's members nevertheless refused to yield to efforts to remove them. Left to their own devices, hundreds applied for work permits in Mexico. Other migrants staying in the sports complex voluntarily established an informal first-come, first-serve system to organize the caravan's thousands of asylum claims, given that the U.S. was processing only approximately thirty per day, making it difficult to track whose lot should be called. It was a sign, to some, that the caravan would become a dependent fixture in Tijuana. To others, it was further evidence of the industriousness that had carried them all the way to the border in the face of steep odds.

On the evening of Wednesday, November 28, however, light rain began to fall on Tijuana. Migrant families housed in the roofless sports complex, which was at three times its capacity, covered themselves and their belongings with tarps and huddled close to keep dry, hoping to wait it out. The next day, the real downpour began, soaking the desert earth and transforming the grounds of the Benito Juarez sports complex into deep puddles and thick mud. Thick streams of water pounded nylon tents and mattresses and swirled into open sewage drains. Men, women, and children sleeping in the open air, wrapped in thin blankets, were forced up to find shelter elsewhere, while an outbreaks of flu-like symptoms, lice, and chicken pox spread through the encampment. Scrambling to save their meager belongings and to keep their children warm and dry, families began uprooting themselves from the complex to seek refuge on the streets outside. That same day, admitting its failure, the city closed the complex down and began moving its occupants to a covered building in Tijuana's southeastern El Barretal colonia, a forty-five minute drive from

the border. Mothers and their children, along with men in their twenties, drifted into the street, unmoored from the group, trying their luck
in the Zona Norte. Though local political opposition and American military force could not dislodge them, the flooding had uprooted the
migrant caravan, just as it had the waste tires from the high canyons and
the drug users in the vents in the canal. They were the latest in a long
line of visitors that saw this border city as a stepping stone, only to find
in it a kind of home.

*

All languages carry implicit assumptions about the worth of the subjects
and objects they seek to represent. We speak of people pejoratively without
intending to—hookers, junkies, dealers, migrants—these words becoming
so deeply embedded in our consciousness that we stop perceiving their
original function, which is to reflexively diminish their subjects so that
we no longer have to care for them. In our language, these words are
loaded with judgment—even "migrant," which was a mostly neutral term
until the denial of immigration as an inalienable part of the history of
the United States became a governing philosophy; since then, it has
become an insult. In English, the power of these words to dehumanize
comes largely from how they are deployed. Nahuatl, the language of the
Aztec people, is more straightforward. In Nahuatl words we can glimpse
a starker truth about meanings and even uncover omens if we listen in
the right way.

The Aztec had many names for sex workers, but almost all of them
contain the noun construction *micqui*, meaning "dead person." Aztec
codices call these women *tlacamicqui* (a dead person), *xochimicqui* (one
that has died), *teomicqui* (a sacrificed captive), or *miccatzintli* (a poor dead
person, a bathed slave). They also call them by another name. *Tenanhuan*:
mothers. This is language direct enough to reveal the contradictions that
arise when men define a woman's worth. This same contradiction drives
business in the Zona, a place that draws men so desperate for a woman's
touch that they will pay for it while also hating the tlacamicqui for
revealing the depths of their own desire. It is a hatred arising out of the
fear of total surrender to a woman—a stranger—who knows you in ways
even your own mother never could, and who perceives the shameful
secret you thought you had kept from the world. The fear is amplified
once it dawns on you what you might be capable of once in her thrall.

Fear and desire have always been shared between Tijuana and the United States. But now, this city, in which Juan Soldado, a convicted rapist, is celebrated as a patron saint, has been forsaken by the country around which it shaped its identity. Eager to please, Tijuana created a kind of tarnished American Dream for migrants seeking a pathway to a better life, while simultaneously offering Americans escape from the moral confines that their dream had imposed. The friction between those opposing desires is the lifeblood of this place. It also feeds the ongoing barter that occurs here at the edge of the empire: drugs pass through the border wall as easily—and frequently—as the squadrons of pelicans that surf the waves beyond its rusty edge, heroin and other opioids providing relief from the stressors of American life. Tens of thousands of Mexicans subject themselves to the random humiliation of border security each day to tend to the homes of Southern Californians. And in the Zona, the women wait for both death and desire—their end and that which prolongs it—with thousands more ready to take their places. Perhaps they'll say furtive prayers for their own protection as they see an officer or narco advancing upon them. Let us hope that Juan Soldado, the city's protector, is truly the saint of the dispossessed, and not just a man who sparked a femicide.

There is a final way in which epidemiology mirrors augury. Both require deaths. In traditions ranging across all of the world's continents, omens are read in entrails and cracked bones, the manner by which the flesh falls to the earth portending some future doom or salvation. In Tijuana, as the femicide rages on, driven by the fear that has spread from America's heart and into the empire's fringes, we dissect the epidemic's data for hints of how the future might unfold for women in the city. And that's where the epidemiologist's burden truly lies. We paint portraits of epidemics, those ruthless phenomena of nature, humanity's constant companions, in order to name the future we hope to avoid. All the facets of this science—its scrupulous attention to detail, its rigorous modeling, the care taken in asking the right questions and recruiting the right people—all of this is done in the hope that from past deaths some meaning, at least, might be gleaned to stave off the deaths to come.

Acknowledgments

I love Tijuana. It's a city beset with deep structural problems, but it's also a place full of energy, richness, and optimism. This book focuses on a particular subpopulation that daily faces down a daunting set of risks. But Tijuana is a much bigger city than the Zona Norte, and there's a reason that, despite the seemingly exponential increase in the homicide rate over the past few years, it's nevertheless experiencing a renaissance in food, visual art, architecture, and fashion. I would encourage everyone who has read this book to visit Tijuana and experience firsthand its transformation from forgotten American outpost to Mexican cultural hub. It is unlike any other city I have visited and like the best cities, it rewards exploration.

I would like to acknowledge the dedication and exceptional skill of my editor, Ben Hyman, under whose firm and friendly guidance this book took shape. I am proud of this work and much of that feeling is due to Ben's tirelessness in nurturing its strengths and gently excising its weaknesses. Kirby Kim, my agent at Janklow & Nesbitt, understood early on both the value of epidemiology as a narrative lens and the importance of telling the story of the victims of the U.S.'s border policies. Kirby's vision was a guiding light and I am lucky to know him. Miranda Elliott has, throughout our relationship, challenged me to better understand what intimacy really means, both in our life together but also in my orientation to the world at large. I am so grateful for that.

Other people helped this book along its journey. I am indebted to Teresita Rocha Jimenez, whose empathy and intelligence were instrumental in forging connections with many of the people profiled in this book and across Tijuana. I also acknowledge Jaime Arredondo Sanchez Lira, whose knowledge of Tijuana's many power brokers and connections with law enforcement helped enormously in my understanding of the city. Linda Spalding and Tessa McWatt both read early sections of the book and provided excellent and constructive feedback. Karolina Waclawiak and Andi Winette edited a longform piece at *The Believer* magazine that became the kernel for *City of Omens*. Lauren Sharp pushed me to improve the clarity of my vision for the book, which paid dividends. John Ortved was instrumental in launching this book along its path to publication. My parents instilled in me a love of reading, and my mother Elly Werb's dedication to writing inspired my own practice. Pat Placzek taught me the value of art for art's sake.

There are a number of agencies and individuals working to effect positive change in Tijuana, particularly among migrants, marginalized women, and people who use drugs. Among those, I am most familiar with Prevencasa (https://donate.icfdn.org/npo/prevencasa), Centro Ser (http://centroser.org/), Las Memorias (http://www.lasmemorias.org/), and Dr. Patty Gonzalez's Wound Clinic (http://globalhealth.ucsd.edu/resources /spotlights/archive/Pages/WoundClinic.aspx). All would benefit greatly from donations.

Notes

Chapter 1: Welcome to El Bordo

11 about 5 percent of people who inject drugs Steffanie A. Strathdee, Remedios Lozada, Victoria D. Ojeda et al., "Differential Effects of Migration and Deportation on HIV Infection Among Male and Female Injection Drug Users in Tijuana, Mexico," *PLoS ONE* 3, no. 7 (2008): e2690.

11 12 percent are believed to be HIV-positive Steffanie A. Strathdee et al., "Reductions in HIV/STI Incidence and Sharing of Injection Equipment among Female Sex Workers Who Inject Drugs: Results from a Randomized Controlled Trial," *PLoS ONE* 8, no. 6 (2013): e65812.

13 "this might explode someday" Kate Callen, "U.S. Navy Tested Tijuana Prostitutes for AIDS," United Press International, 1989.

17 "affords subsistence or lodgment" Miquel Porta, ed., *A Dictionary of Epidemiology*, 6th ed. (New York: Oxford University Press, 2014), 137.

17 "all that which is external to the individual human host." Ibid., 93.

17 literally, causing a pathological process Ibid., 211.

20 raise it as much as fourfold Ming Ding et al., "Long-Term Coffee Consumption and Risk of Cardiovascular Disease: A Systematic Review and a Dose-Response Meta-analysis of Prospective Cohort Studies," *Circulation* 129, no. 6 (February 2014): 643–59.

22 the stakes were too high to produce shoddy science The study on clean needle distribution and injection drug use cessation was eventually published after I got the statistical analysis right. Dan Werb et al., "Patterns of Injection Drug Use Cessation during an Expansion of Syringe Exchange Services in a Canadian Setting," *Drug and Alcohol Dependence* 132, no. 3 (October 2013): 535–40.

Chapter 2: The Price of Something Purchased

28 a state north of Jalisco along the Sea of Cortez Jonathan Marshall, "CIA Assets and the Rise of the Guadalajara Connection," *Crime, Law and Social Change* 16, no. 1 (July 1991): 85–96.

28 a famously corrupt Mexican intelligence agency The DFS was dissolved in 1985 as a result of endemic corruption.

28 profiting handsomely from the international drug trade Dirección Federal de Seguridad (Mexico) Security Reports, 1970–1977, Benson Latin American Collection, University of Texas at Austin. See historical note at https://legacy.lib.utexas.edu/taro/utlac/00200/lac-00200.html.

28 dubbed the Guadalajara Cartel Elaine Shannon, *Desperados: Latin Drug Lords, U.S. Lawmen, and the War America Can't Win* (Bloomington, IN: iUniverse, 2015).

29 the basis for the plaza system Diego Esparza, Antonio Ugues Jr., and Paul Hernandez, "The History of Mexican Drug Policy," paper presented at the annual meeting of the Western Political Science Association (Portland, OR: March 22–24, 2012).

29 "the price of something purchased." Alonso de Molina, Vocabulario en Lengua Castellana y Mexicana (Mexico City: Casa de Antonio de Spinosa, 1571).

31 the central hub of cartel power Carmen Boullosa and Mike Wallace, "How the Cartels Were Born," *Jacobin*, Spring 2015.

31 Ocampo's murder was undertaken by a federal police commando unit Anabel Hernández, *Narcoland: The Mexican Drug Lords and Their Godfathers* (London: Verso, 2013), 25.

31 their pain scoring the city Duncan Tucker, "Young Women Are Getting Abducted off the Streets of Mexico's Second Largest City," *VICE News*, March 28, 2016.

31 the Mérida Initiative, a militarized show of friendship Clare Ribando Seelke and Kristin Finklea, *U.S.-Mexican Security Cooperation: The Mérida Initiative and Beyond*, CRS Report No. R41349 (Washington, DC: Congressional Research Service, 2017).

34 shipped in from Afghanistan through new drug-trafficking routes Glenn Greenwald, *Drug Decriminalization in Portugal: Lessons for Creating Fair and Successful Drug Policies* (Washington, DC: Cato Institute, 2009), 6.

34 offered a slew of services Caitlin Hughes and Alex Stevens, *The Effects of the Decriminalization of Drug Use in Portugal* (London: Beckley Foundation Drug Policy Programme, 2007), 3.

34 use of heroin dropped by about 25 percent Ibid.

34 significantly fewer people were becoming addicted Caitlin Hughes and Alex Stevens, "What Can We Learn from the Portuguese Decriminalization of Illicit Drugs?" *British Journal of Criminology* 50, no 6 (November 2010): 999–1022.

35 the ecology of laws around heroin use that transforms it Tens of thousands of people are injected with morphine—heroin by another name—every day in hospitals around the world by trained specialists using sterile equipment; few people seem to think that's a problem. The value judgment around whether opioids should be used arises, I would argue, when the type of pain being treated is psychic rather than physical.

37 hybrid pig-duck influenza strains K. F. Shortridge, "Pandemic Influenza: A Zoonosis?" *Seminars in Respiratory Infections* 7, no. 1 (March 1992): 11–25.

42 sell the drops to other clients or keep them to use Steffanie A. Strathdee et al., "'Vivo para Consumirla y la Consumo para Vivir' ['I Live to Inject and Inject to Live']: High-Risk Injection Behaviors in Tijuana, Mexico," *Journal of Urban Health* 82, suppl. 4 (December 2005): iv58–iv73.

Chapter 3: The Threshold

48 Francisco Palou erected a cross George W. Hendry, "Francisco Palou's Boundary Marker," *California Historical Society Quarterly* 5, no. 4 (December 1926): 321–27.

48 their rivals to the south, the Dominicans of Baja California In 1926, intrepid historians published an account of finding "Palou's rock," the location of which had been lost to the ages. They buried a bottle of Chianti to mark the spot and posed for photographs on top of the rock while holding a rattlesnake.

49 view impending battles from a safe remove Claire F. Fox, *The Fence and the River: Culture and Politics at the U.S.-Mexico Border* (Minneapolis: University of Minnesota Press, 1999).

51 as if by centrifugal force Javier Osorio, "The Contagion of Drug Violence: Spatiotemporal Dynamics of the Mexican War on Drugs," *Journal of Conflict Resolution* 59, no. 8 (December 2015): 1403–32.

52 a fat gray line representing a threshold of murders Eduardo Guerrero Gutiérrez, "Epidemias de Violencia," *Nexos*, July 1, 2012.

53 over sixteen hundred rapes and sexual crimes were recorded Incidencia Delictiva Registradas ante Procuraduria General de Justicia del Estado: Año 2016. Secretaría de Seguridad Pública del Estado. 2017.

53 The bodies, upon examination, reveal multiple causes of death Michael Lettieri, *Violence against Women in Mexico* (San Diego: Trans-Border Institute, Joan B. Kroc School of Peace Studies, University of San Diego, 2017).

54 shown to increase an individual's risk of being obese Nicholas A. Christakis and James H. Fowler, "Social Contagion Theory: Examining Dynamic Social Networks and Human Behavior," *Statistics in Medicine* 32, no. 4 (February 2013): 556–77.

55 mapping subtle tonal differences in birdsong See, for example, Lewis Petrinovich and Thomas L. Patterson, "The Responses of White-Crowned Sparrows to Songs of Different Dialects and Subspecies," *Zeitschrift für Tierpsychologie* 57, no. 1 (1981): 1–14.

56 "[HIV] is militarily relevant" Edmund Tramont and Donald Burke, "AIDS/HIV in the US Military," *Vaccine* 11, no. 5 (1993): 529–33.

56 "a paper using the data from the global survey" Lydia Temoshok et al., "Risk of HIV Transmission in Infected US Military Personnel," *The Lancet* 347 (1996): 697–98.

56 freed soldiers from "traditional social controls," Soldiers, as a group of people confined within a system of control, systematically put themselves in harm's way after having ceded a certain amount of control over their bodies. From an epidemiologic perspective—that is, in the ways that matter to disease progression —soldiers and sex workers resemble each other.

57 "African militaries would be severely hampered in multiple ways" Robert Ostergard Jr., "HIV/AIDS, the Military and the Future of Africa's Security," (presented at the International Studies Association Annual Conference, March 17–20, Montreal, 2004).

60 English physician John Snow began investigating a cholera outbreak Sandra Hempel, "John Snow," *The Lancet* 381, no. 9874 (April 13, 2013): 1269–70. This correction by *The Lancet*'s editors—155 years after John Snow's death—represents an extremely posthumous and tongue-in-cheek attempt at addressing the fact that the journal had derided Snow's accomplishments during his lifetime.

Chapter 4: The Canyons and the Mesa

73 The maquila program kicked off in 1965 David W. Eaton, "Transformation of the Maquiladora Industry: The Driving Force Behind the Creation of a NAFTA Regional Economy," *Arizona Journal of International & Comparative Law* 14 (Fall 1997): 747–837.

74 forty million or so flat-screen televisions bought by Americans each year Robbie Whelan and Santiago Pérez, "Why Your Flat-Screen TV Would Cost More if Nafta Ends," *Wall Street Journal*, November 27, 2017.

74 roughly one hundred thousand women, many of whom are migrants Kate Gallagher, *Tijuana Regional Profile* (San Diego: San Diego Regional EDC, February 13, 2017).

74 almost every single pacemaker sewn into the hearts of Americans Sarah Varney, "Also Made in Mexico: Lifesaving Medical Devices," *New York Times*, March 31, 2017.

75 the number of migrants coming to the city far exceeds the number of jobs All data from the Instituto Nacional de Estadística y Geografía. Available at http://www.inegi.org.mx.

76 Fordlândia was meant to house ten thousand workers Greg Grandin, *Fordlandia: The Rise and Fall of Henry Ford's Forgotten Jungle City* (New York: Metropolitan Books, 2009).

78 California drivers burn through forty-two million tires a year Zach St. George, "Unwanted California Tires End Up in Rivers and Beaches," *High Country News*, March 30, 2015.

79 eighty thousand pounds of waste tires removed Ibid.

79 CalRecycle can only act as a middleman Ibid.

79 end up being resold or dumped in Mexico Wendy Fry, Alejandro Alejandre, and Lynn Walsh, "Money in California Tire Recycling Management Fund Isn't Used for Recycling," NBC San Diego, February 12, 2015.

81 studied the pollution's effect on local communities Wael K. Al-Delaimy, Catherine Wood Larsen, and Keith Pezzoli, "Differences in Health Symptoms Among Residents Living Near Illegal Dump Sites in Los Laureles Canyon, Tijuana, Mexico: A Cross Sectional Survey," *International Journal of Environmental Research and Public Health* 11, no. 9 (September 2014): 9532–52.

83 why clinicians were seeing different symptoms cluster Harvey J. Alter et al., "Detection of Antibody to Hepatitis C Virus in Prospectively Followed Transfusion Recipients with Acute and Chronic Non-A, Non-B Hepatitis," *New England Journal of Medicine* 321, no. 22 (November 30, 1989): 1494–1500.

83 the virus may retreat and lie dormant Harvey J. Alter and Leonard B. Seeff, "Recovery, Persistence, and Sequelae in Hepatitis C Virus Infection: A Perspective on Long-Term Outcome," *Seminars in Liver Disease* 20, no. 1 (2000): 17–35.

84 it "confounded" the relationship between coffee and lung cancer Richard Riegelman, *Studying a Study and Testing a Test: How to Read the Medical Evidence*, 10th edition (Netherlands: Wolters Kluwer, 2004).

85 Actuaries, because they are obsessed For a great introduction to this subject, see Shane Whelan, "Chapter 1: Introduction to (Actuarial) Modelling," in *Lecture Notes: Models/Stochastic Models*, 2006. Available at docuri.com /download/1introduction-to-modelling_59bf3b3cf581716e46c54cf0_pdf.

Chapter 5: The Beat

91 kidnappings spiked to 92 These data are all produced by the Secretaría de Seguridad Pública del Estado de Baja California. Annual reports on crimes registered in the state's major cities are available at http://www.seguridadbc .gob.mx/contenidos/estadisticas2.php.

92 Zeta, a fierce and sensational weekly magazine Andrea Noel, "Suicide Journalism on the Crazy-Mean Streets of Tijuana," *Daily Beast*, December 10, 2016.

92 ranked the most dangerous country in the world for journalists Steven M. Ellis, "Mexico Most Deadly Country for Journalists in 2017," International Press Institute, December 19, 2017.

93 a vest made out of Xolo skin Matthew T. Hall, "Ex-Tijuana mayor, Xolos Owner Jorge Hank Has a Dogskin Vest," *San Diego Union-Tribune*, May 1, 2013.

93 traffic a Siberian white tiger cub Josh Kun, "The Island of Jorge Hank Rhon," *LA Weekly*, February 15, 2006.

93 "Law Enforcement High Jinks in TJ" Available at wikileaks.org/plusd /cables/09TIJUANA709_a.html.

93 shot and killed while waiting in traffic Kevin Sullivan, "Gunmen Kill Editor of Tijuana Newspaper," *Washington Post*, June 23, 2004.

94 sent back to the police academy for training Richard Marosi, "500 Police Officers Replaced in Tijuana," *Los Angeles Times*, November 19, 2008.

94 Capella Ibarra was fired Jo Tuckman, "Tijuana Police Chief Fired after Weekend of Violence," *Guardian*, December 2, 2008.

95 El Teo, a high-ranking capo Lizbeth Diaz, "Tijuana Violence Slows as One Cartel Takes Control," *Borderland Beat*, September 6, 2011.

95 El Pozolero [the Soup Maker] Marc Lacey, "Mexican Man Admits Using Acid on Bodies, Army Says," *New York Times*, January 24, 2009.

95 Cartel Tijuana Nueva Generación Christopher Woody, "Cartels Are Leaving Grisly Displays as a Warning at a Major US-Mexico Border Crossing," *Business Insider*, November 4, 2016.

96 over one hundred thousand Mexicans have been killed Associated Press, "100,000 Dead, 30,000 Missing: Mexico's War on Drugs Turns 10," CBSNews .com, December 11, 2016.

98 the leading cause of unintentional injury Deborah Dowell et al., "Contribution of Opioid-Involved Poisoning to the Change in Life Expectancy in the United States, 2000–2015," *Journal of the American Medical Association* 318, no. 11 (September 19, 2017): 1065–67.

98 might relapse three times James Bell et al., "Cycling In and Out of Treatment; Participation in Methadone Treatment in NSW, 1990–2002," *Drug and Alcohol Dependence* 81, no. 1 (January 2006): 55–61.

99 the most effective tool we have to treat addiction Laura Amato et al., "An Overview of Systematic Reviews of the Effectiveness of Opiate Maintenance Therapies: Available Evidence to Inform Clinical Practice and Research," *Journal of Substance Abuse Treatment* 28, no. 4 (June 2005): 321–29.

99 8 percent of people eligible for methadone Louisa Degenhardt et al., "What Has Been Achieved in HIV Prevention, Treatment and Care for People Who Inject Drugs, 2010–2012? A Review of the Six Highest Burden Countries," *International Journal of Drug Policy* 25, no. 1 (January 2014): 53–60.

99 less than four thousand people are officially enrolled Bradley M. Mathers et al., "HIV Prevention, Treatment, and Care Services for People Who Inject Drugs: A Systematic Review of Global, Regional, and National Coverage," *The Lancet* 375, no. 9719 (March 20, 2010): 1014–28.

107 making Tijuana the most dangerous big city All data from annual reports of the Secretaría de Seguridad Pública del Estado de Baja California: "Incidencia Delictiva Registradas ante Procuraduria General de Justiciar del Estado."

Chapter 6: Shore Leave

111 one in five American servicemen sent to fight M. Duncan Stanton, "Drugs, Vietnam, and the Vietnam Veteran: An Overview," *American Journal of Drug and Alcohol Abuse* 3, no. 4 (1976): 557–70.

111 doctors refused to interpret drug use within a social context Hannah Cooper, "Medical Theories of Opiate Addiction's Aetiology and Their Relationship to Addicts' Perceived Social Position in the United States: An Historical Analysis," *International Journal of Drug Policy* 15, no. 5–6 (December 2004): 435–45.

112 "psychopathology and addiction coincide fairly well" Granville W. Larimore and Henry Brill, "Epidemiologic Factors in Drug Addiction in England and the United States," *Public Health Reports (1896–1970)* 77, no. 7 (July 1962): 555–60.

112 the Framingham Heart Study Syed S. Mahmood et al., "The Framingham Heart Study and the Epidemiology of Cardiovascular Diseases: A Historical Perspective," *The Lancet* 383, no. 9921 (March 15, 2014): 999–1008.

114 "no correlation between psychiatric diagnosis and drug used" Peter L. Putnam and Everett H. Ellinwood Jr., "Narcotic Addiction among Physicians: A Ten-Year Follow-Up," paper presented at the 121st Annual meeting of the American Psychiatric Association (New York: May 3–7, 1965).

114 twice as many of the then-physicians had used drugs George E. Vaillant, Jane R. Brighton, and Charles McArthur, "Physicians' Use of Mood-Altering Drugs: A 20-Year Follow-Up Report," *New England Journal of Medicine* 282, no. 7: 365–70.

114 doctors were primed to self-medicate Patrick H. Hughes et al., "Resident Physician Substance Use, by Specialty," *American Journal of Psychiatry* 149, no. 10 (October 1992): 1348–54.

115 otherwise known as the epidemiologic triangle Council on Mental Health, "Narcotics and Medical Practice: Medical Use of Morphine and Morphine-like Drugs and Management of Persons Dependent on Them," *Journal of the American Medical Association* 218, no. 4 (October 25, 1971): 578–83.

115 between 100,000 and 200,000 Americans had started using opioids William M. Compton and Nora D. Volkow, "Major Increases in Opioid Analgesic Abuse in the United States: Concerns and Strategies," *Drug and Alcohol Dependence* 81, no. 2 (February 2006): 103–7.

115 "the infectious agent is heroin" Mark H. Greene, "An Epidemiologic Assessment of Heroin Use," *American Journal of Public Health* 64, suppl. 12 (1974): 1–10.

115 "Dope? Do you think the Russians allow dope? Hell no" Sunil Kumar Aggarwal, "Health Scientist Blacklisting and the Meaning of Marijuana in the Oval Office in the Early 1970s," *Medium*, July 1, 2015.

118 The kids, by and large, had started injecting within the very same neighborhood where I worked Dan Werb et al., "Drug-Related Risks Among Street Youth in Two Neighborhoods in a Canadian Setting," *Health & Place* 16, no. 5 (September 2010): 1061–67.

118 a murder-suicide a few days after a trip across the border to the Zona Vincent Cabeza de Baca and Juan Cabeza de Baca, "The 'Shame Suicides' and Tijuana," *Journal of the Southwest* 43, no. 4 (Winter 2001): 603–35.

119 *Pollero*, or "chicken farmer" All of the information in this section comes from polleros in Tijuana who declined to consent to have their names or identifiers used.

120 "there's a lot more people that have drowned" Sebastian Rotella, "A River of Hope Becomes River of Tears," *Los Angeles Times*, February 22, 1993.

125 more than five million Americans who crossed the border seeking alcohol, prostitution, and horseraces "Tijuana—Evolucion de la Poblacion 1900 hasta 2010." Foro Mexico. Last updated on April 4, 2018. Available at: https://www.foro-mexico.com/baja-california/tijuana/mensaje-354925.html.

126 "the letting down of moral conduct" Dominique Brégent-Heald, "The Tourism of Titillation in Tijuana and Niagara Falls: Cross-Border Tourism and Hollywood Films between 1896 and 1960," *Journal of the Canadian Historical Association* 17, no. 1 (2006): 179–203.

126 Butter, coffee, sugar, cooking fat, and gasoline were all closely rationed Arthur Herman, *Freedom's Forge: How American Business Produced Victory in World War II* (New York: Random House, 2012), 153, 162–65, 171.

127 "wander into a book store and study pornographic books" Keith Monroe, "Tijuana: Border Hell Town," *Coronet*, September 1956.

127 "and other American vermin" Roberta Ridgely, "The Man Who Built Tijuana," *San Diego Magazine*, 1966.

127 "Its sailors visit Tijuana every weekend" Kate Callen, "U.S. Navy Tested Tijuana Prostitutes for AIDS," UPI, February 10, 1989.

128 "The intent is just to look out for the Marines' safety" William M. Welch, "Tijuana Off-Limits to U.S. Marines," *USA Today*, January 22, 2009.

Chapter 7: Mythmaking

135 people in one setting susceptible to an epidemic Incidentally, one of the reasons why the U.S.'s current opioid overdose crisis took so long to be recognized is exactly because of a failure to generate a comparison group in the areas affected by the crisis. Since the Nixon presidency, the American system of drug use and disease surveillance has focused primarily on inner cities, where addiction and HIV have pooled disproportionately among communities of color. As levels of opioid use rose precipitously in rural areas among majority white populations, it took a massive reorientation of the public health apparatus to arm epidemiologists with the basic surveillance tools they needed to identify the expanded contours of this modern opioid epidemic, which was necessary before anyone could start to respond. The inevitable lag that accompanied this retooling was one of many key reasons that the crisis accelerated out of control before anyone could take action.

136 over 170,000 victims, with over 280,000 people internally displaced Diego Oré, "Mexico Overturns Law Meant to Regulate Troops in Drug War," Reuters, November 15, 2018; Jo Tuckman, "Thousands Displaced by Mexico's

Drug Wars: Government Is 'Deaf and Blind' to Our Plight," *Guardian*, April 3, 2015.

138 an ethical imperative not to share HIV test results Dermot Maher, "The Ethics of Feedback of HIV Test Results in Population-Based Surveys of HIV Infection," *Bulletin of the World Health Organization* 91, no. 12 (December 2013): 950–56.

139 scientists and their funders had engaged in major ethical lapses Jerome A. Singh and Edward J. Mills, "The Abandoned Trials of Pre-exposure Prophylaxis for HIV: What Went Wrong?" *PLoS Medicine* 2, no. 9 (2005): e234.

143 a clearance rate of 12 percent Sandra Dibble, John Gibbins, and Alejandro Tamayo, "The Deadliest Year," *San Diego Union-Tribune*, August 27, 2017.

143 made up of eight separate genetic segments Hannah Hoag, "Study Revives Bird Origin for 1918 Flu Pandemic," *Nature*, February 16, 2014.

143 an 1872 horse flu epidemic Ibid.

143 even responsible for the Great Boston Fire Tara Smith, "The 1872 Equine Influenza Epidemic That Sickened Most U.S. Horses," *Mental Floss*, July 1, 2015.

144 two rogue sailors killed a sex worker in a hotel "Soldiers Formally Charged in Tijuana Prostitute Attack," KGTV-TV San Diego, February 9, 2009.

Chapter 8: Modes of Control

145 the incestuous coupling of the Sun and his sister the Moon Constance Goddard DuBois, "The Story of the Chaup: A Myth of the Diegueños," *Journal of American Folklore* 17, no. 67 (October–December 1904): 217–42.

146 in 1990, around five hundred maquiladora firms operated Per Strömberg, *The Mexican Maquila Industry and the Environment: An Overview of the Issues* (New York: United Nations Publications, 2002).

147 a time when the number of women killed in the city was relatively low These rates are all derived by cross-referencing homicide data stratified by gender from Mexico's Instituto Nacional de Estadística y Geografía with publicly available data on Tijuana's population demographics.

148 What was a "pathological process"? Jonathan D. Sleath, "Diseases Are Really Just Examples of Pathological Processes," *BMJ* 342 (May 3, 2011): d2548.

157 female murders among the city's total homicides had dropped Instituto Nacional de Estadística y Geografía, "Porcentaje de Muertes por Homicidio con Respecto al Total de Muertes Violentas por Entidad Federativa y Sexo, 2004 a 2015," November 17, 2016.

157 at least 12 percent acquired the virus Steffanie A. Strathdee et al., "Reductions in HIV/STI Incidence and Sharing of Injection Equipment Among Female Sex Workers Who Inject Drugs: Results from a Randomized Controlled Trial," *PloS ONE* 8, no. 6 (2013): e65812.

163 as with many myths, there is another version Dubois, "The Story of the Chaup," 217–18.

Chapter 9: Causation

170 people who paid a bribe to police were more likely, not less, to access methadone Dan Werb et al., "Police Bribery and Access to Methadone Maintenance Therapy Within the Context of Drug Policy Reform in Tijuana, Mexico," *Drug and Alcohol Dependence* 148 (2015): 221–25.

171 only 8 percent of the sample— less than fifty people in total—had actually been enrolled Ibid.

175 action within that buffer was likely to discourage people Dan Werb et al., "Spatial Patterns of Arrests, Police Assault and Addiction Treatment Center Locations in Tijuana, Mexico," *Addiction* 111, no. 7 (July 2016): 1246–56.

178 city-wide systems leading to the death of women Sergio González Rodríguez, *The Femicide Machine*, trans. Michael Parker-Stainback (Cambridge, MA: MIT Press, 2012).

181 83 million crossings recorded Border crossing entry data, Bureau of Transportation Statistics, United States Bureau of Transportation. Available at: https://www.bts.gov/content/border-crossingentry-data.

183 a discontinuous outcome, a sudden jarring shift Catastrophe theory, also known as chaos theory, is a branch of mathematics that links system-wide events to minute alterations in variables that might seem, at first glance, irrelevant. It's a useful way to track the unpredictable spread of certain epidemics, and it is one of the few epidemiologic methods that has also made the leap from the annals of scientific journals to the epicenter of pop culture. This is the theory popularly captured by the so-called butterfly effect, which posits that a butterfly flapping its wings in China can cause a tornado in New Mexico. While that's a fanciful notion, catastrophe theory has some very real implications for how epidemiologists track outbreaks and disease. A catastrophe, in formal epidemiologic terms, is a sudden change resulting from a discontinuous process. One example of catastrophe theory in practice (pulled from the John Last's *Dictionary of Epidemiology*, of course) is the boiling point of water: if we only observed water heating to 211 degrees Fahrenheit, we would assume that adding more heat would simply make the water hotter. At 212 degrees Fahrenheit, though, water begins to boil. The linear association between adding energy and seeing an increase of one degree in the heat of water is suddenly interrupted by the discontinuous process of water turning to steam. While it's obvious after the fact, it's difficult to predict that a difference of just one degree will suddenly turn liquid into vapor until you observe it happening. Catastrophe theory isn't the predictable increase in traffic on the Vía Rápida during rush hour. It's the collision of that traffic with a woman, like Angie, who has been running along her own linear path over the canal's low walls.

185 moved the femicide from outbreak to epidemic All data from the Instituto Nacional de Estadística y Geografía. Available at http://www.inegi .org.mx.

185 well below the threshold of 5 percent José Luis Valdespino-Gómez et al., "Las Enfermedades de Transmisión Sexual y la Epidemia de VIH/SIDA," *Salud Pública de México* 37 (1995): 549–55.

185 prevalence of HIV doubled among a sample of women Annick Borquez et al., "The Effect of Public Health-Oriented Drug Law Reform on HIV Incidence in People Who Inject Drugs in Tijuana, Mexico: An Epidemic Modelling Study," *Lancet Public Health* 3, no. 9 (September 1, 2018): e429–37.

185 only 2.5 percent of men who injected drugs were infected Esmeralda Íñiguez-Stevens et al., "Estimaciones de Prevalencia del VIH por Género y Grupo de Riesgo en Tijuana, México: 2006," *Gaceta Médica de México* 145, no. 3 (May 2009): 189–95.

186 equivalent to 263 HIV cases per 100,000 women Kimberly C. Brouwer et al., "Estimated Numbers of Men and Women Infected with HIV/AIDS in Tijuana, Mexico," *Journal of Urban Health* 83, no. 2 (March 2006): 299–307.

Chapter 10: And Yet They Love Them

191 post-Enlightenment scientific positivism Tom Steele, "The Role of Scientific Positivism in European Popular Educational Movements: The Case of France," *International Journal of Lifelong Education* 21, no. 5 (2002): 399–413.

191 meticulously planned neighborhoods Vukan R. Vuchic, *Urban Transit Systems and Technology* (Hoboken, NJ: Wiley & Sons, 2007).

192 muscardine, a fungal disease that afflicted silkworms M. Schwartz, "The Life and Works of Louis Pasteur," *Journal of Applied Microbiology* 91, no. 4 (October 2001): 597–601.

192 age-old dilemma of rural Europe's most tenacious plague Louis Pasteur, Chamberland, and Roux, "Summary Report of the Experiments Conducted at Pouilly-le-Fort, Near Melun, on the Anthrax Vaccination, 1881," *Yale Journal of Biology and Medicine* 75, no. 1 (January–February 2002): 59–62.

194 HIGHLY EFFECTIVE AGAINST ANTHRAX Greg Winter, "A Nation Challenged: The Pharmacies; Sí, We Have Cipro; the Panicky and the Profiteers Head to Mexico," *New York Times*, October 20, 2001.

196 typically fund fewer than one in five projects "Research Project Success Rates by NIH Institute for 2017," National Institutes of Health Research Portfolio Online Reporting Tools. Available at https://report.nih.gov/success _rates/Success_ByIC.cfm. Studying the varying levels of funding success at different institutions is one way that savvy researchers look to improve their chances of securing support for their work. Often, there is at least some overlap between the aims of the various bodies that make up the National Institutes of Health. A scientist can take advantage of that fact by framing their research proposals to respond to the goals of whichever institute currently has the higher chances of providing funding.

199 4 percent of the clients he interviewed tested positive for HIV Thomas L. Patterson et al., "Correlates of HIV, STIs and Associated High Risk Behaviors Among Male Clients of Female Sex Workers in Tijuana, Mexico," *AIDS* 23, no. 13 (August 24, 2009): 1765–71.

200 anxiety and isolation of these deportees Shira Goldenberg et al., "'Over Here, It's Just Drugs, Women and All the Madness': The HIV Risk Environment of Clients of Female Sex Workers in Tijuana, Mexico," *Social Science & Medicine* 72, no. 7 (April 2011): 1185–92.

202 as many as 12 percent were infected after 2006 Steffanie A. Strathdee and Carlos Magis-Rodriguez, "Mexico's Evolving HIV Epidemic," *Journal of the American Medical Association* 300, no. 5 (2008): 571–73.

203 they served foreign clients, used drugs with their clients, and worked on the street Erin E. Conners et al., "Structural Determinants of Client Perpetrated Violence among Female Sex Workers in Two Mexico-U.S. Border Cities," *AIDS and Behavior* 20, no. 1 (January 2016): 215–24.

209 Tijuanenses reported that they did not trust the force Esther Hernández, "Policías de BC Tienen el Mejor Salario del País," Frontera.info, July 12, 2017. Available at https://www.frontera.info/EdicionEnLinea/Notas /Noticias/12072017/1235394-Policias-de-BC-tienen-el-mejor-salario-del-pais .html.

211 sex workers who used drugs in Tijuana more likely to have their syringes confiscated Leo Beletsky et al., "Syringe Confiscation as an HIV Risk Factor: The Public Health Implications of Arbitrary Policing in Tijuana and Ciudad Juarez, Mexico," *Journal of Urban Health* 90, no. 2 (2013): 284–98.

Chapter 11: The Bottom Line

217 thirty thousand pills worth tens of millions of dollars—destined first for Tijuana Sandra Dibble, "Record Fentanyl Seizure by Mexican Military Was Headed for Tijuana," *San Diego Union-Tribune*, August 25, 2017.

220 eight thousand women initially signed up to receive registration cards James C. McKinley Jr., "A New Law in Tijuana Regulates the Oldest Profession," *New York Times*, December 13, 2005.

221 shipping eight hundred thousand condoms per month into the Zona Kate Callen, "U.S. Navy Tested Tijuana Prostitutes for AIDS," United Press International, 1989.

221 zero cases of HIV among the Zona's sex workers Patrick McDonnell, "Study by U.S. Navy, Mexicans Shows No AIDS in 357 Tijuana Prostitutes," *Los Angeles Times*, February 11, 1989.

223 about 50 percent fewer women in the Tijuana group Steffanie A. Strathdee et al., "Reductions in HIV/STI Incidence and Sharing of Injection Equipment Among Female Sex Workers Who Inject Drugs: Results from a Randomized Controlled Trial," *PLoS ONE* 8, no. 6 (2013): e65812.

225 they have proven to be spectacularly successful Chloé Potier et al., "Supervised Injection Services: What Has Been Demonstrated? A Systematic Literature Review," *Drug and Alcohol Dependence* 145 (December 2014): 48–68.

225 not a single person has died after overdosing Jo Kimber, Kate Dolan, and Alex Wodak, *International Survey of Supervised Injecting Centres (1999–2000)*, Technical Report 126 (Sydney: National Alcohol and Drug Research Centre, 2001). Available at https://ndarc.med.unsw.edu.au/resource/international-survey-supervised-injecting-centres-1999-2000. Since the publication of this report, no deaths have been reported at any supervised injection sites in the world.

225 almost 25 percent of people who injected drugs in the neighborhood were HIV-positive Steffanie A. Strathdee et al., "Needle Exchange Is Not Enough: Lessons from the Vancouver Injecting Drug Use Study," *AIDS* 11, no. 8 (July 1997): F59–65.

226 Insite, in the midst of the Downtown Eastside, meant being at the epicenter of a success story Despite the effectiveness of Insite in reducing injection-related risks among its clients, Vancouver still faces long odds in controlling an epidemic of opioid overdose deaths that in 2017 claimed 432 people, roughly equivalent to an annual overdose death rate of 35 per 100,000 people. It is a truly horrifying—and preventable—epidemic that likely requires a major policy shift (the regulation of the illegal opioid market) to control.

229 drug law enforcement usually ended up increasing drug market violence Dan Werb et al., "Effect of Drug Law Enforcement on Drug Market Violence: A Systematic Review," *International Journal of Drug Policy* 22, no. 2 (March 2011): 87–94.

229 many supposed "clinics" were no better than labor camps Dan Werb et al., "The Effectiveness of Compulsory Drug Treatment: A Systematic Review," *International Journal of Drug Policy* 28 (February 2016): 1–9.

230 almost four hundred new HIV cases attributable to drug injecting across the province of British Columbia Mark W. Hull and Julio Montaner, "HIV Treatment as Prevention: The Key to an AIDS-Free Generation," *Journal of Food and Drug Analysis* 21, no. 4 (December 2013): S95–S101.

230 By 2016, there were only sixteen BC Centre for Disease Control, *HIV in British Columbia: Annual Surveillance Report 2016* (Vancouver: British Columbia Centre for Disease Control, 2018). Available at http://www.bccdc .ca/search?k=hiv%20percent20annual%percent20report.

Chapter 12: Endless Variation

233 This linear narrative, though, conceals a murkier story For details of Soldado's story, I've relied on Paul J. Vanderwood, *Juan Soldado: Rapist, Murderer, Martyr, Saint* (Durham, NC: Duke University Press, 2004).

234 "the lawyer of the impossible" Luis D. León, "Metaphor and Place: The U.S.-Mexico Border as Center and Periphery in the Interpretation of Religion," *Journal of the American Academy of Religion* 67, no. 3 (September 1999): 541–71.

235 reporting on an outbreak of HIV infection in Chicago Ethan Morgan et al., "HIV-1 Infection and Transmission Networks of Younger People in Chicago, Illinois, 2005–2011," *Public Health Reports* 132, no. 1 (January–February 2017): 48–55.

236 after thousands of Haitians had successfully crossed into the United States through Tijuana Kirk Semple, "Haitians, after Perilous Journey, Find Door to U.S. Abruptly Shut," *New York Times*, September 23, 2016.

237 "what we need is someone with a stronger hand" Sandra Dibble, "Tijuana's Top Cop Steps Down," *San Diego Union-Tribune*, February 26, 2016.

237 a sign of just how violent the city was about to become Within a year of leaving his post, Alex found a job as the chief of the State Public Safety Commission in Morelos, a small mountainous state just south of Mexico City where a mass grave of fifty bodies had been unearthed in 2016. They had been dumped there by morgue officials in what some called an act of incompetence and others labeled an act of complicity with the cartels.

237 In 2018, over 2,300 people were killed in Tijuana Alejandra Sánchez Inzunza and José Luis Pardo Veiras, "Tijuana's Tourism Is Booming Even as the Homicide Rate Spikes," *Vice*, December 11, 2018.

244 people who inject with black tar heroin are also less likely to become infected with HIV Daniel Ciccarone and Philippe Bourgois, "Explaining the Geographical Variation of HIV Among Injection Drug Users in the United States," *Substance Use & Misuse* 38, no. 14: 2049–63.

250 average life expectancy of Americans had declined for the first time Lenny Bernstein and Christopher Ingraham, "Fueled by Drug Crisis, U.S. Life Expectancy Declines for a Second Straight Year," *Washington Post*, December 21, 2017.

Epilogue

254 Trump likening them to an invading army Matthew Choi, "Trump: Military Will Defend Border from Caravan 'Invasion,'" *Politico*, November 10, 2018.

255 "human rights are only for upstanding humans" Robert Valencia, "Migrant Caravan: Donald Trump Earns Apparent Support of Mexican Mayor, Who Wears 'Make Tijuana Great Again' Hat," *Newsweek*, November 21, 2018.

255 a crowd decried the flow of irregular migration, seeking, it seemed, to rewrite Tijuana's reputation James Fredrick, "Shouting 'Mexico First,' Hundreds in Tijuana March against Migrant Caravan," NPR, November 19, 2018.

255 Gastelúm's approval rating was mired at 4 percent Robert Valencia, "Migrant Caravan: Donald Trump Earns Apparent Support of Mexican Mayor."

256 the Mérida Initiative, which has to date provided more than $1.6 billion The Mérida Initiative: Overview. U.S. Embassy & Consulates in Mexico. Available at: https://ms.usembassy.gov/our-relationship/policy-history /the-merida-initiative/.

257 19 percent of the world's foreign-born population United Nations Department of Economic and Social Affairs, "Trends in International Migration, 2015," United Nations Population Division, December 2015. Available at http://www.un.org/en/development/desa/population/migration/publications /populationfacts/docs/MigrationPopFacts2015.4.pdf.

257 hundreds applied for work permits in Mexico Christine Murray, "Handful of Caravan Migrants Launch Hunger Strike at U.S. Border," Reuters, November 29, 2018.

257 the U.S. was processing only approximately thirty per day Jonathan Blitzer, "The Long Wait for Tijuana's Migrants to Process Their Own Asylum Claims," *New Yorker*, November 29, 2018.

257 the industriousness that had carried them all the way to the border Ibid.

257 outbreaks of flu-like symptoms, lice, and chicken pox spread through the encampment Christine Murray, "Handful of Caravan Migrants Launch Hunger Strike at U.S. Border."

257 moving its occupants to a covered building in Tijuana's southeastern El Barretal colonia Leyla Santiago, Deborah Bloom, and Duarte Mendonca, "Main Migrant Shelter in Tijuana Closed 'Due to Health Issues,'" CNN, December 4, 2018.

258 "migrant," which was a mostly neutral term Beginning as early as 2015, news organizations including *Al Jazeera English* and the *Washington Post* both questioned whether "migrant" could be used, given that "it has evolved from its dictionary definitions into a tool that dehumanises and distances, a blunt pejorative." See Adam Taylor, "Is It Time to Ditch the Word 'Migrant'?" *Washington Post*, August 24, 2015.

258 *micqui*, meaning "dead person" Lisa Sousa, *The Woman Who Turned into a Jaguar, and Other Narratives of Native Women in Archives of Colonial Mexico* (Stanford, CA: Stanford University Press, 2017).

Index

A NOTE ON THE AUTHOR

Dan Werb, PhD, is a science writer and epidemiologist. He is an assistant professor in the Division of Infectious Diseases and Global Public Health at the University of California San Diego and at the University of Toronto's Dalla Lana School of Public Health, and is a research scientist at St. Michael's Hospital in Toronto. For his research, he has received the U.S. National Institute on Drug Abuse's Avenir Award, a Pierre Elliott Trudeau Foundation Scholarship, and other honors. His journalism has appeared in many publications, including *The Believer*, *HuffPost*, and *The Walrus*, where his feature "The Fix," on new tactics for treating injectable drug abuse, won a Canadian National Magazine Award. He lives in Toronto and San Diego, California.